MONTESSORI

IN

CONTEMPORARY

AMERICAN

CULTURE

MONTESSORI
IN
CONTEMPORARY
AMERICAN
CULTURE

MARGARET HOWARD LOEFFLER
Editor
OKLAHOMA CITY UNIVERSITY

HEINEMANN
PORTSMOUTH, NH

Heinemann Educational Books, Inc.
361 Hanover Street   Portsmouth, NH 03801
Offices and agents throughout the world

Library of Congress Cataloging-in-Publication Data
Montessori in contemporary American culture / [edited by] Margaret
   Howard Loeffler.
         p.   cm.
   Based on a series of papers presented at a symposium on
"Montessori in the Contemporary American Culture", held in
Arlington, Va., in April 1990, and sponsored by the American
Montessori Society.
   Includes bibliographical references and index.
   ISBN 0-435-08709-6
   1. Montessori method of education—United States—Congresses.
I. Loeffler, Margaret Howard, 1921–
LB775.M8M56   1992
371.3'92'0973—dc20

                                                        92–523
                                                        CIP

Designed by Adrianne Onderdonk Dudden.
Printed in the United States of America.
92   93   94   95   96   9   8   7   6   5   4   3   2   1

This book is dedicated to the memory of Ann Burke Neubert, a bright and energetic young teacher and researcher who recognized the importance of objective examination of educational ideas and made a significant contribution to the symposium and to this book.

CONTENTS

NOTES ON CONTRIBUTORS

Marlene Barron, M.S., is head of West Side Montessori School in New York City, a member of the graduate faculty at New York University, director of the Montessori Teacher Education Program at NYU, and past president of the American Montessori Society. She has served as a school consultant in both the public and private sectors and is a nationally known lecturer and author of numerous articles and books. Her most recent book, *I Learn to Read and Write the Way I Learn to Talk: A Very First Book About Whole Language,* was published in 1990.

Elizabeth Bronsil, M. Ed., is director of the Montessori Teacher Education Program and laboratory school at Xavier University in Cincinnati, Ohio, past secretary of the Teacher Education Committee of the American Montessori Society, and a member of the Commission of the Accreditation Council for Childhood Education Specialist Schools. She teaches at the preschool and elementary levels, consults for schools, and has served in the Headstart Migrant Education Program.

Eileen Wilms Buermann, M.Ed., is program coordinator at Bennett Park Montessori Center, a public Montessori magnet school program in Buffalo, New York, which has been operating successfully since 1977. She also is director of the Buffalo Montessori Teacher Education Program, a school consultant and workshop presenter, and a member of the Teacher Education Committee of the American Montessori Society.

John Chattin-McNichols, Ph.D., is associate professor of education at Seattle University and director of the Montessori Institute of the Pacific Northwest. He was a Fulbright fellow to the University of the West Indies, Trinidad, 1987–88; serves as codirector of the Teachers' Research Network; and is president of the Accreditation Council of the Childhood Education Specialists Schools. He is the author of many articles on teacher-education research and on computers in education. His latest book, *The Montessori Controversy* was published in 1992 by Delmar.

Carol Chomsky, Ph.D., is a psycholinguist and lecturer on education at the Harvard Graduate School of Education, Cambridge, Massachusetts. She teaches linguistics and education, psycholinguistics, reading and language research, and microcomputers and language. She is currently working on development of computer software for reading and language instruction, including use of laser disks.

Elisabeth Johnston Coe, Ph.D., is director of the middle school program for twelve-to fourteen-year-olds at School of the Woods, Houston, Texas, and a staff member of the Houston Montessori Center. She is currently president of the American Montessori Society, serves as a consultant to public schools in Minnesota and Texas and private schools throughout the country, and is a member of the Teacher's Research Network.

William Crain, Ph.D., is professor and chair of the Department of Psychology at City College and a member of the Teaneck, New Jersey, Board of Education. He is the author of many articles and books on developmental psychology, including *Theories of Development: Concepts and Applications* (Prentice-Hall, 1992).

David Elkind, Ph.D., is professor of child study and former senior resident scholar at the Lincoln Filene Center, Tufts University. He is past president of the National Association for the Education of Young Children. Dr. Elkind is an internationally recognized lecturer and author of many articles and twelve books, including *Miseducation of Children, The Hurried Child,* and *All Grown Up and No Place to Go.*

David Kahn, B.A., is the executive director of the North American Montessori Teacher's Association and the editor of its journal, both affiliated with the Association Montessori International (AMI) headquartered in the Netherlands. He is the administrative director of the Ohio Montessori Training Institute associated with Cleveland State University and is the author of numerous articles and a book on Montessori in the public schools.

Lilian G. Katz, Ph.D., is professor of early childhood education at the University of Illinois, Urbana, Illinois, and has served as director of the Educational Resources Information Center clearinghouse on elementary and early childhood education since 1968. She is president-elect of the National Association for the Education of Young Children, an internationally known lecturer, and the author of many articles and books, including *Engaging Children's Minds: The Project Approach.*

Margaret Howard Loeffler, Ph.D., is an anthropologist and former director of the Primary Division of the Casady School in Oklahoma City, Oklahoma. She is presently a member of the graduate faculty and academic director of the master of education in early childhood program at Oklahoma City University, which offers an AMS credential. She is founder and codirector of the Teachers' Research Network, an association of teachers carrying out research in their own classrooms. She developed and chaired the symposium "Montessori in Contemporary American Culture."

Antonia Lopez, M.Ed., is education and staff development director of the Foundation Center for Phenomenological Research, an organization that sponsors Spanish-language Montessori teacher training for mothers of migrant worker families and Montessori childcare programs for their children. Ms. Lopez is a member of the board of directors of the American Montessori Society and a nationally known speaker and consultant on issues related to migrant families.

Ann Burke Neubert, M.Ed., until her sudden and recent death, was director of the northeast Montessori Institute and founder/president of the Early Education Company. A member of the American Montessori Society Board, Ms. Neubert also was chairperson of the AMS Teacher Education Committee and president of the Accreditation Council of the Childhood Education Specialist Schools. She was a university instructor and consultant for early education, Headstart, and Montessori classes. Ms. Neubert was the author of numerous articles on Montessori education and early childhood topics.

Nancy McCormick Rambusch, Ph.D., was instrumental in the rebirth of Montessori in the United States in the 1950s. In 1958, she headed the Whitby School in Greenwich, Connecticut, where the American Montessori Society started in 1960. She has directed early education programs, trained teachers, and consulted in both the public and private sectors. Dr. Rambusch was director of Early Childhood Education at the Agency for Child Development in New York City before accepting her current post at the State University of New York at New Paultz. She is an internationally known lecturer and author.

Sylvia O. Richardson, M.D., is professor of communicology and clinical professor of pediatrics at the University of South Florida. She holds an M.A. in the education of the exceptional, is a certified speech/language pathologist, and an accredited Montessori teacher. She has been president of ASHA and the International Orton Dyslexia Society. She is an internationally known writer and lecturer.

Joy Starry Turner, M.A., is director of the Montessori Western Teacher training Program and the Montessori Greenhouse School and is currently editor of the American Montessori Society quarterly magazine *Montessori Life.* Ms. Turner has written all teacher training and school accreditation manuals used by AMS. She is a member of the AMS Teacher Education Committee, current president of the Montessori Accreditation Council for Teacher Education, and past president of the Accreditation Council of the Childhood Education Specialist Schools. She is the author of *The Montessori Western Teacher Resource Book, Unit Studies for Early Childhood,* and numerous professional articles.

PREFACE

This book is based on a series of papers presented at a three-day symposium on "Montessori in Contemporary American Culture" held in Arlington, Virginia, in April 1990 and sponsored by the American Montessori Society under a grant from the Island Foundation of Massachusetts. The symposium examined the influence of Dr. Maria Montessori's ideas on the current American cultural and educational scene, more than eighty years after the initial introduction of her ideas in 1907 and thirty years after their second American entry in the late 1950s.

Maria Montessori was an unusual woman. An early advocate of women's rights, she became a well-known and much sought-after speaker on this subject in Europe in the late 1890s. She was the first woman in her native Italy to be accepted into medical school and to be granted an M.D. degree.

Her interest in education grew out of her work as a physician in mental retardation. Appointed director of the State Orthophrenic School in Rome, she began a careful study of students considered mentally defective and of mentally retarded children who for lack of more suitable placement had been housed in adult insane asylums. Montessori believed that many of these children were able to learn and consequently could become more productive members of society.

Her first educational success was in devising methods for these children's education, adapted from the earlier work of Jean Itard and Edward Sequin, French physicians and educators of developmentally disabled children. The educational experiment was a great success: many of these children learned to read and write as well as normal children in the early grades of the traditional schools.

Montessori's success at tapping the inherent potential of these developmentally disabled children so that they could function at higher levels laid the groundwork for the next fifty years of her career. Although she continued her work as a university professor and a practicing physician, Montessori began to apply what she had learned to the education of "normal" children, and that became a consuming interest for the rest of her life.

Montessori was an idealist, and she believed that children were the major hope for a better and more peaceful world. She thought that education could be a vital force in creating more responsible and caring individuals who would be able to overcome the prejudices and tensions leading to conflict in the world. She also believed that children were inherently good and that if their true natures were understood and allowed to develop, instead of being inhibited and distorted by adult misdirection, they would grow into adults who would work toward peace and understanding others.

Montessori was also a practical activist who recognized that it was important to translate her beliefs into practical methods. She drew on her background in medical sciences, anthropology, and psychiatry in her astute observations of young children; like Piaget, she based her ideas on young children's development. Unlike Piaget, however, Montessori emphasized the need to educate teachers directly in order to bring about the changes that she felt were necessary to accomplish her goals.

Montessori's activist approach brought her into conflict with some of her staunchest advocates. She found it difficult to delegate her authority to others in teacher training despite the pressing need worldwide for teachers trained in her method. Her approach also moved her from being seen primarily as a theorist and scientist in child development into the role of an educational entrepreneur.

On a more positive note, this strong desire to see her ideas implemented as she envisioned them has, no doubt, even more than her writings, enabled her major ideas to survive essentially unchanged for more than eighty years in a variety of cultures. Not only have these ideas survived, but many of them have become widely accepted concepts in child development settings of all types.

The importance of this maintenance of the "Montessori model of education," with its core concepts, adapted as it has inevitably been to meet the needs of different cultures including the American one, cannot be overestimated in explaining the durability of her insights. Eighty years of practice have subjected these concepts to cultural differences, individual teachers' idiosyncrasies, and thousands of children's daily challenges, attesting to the universality and validity of her observations and provide important research data regarding the authenticity of her insights.

This book is an attempt to bring to the general reader a view of Montessori's influence in the present American culture. The authors of these chapters (which were papers presented at the symposium) come from many disciplines and have approached Montessori's ideas from many viewpoints. Together they provide a comprehensive view of Montessori's influence on the American culture of the 1990s while at the same time generating a discussion of those issues and questions that her ideas still pose for many contemporary educators.

As editor, I hope that this book will provide an important and long overdue resource about Maria Montessori's work and its current applications and will meet the needs of psychologists, educators, social workers, physicians, parents, and others interested in the development of children. Perhaps this publication can mark the beginning of a new era in the evaluation of Montessori's work—one marked by a greater objectivity and a separation of her work from her personality.

Margaret Loeffler

ACKNOWLEDGMENTS

The symposium from which this book was derived would not have occurred without a grant from the Island Foundation of Massachusetts and the interest and support of its board and president, Lucy Nesbeda, and its executive director, Jenny Russell. My sincere thanks to them for their belief in the importance of this work.

The executive director of the American Montessori Society, Bretta Weiss, provided enthusiasm and support for the project from its earliest planning stages through its final implementation including a constructive reading of many parts of this manuscript. This project owes its existence to the work and support of Ms. Weiss, and a mere thank you seems inadequate for such a contribution.

Carole Korngold, the immediate past president of the American Montessori Society, also lent her energy and enthusiasm to the project, and her leadership (and humor) added much to the success of the symposium and, consequently, to this book. The board of the American Montessori Society provided additional funds for the symposium as well as assistance in all phases of the project and their support is greatly appreciated.

A sincere thanks, of course, must go to the presenters and participants in the symposium. The participants' questions and comments in response to the papers as they were presented contributed a great deal to their constructive revision. It is with sincere regret that, due to publishing constraints, we have had to limit the number of papers from the symposium panels on childcare and public school Montessori programs. The panel papers not published in this book will be published in booklet form by the American Montessori Society.

A final thanks to the professional editors who have provided invaluable support and expertise in the preparation of this book.

Margaret Loeffler

PART ONE
CURRENT VIEWS
INSIDE
MONTESSORI

INTRODUCTION

The book begins with Nancy Rambusch's recollections of Montessori's second introduction into the American culture in the early 1960s. Rambusch was the major player in Montessori's reintroduction, and her chapter explains some of the conflicts that occurred as Montessori's innovative ideas were adapted to American culture.

The schism with the European Montessori community, which Rambusch discusses, in retrospect seems inevitable given the personal ties that bound many Europeans to Montessori as a charismatic leader of a movement rather than as an astute child developmentalist. The Americans who were the primary movers of the Montessori revival had not known Dr. Montessori as an individual; consequently, they were free to examine her ideas objectively and to recognize both their strengths and their weaknesses.

One difficulty that occurred in the early phases of this reexamination, however, was the importation of many Montessori-trained teachers from Europe and Asia who were unfamiliar with American culture and who had been thoroughly imbued with the European Montessori view. Although Americans established training centers for American teachers from the beginning, only a small number of teachers could be handled in the first few years and schools were impatient for staff. In addition, Montessori faculty for these training centers often were recruited, by necessity, from European and Asian Montessorians, leading to many philosophical and cultural misunderstandings between faculty and students. These were some of the basic reasons that led to the severing of ties between the majority of the American Montessori group and the European Montessori hierarchy in 1965.

As centers for the education of American Montessori teachers—many with university affiliations—appeared in all areas of the United States in the late 1960s and early 1970s, Montessori classrooms were Americanized and evolved to meet the needs of a changing American culture.

The next two chapters in part I examine in some detail the fit between Montessori's writings and current classroom practices.

In "Montessori's Writings Versus Montessori Practices," Joy Turner, the current editor of *Montessori Life,* a major publication of the American Montessori Society, carefully delineates the major concepts in Montessori's own writings and compares them with contemporary American Montessori practices. Her views are based on her own classroom observations as well as her knowledge of the content of accredited Montessori teacher education programs as indicated by the published standards of the national accrediting agency. In addition, she has interviewed graduates of a range of Montessori teacher education programs including those associated with the most traditional views of Montessori methodology.

Turner sees Montessori education as a system with three interactive elements: the child, the environment, and the adult. She concludes that although the view of the child has changed less than the views of the environment and the adult teacher, cultural accommodation has occurred in all of these elements. Because response to the child is a basic Montessori tenet affecting all the elements, Turner suggests that such accommodation may be inherent in the Montessori system itself.

Chapter 3, "Is There an American Montessori Model?" is an analysis by Ann Neubert of the Americanization process in the classroom, based upon a study done at the University of Michigan. To supplement the earlier study, questionnaires were also sent to American Montessori teachers.

The Neubert study compares the stated goals of American Montessori teachers with what is actually observed in the classrooms. The data suggest cultural adaptation of curricular content and a change in the amount of time teachers spend observing children in their own classrooms. Other basic Montessori principles—for instance, the aim for student autonomy and self-reliance, and avoidance of large group instruction—seem to be intact in American classrooms.

In "What Does Research Say About Montessori?" John Chattin-McNichols reports on research carried out in American Montessori programs. Chattin-McNichols has divided the research into two types: process research and outcome research. Congruent with the recent move toward more ethnographic research, he suggests the need for more process research, which would reveal most clearly the social interactions and personal development said to be important goals of Montessori education.

Chattin-McNichols examines several studies on the occurrence of fantasy play in Montessori classrooms—a problematic area for many teachers because of Montessori's writings on this subject. The author's review of outcome research suggests many positive outcomes of Montessori education in comparison with other methods. In many cases, however, special programs—focused on specific outcomes—can produce better scores in these specific areas than Montessori programs, at least in the short term. Chattin-McNichols suggests that this may be due to the broader and more process-oriented goals of Montessori education, which indicate effectiveness on long-term measures. The author also notes evidence of the continuation of positive Montessori preschool outcomes into the elementary years.

The author sees the growing cadre of Montessori teachers who are undertaking action research in their own classrooms as a very positive development, which will add to the research base. In addition, the public school Montessori programs, which are accumulating a growing data base on outcomes, will be new and important sources of information in evaluating Montessori's effectiveness.

The final chapter in part I, "Montessori and Constructivism," compares Montessori's and Piaget's views of the child. Loeffler attempts to dispel some myths about Montessori as well as to demonstrate similarities with Piaget's views. She examines the role of the didactic apparatus in Montessori education, both supporting and questioning the usefulness of these "efficient experiences." The author also discusses such issues as Montessori's view of control of error in the learner and individual as opposed to group learning.

The author's conclusion, which may generate controversy, is that the essence of Montessori education lies in the social and psychological environment created for the learners, rather than in the more visible and unique artifacts of the method.

1

MONTESSORI IN AMERICA: A HISTORY

Maria Montessori (1870–1952), the Italian physician turned educational innovator, was once described as "a woman who looks at children as a naturalist looks at bees." This description derived from the emphasis Montessori's pedagogical method placed on the observation of individual children. Montessori's strategies for educating young children in group settings rivaled those of German educator Frederick Froebel's in novelty and far exceeded Froebel's in responsiveness to individual children's needs.

As a physician rooted in the study of biology and as a clinician immersed in firsthand experience with young children, Montessori devised an approach to early education based upon an intuitive as well as a rational understanding of children's cognitive growth and development. She was to the emergent field of child development what Claude Monet was to nineteenth-century painting—an impressionist. Like Monet, Montessori illumined what she saw. Despite her often archaic vocabulary, Montessori has proved to be astonishingly modern in her outlook (Hornberger, 1982). Her modernity explains why two different generations of American parents, widely separated in time, found her ideas compelling enough to involve their own youngsters in American Montessori education.

INTRODUCTION OF MONTESSORI'S WORK INTO AMERICA

Montessori's educational experiment became known to Americans almost as soon as it began. In 1906, while the young Roman physician was organizing her first Children's House in the San Lorenzo slums, Dorothy

Canfield Fisher, the Vermont children's author who wintered in Rome, was writing home about Montessori's educational practices. Fisher advised American parents to pay particular attention to what Montessori was saying about the nature of young children's learning.

S. S. McClure, the editor of *McClure's Magazine* and a promoter, saw in Dr. Montessori's work and the American interest in it an opportunity to further his own ambitions and joined forces with her. McClure organized an American tour for Montessori in 1911. She arrived in America just two years after Sigmund Freud. Her visit was duly noted in educational circles. She was deliriously welcomed by the small band of American teachers whom she had trained earlier in Rome. Chief among these was Anne George, who later translated Montessori's book on her "method of scientific pedagogy as it applied to the children in Children's Houses." In America, the title of this best-seller was shortened to *The Montessori Method* (1912).

Well before Montessori arrived in New York for her 1911 tour of major American cities, Americans with a great deal of influence had expressed interest in her ideas. The Alexander Graham Bells would seem to have been the ideal American sponsors of Dr. Montessori's work. Dr. Bell, world renowned as the inventor of the telephone, was also a noted educator of the deaf. He had opened a school for training teachers of the deaf in Boston in 1872 and had been a professor of vocal physiology at Boston University. He was the founder of the American Association to Promote Teaching to the Deaf. His experience in organizing support for a new educational idea in America far outstripped Montessori's. Bell and his wife were also the concerned grandparents of seven youngsters of an age to respond to the kinds of experiences that Dr. Montessori's education promised. What could be more natural than for them to organize a Montessori school in their Washington, D.C. home and in addition, a society to train teachers in furtherance of Dr. Montessori's interests in America?

The major difficulty Americans interested in Montessori education were experiencing was finding teachers appropriately trained in the "method." The Bells were confident that they and Dr. Montessori could organize cooperatively a way around this roadblock. The Bells were wrong.

When Montessori arrived in America and was told of the work that the Bells had already done, she was enraged. She reserved to herself the power to train teachers in her method, as well as the power to designate those, other than herself, who might train them. Further, Montessori could conceive of no way that any movement bearing her name and devoted to her ideas, in any country, could proceed without her presence at its center and without her express permission regarding its organization.

Americans, then as now, had a hard time understanding why Dr. Montessori believed that her educational insights belonged to her alone. Typically, notions about child development have always been debated in a free market of inquiry, to be accepted or rejected by adherents or critics as each sees fit. The notion that Dr. Montessori's ideas, once articulated, were *her* personal property never occurred to the Bells or to any of the other interested Americans outside those of Montessori's intimate circle of adherents. Neither had it occurred to them that Montessori herself intended to direct and manage personally the worldwide diffusion of her method.

THE MOVEMENT OF IDEAS BETWEEN CULTURES

When ideas move from one culture to another, they often follow a predictable path. First, the particular idea is transported or carried from the host to the receiving culture. As far as Montessori's ideas are concerned, this work was accomplished the first time by such voluntary American publicists as Dorothy Canfield Fisher and S. S. McClure. Fisher's book, *A Montessori Mother* (1912), not only reported Dr. Montessori's work in Rome, but situated that work in the context of middle-class American family life. In *McClure's Magazine*, following the enthusiastically received article by Josephine Tozier on Montessori as an educational wonder worker (1911), the magazine featured a section called "The Montessori Movement in America" and printed frequent bulletins regarding the method and ways to effect its American implementation.

Once an idea has been transported, it requires translation. This is most effectively done by those receiving the idea, not by those sending it. Thus, when Fisher, McClure, and the Bells became interested in Montessori education, they began immediately to situate it in an American context. Who better to do this, in America, than Americans?

Finally, when a received idea is translated into a new culture, it reshapes the culture, even as it is reshaped by the culture. Once this has occurred, one can fairly describe the particular idea as "naturalized."

The first time around in America, Montessori's ideas got only as far as the translation stage. Retrospectively considered, there were a few plausible reasons for this. One was that Montessori, a person of immense personal vanity, was unable to recognize friendly support when she encountered it (Cohen, 1964). Another was that the Americans themselves bungled the diffusion effort.

MONTESSORI'S SECOND CHANCE IN AMERICA

It took another half-century to bring Montessori's ideas to the point where they became transformed and "naturalized." The cultural and psychological climates in America after the Second World War were radically different from those of Montessori's 1911 visit (Hunt, 1964).

In the early 1960s Montessori was granted the hearing she had earlier denied herself. A group of American parents who believed that her ideas had particular relevance for their children's lives, enthusiastically seized upon her thought and pedagogical practice. Some were Catholic and were persuaded that the parochial education awaiting their children was as monolithic in content as it was in intent. Others early attracted to Montessori education were among those who went into orbit with Sputnik, and rebelled against what the Council for Basic Education characterized as the "life adjustment" curriculum in the schools. Yet other parents, looking retrospectively upon barren childhoods, were determined to provide their youngsters with a golden time they themselves had not known.

Only during Montessori's lifetime did her method remain wholly her own. After her death, in 1952, it belonged, not to her designated son and heir, Mario Montessori, but to anyone, anywhere, determined to explore its implications and practices. The organization Montessori had founded, the Association Montessori Internationale (AMI) and the network personally established by her to further her work had no special relevance for Americans interested in Montessori education.

Mario Montessori, as his mother's heir, tried to control teacher training much as Montessori had done in her lifetime. The resources and energies of the AMI, from an American perspective, appeared to be centered on endless squabbles with possible usurpers and polluters of the method. E. M. Standing (1962), one of Montessori's biographers, described Mario's "work" thus:

> At Montessori's death, her son, Mario, was bequeathed the "delicate" task of safeguarding the integrity of the Montessori movement . . . by recognizing only such Montessori schools and training courses as faithfully interpret both in spirit and practice, the Montessori principles. (p. 72)

The American adopters turned adapters wanted more than simply to transpose Montessori education from Europe to America. American Montessori education needed to be as diverse and pluralistic as America itself.

The position of the fledgling American Montessori Society (AMS), founded in 1960, was not that of a branch office of the International Montessori Association (AMI). The AMS, given the size of the continent and the complexity of the culture, became regionalized. It represented a congeries of possibilities for early education, all inspired by the thought and practices of Maria Montessori, but not all following an identical path. There would be American Montessori preschools, kindergartens, and day-care programs. There would be Montessori public, parochial, and independent school elementary programs as well as parent cooperatives.

THE "DISPLACEMENT OF CONCEPT" NOTION

When an idea or concept is transformed in reciprocal contact with a particular culture, its original definition is often dislocated or displaced. Schon (1963) calls this state of affairs the "displacement of concept." An American Montessori education proved to be a valid instance of this phenomenon, making of "Montessori" education "American Montessori" education. The American Montessori Society has, from its beginnings, supported this definitional shift.

Schon (1963) sees displacement of concept as a large-scale metaphor—one that is central to the development of all new concepts and theories, whether bearing on science, invention, or philosophy. In displacement, the familiar is brought to bear on the unfamiliar in such a way as to yield new concepts, while at the same time retaining as much as possible of the past.

The evolution of a theory is very much like the process of invention and product development as it occurs in industry. New concepts are framed only in terms of concept displacement. The emergence of the new concept involves, in some sense, treating the new in terms of the old. After all, we have nothing else. But the processes that seem at first to involve treatment of the new in terms of the old do not always lead to the formation of new concepts. Old concepts may be used that do not generate change.

The process whereby an old concept is shifted to a new situation in such a way as to change and extend it is Schon's "displacement of concept." That is precisely what occurred in the second American iteration of "Montessori" education, transforming it and making of it "American Montessori" education.

HOW A CONCEPT IS DISPLACED

The steps in the displacement are as follows:

1 Aspects of the old theory are transposed to the new situation.
2 "Old" aspects of the theory are interpreted in the new situation.
3 Areas of communality and difference between the old and the transposed theory are spelled out. Schon (1963) argues that symbolically the old theory comes to function as a protective model for the new situation. Asked to find the old theory in the new situation, one comes to see the old theory in a different way.

The transformation of Montessori education in America to American Montessori education resided in the radical change wrought on the European Montessori educational model by its American context. The term *Montessori* was rich in the connotations of the historical personage, the social movement, and the pedagogical practices. *American* was redolent of size, plurality, complexity, and ambiguity. By intentionally linking the two notions as equivalent terms, as the American Montessori Society did, one could not have easily said which context was central. The boundaries and the internal structure of the concept were changing and indistinct (Schon, 1963).

The four stages of the displacement concept are

1 transposition
2 interpretation
3 correction
4 spelling out

The transposition stage is not a once-and-for-all affair. It goes on indefinitely as more and more notions of the old idea cluster are shifted to the new situation. Over time, the concept "fills out."

Transposition is inseparable from interpretation. Interpretive transposition—the assignment of a concept from the old cluster to a specific aspect of the new situation—does not necessarily proceed smoothly. The new situation already had a conceptual structure before any of the old theory was displaced to it. This preexisting structure resists transposition and interpretation. The resultant adjustment is displacement.

Once Montessori education had been announced in America, in the 1960s, some European-trained teachers arrived, and the first schools were established. Understandably the AMI resisted the notion that the

American situation was unique, arguing that every national group was unique principally by virtue of its geography. Those within the AMS innocent of notions of cultural complexity also resisted the view of cultural change assuming that the old theory could be placed like a stencil over the new situation. Instead, transposition is a case of mutual adaptation, in which both old and new are modified in various ways to suit one another. Some aspects of the old theory may not "travel" to the new situation; they may even be dropped from the old theory. The interpretation given to aspects of the old concept may be changed.

Over time, the novelty of the metaphor dies. The new term, in this case American Montessori, comes into use as a literal, not a figurative, term. The concept has now been displaced.

The final stage is the "spelling out," which comes from the culture in which the old idea is now newly embedded.

THE AMERICAN MONTESSORI SOCIETY'S INTENTIONS

The American Montessori Society intended to build a national network of Montessori schools and teacher preparation programs. In its early years, the AMS had far too few resources to realize its ambitions fully. It faced a growing constituency with apparently limitless needs.

In America, two groups, the International Montessori Association and the American Montessori Society, were interpreting very differently their right to speak on behalf of Montessori education.

When Mario Montessori engaged in controversy with the American Montessori Society, the underlying issue was always one of legitimacy: "Who has the right to speak for Montessori?" The American response was that, once dead, Montessori was better able to speak for herself through her writing than were many of her uncritical disciples able to speak for her. While the AMI patrolled the borders of international pedagogical integrity, the AMS saw itself as a legitimate indigenous purveyor of Montessori insights and teacher training.

DIFFICULTIES WITHIN THE SOCIETY

The real drama within the American Montessori movement occurred as those seeking answers to educational problems looked to Montessori education as a short-term American panacea. Many parents interpreted Montessori education as guaranteeing immeasurably superior outcomes for children by the children's mere attendance at such programs. The demands made on the fledgling AMS by its member schools were crushing. The impact of positive media coverage nearly destroyed the society. As a defense, it erected a "facade."

Smith and Keith (1971) define a facade as the image an organization presents to its several publics. When an organization is forced to make premature statements concerning its aims and structure, its formal description rarely matches its emergent reality. What results is a biased or partial picture that tends to be interpreted literally and that serves subsequently as a referent. An organization is hard put to defend its "unfinished" state and that of its work when both the organization and the work have been reported in the media as already "finished."

Because, by its own conscious choice, the AMS was "unfinished," in contradistinction to AMI, the major difficulty that it encountered through publicity was an inadequate discrimination between its intentions and its reality.

The AMS commitment to culturally relevant versions of Montessori education was a self-imposed task of enormous complexity. In all of its literature, the society's intention was made clear. The first American Montessori teacher-training course was thus described:

> Through lectures on the theory and practice of Montessori education, as well as through exposure to the educational and developmental trends in (American) Early Childhood Education, a Montessorian learns to relate the insights of Montessori to those of American educators. (Rambusch, 1962, p. 1)

The distinction between the "old" and the "new" Montessori focus was expressed early on:

> Very simply, the Montessori ideas today are meeting the same "Americanization" test as did those of Frederick Froebel fifty years ago. . . . There is good reason to believe that the American Montessori movement will be destroyed as intellectually and pedagogically substantive if it is representative of the fossilized outlook of those Europeans whose fidelity to Dr. Montessori's memory is as unquestioned as is their innocence of the complexity of American culture. (Rambusch, 1963, p. 3)

Placing Montessori education in a viable American context was a recurrent theme in the early organization and conduct of the AMS. Applebaum (1972) compares the objectives of the AMS and the AMI:

The AMS goal [was] to insert Montessori insights into American culture as opposed to the AMI goal (which was) simply to establish Montessori classes in America.

The impetus of the reiterated American movement sprang from two sources. Its organizers had no need to accept Dr. Montessori's proprietary view of her work and none of the founders of the American Montessori movement had known Dr. Montessori in life. Thus all were free to make the life of the movement their motive force rather than the memory of a cherished, lost leader.

The stabilization of the American Montessori movement occurred as much by default as by design. The resources of the AMS were far too meager to solve all of the problems posed by its clients. Many clients simply solved their own problems. Understandable conflicts within the AMS leadership concerning the self-imposed role of the Society erupted and abated periodically.

In the past thirty years, beyond the AMI and the AMS, other groups interested in Montessori education in America have developed. The very name "Montessori" now evokes a generic response as a kind of early childhood educational experience.

The initial goal that the American Montessori Society set for itself, more than three decades ago—the "naturalization" of Montessori education—has been realized. The realization of indigenous American Montessori models seems indicated by the title of this book, *Montessori in Contemporary American Culture,* and by the variety of areas influenced by Dr. Montessori's work as described in its pages.

REFERENCES

Applebaum, P. (1972). *The growth of the Montessori movement in the United States: 1909–1970.* Ann Arbor: University Microfilms.

Cohen, S. (1972). Montessori comes to America, 1911–1917. *Notre Dame Journal of Education,* 2, 358–372.

Fisher, D. C. (1912). *A Montessori mother.* Chicago: Richardson and Co.

Hornberger, M. A. (1982). *The developmental psychology of Maria Montessori.* Ann Arbor: University Microfilms.

Hunt, J. M. (1964). Introduction. In M. Montessori, *The Montessori method.* New York: Schocken.

Montessori, M. (1912). *The Montessori method.* New York: Frederick C. Stokes.

Rambusch, N. M. (1962). *Learning how to learn: An American approach to Montessori.* Baltimore: Helicon.

———. (1963). The American Montessori picture: Some reconsiderations. *American Montessori Society Bulletin.*

Schon, D. A. (1963). *The displacement of concepts.* London: Tavistock Press.

Smith, L. M., and Keith, P. M. (1971). *Anatomy of educational innovation.* New York: Wiley.

Standing, E. M. (1962). *Maria Montessori: Her life and work.* New York: New American Library.

Tozier, J. (May, 1911). An educational wonder worker: The methods of Maria Montessori. *McClure's.*

2

MONTESSORI'S WRITINGS VERSUS MONTESSORI PRACTICES

ISSUES AND SOURCES OF INFORMATION

What is Montessori? Is it a social movement, a philosophy, or a theory of development? A method, a curriculum, or a set of educational materials? Or is it, as some seem to believe, a cult? How was (or is) the work of Dr. Maria Montessori different from what came before? Is the Montessori approach to education the same today as when initiated almost ninety years ago—or has it changed? Is it still viable? In this study I seek to answer these questions by judging the congruence between Montessori's writings and Montessori practices.

DEFINITIONS

Montessori wrote and lectured in Italian, over a period of more than forty years. At least fifteen books in English have been published under her name, but a biography by Kramer (1976) warns that some of the later works were based on translated notes taken by teachers in training, and not reworked by Montessori herself; it is hard to estimate, she contends, "what exactly has been lost in the multiple stages of transcription and translation" (p. 356).

Acting conservatively with regard to authenticity, I limited this study to seven books of unquestioned authorship, which also span Montessori's own period of development from 1912 to 1949:

- Montessori's first description of her educational experiments with normal children: *The Montessori Method* (1964)

- The following three books, in which she elaborated details: *Dr. Montessori's Own Handbook* (1965a); *Spontaneous Activity in Education* (1965b); and *The Montessori Elementary Material,* vol. 2 (1965c)

- Her first book with advice specific to parents: *The Child in the Family* (1970)

- Her most detailed discussion on the theme of deviations: *The Secret of Childhood* (1966)

- Her last book, *The Absorbent Mind* (1967)

Montessori practices, for purposes of the study, include both the "traditions" of Montessori teacher preparation and the performance of teachers in Montessori schools. It has certainly not been possible for me to observe firsthand all or even most of the eight Montessori associations or the estimated ninety teacher training programs and five thousand Montessori schools in this country. But in the past twenty-five years I have had some experience with most of the training courses—as student, instructor, reviewer, on-site evaluator, accreditation council member, or committee representative. As consultant or evaluator, I have made formal observations in perhaps three hundred different Montessori, public, or other early childhood classrooms. For this study, I also interviewed three teacher educators from the most traditional Montessori training group, the AMI. Despite my experience, my resulting assessment of what constitutes "Montessori practices" has, of course, all the limitations of an individual view.

MONTESSORI AS A SYSTEM

By the time Montessori arrived on the scene, Europe had acknowledged many innovators in education—and had survived them all relatively intact. Among her pedagogical predecessors were the philosophers Locke and Rousseau; the educators Pestalozzi, Herbart, and Froebel; and the doctor-therapists Itard and Seguin. But Montessori's visits to the schools of western Europe in the early 1900s found the actual conditions relatively unchanged over the past two hundred years: enforced immobility, inadequate light and ventilation, rote methodology—to Montessori, these conditions added up to a form of slavery. "The children, like butterflies mounted on pins, are fastened each to his place, the desk, spreading the useless wings of barren and meaningless knowledge" (1964, p. 14).

not muched changed then. scary [handwritten marginal note]

Was Montessori's approach different from what came before? Its unique synthesis of previous ideas has survived in more than eighty countries after almost ninety years and two world wars. As Kramer (1976) puts it, many of Montessori's ideas have become "part of our common language of discourse about the subject of educating the young" (p. 373). Kramer's list of Montessori innovations now accepted as standards for effective learning includes our recognition of the critical importance early childhood has for individual potential, furniture sized to the children who use it, and the idea of individualized instruction based on child needs. For those who know it well, Montessori is a hallmark of excellence in education—and yet that is something of a paradox. As a physician and biologist, Montessori's first concern was the quality of a child's life; a child's *learning* was more a by-product than a goal, though her goals went far beyond the immediate, to nothing less than world reconstruction.

What is Montessori? A person, but also a social movement, a philosophy, a theory of development, a curriculum model, and a set of methodological strategies. Montessori called her approach either a "method" or a "system" of education. In fact, *system* seems an appropriate term, for it includes all facets of a dynamic whole; and when the parts of the Montessori system are working well, the whole becomes more than their sum—a *synergy*.

Taken together, Montessori's books constitute the most extensive description of an educational system produced by a single person. A view of the whole requires us to sort through a forty-year span of ideas clothed in yesterday's language and to identify the basic elements of an educational process of philosophy by a deduction—for most people a task that lacks appeal. And thus truly comprehensive statements of the Montessori system are rare.

Montessori teacher education has addressed the problem by representing the system as "the Montessori triangle" (See Figure 2–1). The image helps us to examine the dynamics of relationship among three basic components: child, environment, and adult (Standing, 1984, p. 266). We'll begin with the concept of "the child."

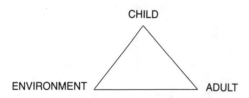

CHILD

ENVIRONMENT   ADULT

Figure 2–1   Montessori Triangle.

THE CHILD

HISTORY

As more than one scholar has pointed out, through most of history there has been no awareness of the particular nature that distinguishes the child from the adult (Ausubel, 1958; Ariès, 1962; DeMause, 1974; Crain, 1980). Not until the 5th century A.D. did people begin to conceive of the child as having a soul. For the next thousand years, most people believed children came into the world "preformed" as miniature adults. Moralists of the sixteenth century described the child as impressionable—as wax, plaster, or clay to be molded (or, more likely, beaten) into shape. Divided on whether goodness or evil, innocence or depravity were innate, they nonetheless agreed on the vital importance of education. Even Locke's doctrine of the *tabula rasa,* though insistent on the neutrality of the newborn's moral and intellectual character, reflected the "pliability" concept of his time. In the eighteenth century, Rousseau provided the first truly positive and developmentalist statement that children are different from adults, with their own modes of feeling and thinking. Pestalozzi and Froebel added a dimension of spirituality with their metaphors of the child like a plant unfolding as it grows.

Throughout this history, however, the child was regarded as a possession of the parents—a chattel, and therefore an object. This view still holds, although increasing numbers of children taken away from abusive or neglectful parents may indicate a movement toward children's rights of self-ownership.

I belabor the history of the concept of the child because I believe, with Elkind, that it has a central influence on how we educate children. He writes:

In addition to a set of values and a theory of instruction, every philosophy of education presupposes a particular image of the child which dominates the other components . . . Calvinistic theology postulated that the child was imbued with original sin, [and] the corresponding educational values and teaching practices were oriented accordingly . . . aimed at developing self-control and discipline with the use of fear, threat, and punishment as motivational aids. Centuries later, when Freud described childhood as the period of neurotic and psychotic formations, a different educational philosophy arose . . . aimed at freeing the child from inhibitions and repressions, and the educational mode was permissiveness and freedom from constraint. (1974, p. 106)

Our contemporary culture seems to hold a dichotomous view of the child. Sputnik punctured our confidence that the balloon of "American know-how" would automatically and forever rise above the rest, awakened us to the possibility that our schools were failing, and made us ripe for a new hope we found in the potential of the young child. The Headstart experiment held the seeds of today's dual image. On one hand we have the damaged child: culturally deprived, handicapped, and most recently, physically or sexually abused. Yet we also think that with the right environment we can produce "the better baby," superkid, or as White and Montessori would call it, the "competent child."

Montessori's written discussions of the child occur in two contexts: one general, describing the child's basic nature and needs, and the other focusing on the child's response to the educative environment.

CHILD'S NATURE AND NEEDS

Writings

It is possible to identify a "Montessori theory of development" with at least four basic principles regarding the child's nature and needs:

1 Development is hierarchical and unfolds in a series of stages.

2 The child is different from the adult—in purpose, pace and rhythm, mentality, and needs.

3 The mechanism of development is both genetic and constructive; the child is innately motivated to fulfill both physical and psychic potentialities through activity and interaction with the environment.

4 The child in the formative stage has special characteristics.

Hierarchy of Development. Montessori's central image endows the child with an innate drive for competence and the ultimate in creativity: the child creates the adult he or she will become. Like Pestalozzi and Froebel, she speaks of the child unfolding according to natural laws of development, but her reference is to a biological process.

"Development," Montessori tells us, "is a series of rebirths. There comes a time when one psychic personality ends, and another begins" (1967, p. 19). She speaks of four periods or planes of development: birth to age 6, the period of formation for both character and intelligence; from 6 to 12, the acquisition of the culture; 12 to 18, the acquisition of independence through physical and psychic transformations; and 18 to 24, maturity through practical work and experience.

For Montessori the most important period of life is the first one: "For that is the time when our intelligence itself, our greatest implement, is being formed [together with] the full totality of our psychic powers" (1967, p. 27). At the age of 3 an educational setting becomes appropriate: "Consciousness shines forth in all its fullness and glory . . . [With its advent] we have unity of the personality, and therefore the power to remember" (1967, p. 166).

Movement is basic to Montessori's sequence of development. She tells us that behind all a child's activities is a reason or motive, that movements are not due to chance, that because a child develops through personal effort and engagement, movement is an essential factor in intellectual growth.

> The child who does not do, does not know how to do. (1964, p. 97)

> Through movement we come in contact with external reality. . . . Physical activity connects the spirit with the world. (1966, pp. 85, 102, 118)

> The starting point of mobility is not motor, but mental. [Yet] movement has great importance in mental development itself, provided that the action . . . *is connected with the mental activity going on* . . . It is not enough that the body should grow in actual size; the most intimate functions of the motor and nervous systems must also be established: the motor functions to secure balance and coordinate the movements; and the sensory functions through which . . . [the child] lays the foundations of intelligence by a continual exercise of observation, comparison, and judgment. . . . To give them their right place, movements must be coordinated with the center—with the brain. Not only are thought and action two parts of the same occurrence, but it is through movement that the higher life expresses itself . . . to serve the whole person and one's life in relation to the outside world. (1967, pp. 71, 142)

Differences. The adult's work, Montessori tells us, is to build up a transcendent environment, whereas the child's purpose is to produce an adult (1970, pp. 233–36). An adult is motivated by thought, but the child has "a driving force that compels him to construct a unity between thought and action" (p. 158), with the result that he grows by working (p. 241). Adult irritation and attempts to speed up the child's slower pace and rhythm can disrupt development (1964, p. 358; 1966, p. 109).

The small child is naive, credulous, uncomprehending of adult notions of morality (1965b, p. 259). Lack of knowledge and experience render the child an "asocial being . . . prey to impulses and inhibitions," foreign to organized adult society (1970, p. 236; 1965b, p. 173).

What a child needs is freedom to move and do, to follow biological rhythms (1966, p. 92), to learn by handling his or her own "real possessions" (1965b, p. 264; 1966, pp. 102–3). The child also needs "rest and a peaceful sameness" (1970, p. 127), an orderly and consistent environment with reasonable limits to keep the child safe.

> To "let the child do as he likes," when he has not yet developed any powers of control, is to betray the idea of freedom. (1967, p. 205)

> [Order] is like the land upon which animals walk or the water in which fish swim. In the first year [the child] derives [his] principles of orientation from [his] environment [and] needs precise and determined guides. (1966, p. 66)

Through participating in our lives, doing and being shown how to do, the child's needs for both social connection and feelings of success can be fulfilled. But for Montessori, the ultimate need which the child strives to meet directly and energetically is independence: "Natural development can be defined as the gaining of successive levels of independence . . . No one can be free without [it]" (1964, p. 95).

When basic needs are not met, when there is, in Montessori's words, "insufficient nourishment for the life of the mind," the child's energies become divided and the personality fails to organize itself, giving rise to defective and deviated growth.

> An adult resigns himself to his lot; a child creates an illusion. (1965b, p. 257)

> A child's tantrums and rebellions are nothing more than aspects of a vital conflict between his creative impulses and his love for an adult who fails to understand his needs . . . With the appearance of psychic deviations individuals lose the sensibilities which would protect them and assure their state of health . . . The instinct for self-preservation, the vital interior force is weakened and disappears. (1966, pp. 127, 218)

> *We serve the future by protecting the present.* The more fully the needs of one period are met, the greater will be the success of the next. (1967, p. 195)

The *mechanism of development* is both genetic and constructive. Nature and nurture interact in the child's process of fulfilling potential.

> The child constructs the mind step by step till it becomes possessed of memory, the power to understand, the ability to think . . . [he] creates his own "mental muscles," using for this what he finds in the world about him. (1967, p. 26–27)

> It would not be possible to conceive liberty of development, if by its very nature the child were not capable of spontaneous organic [growth], if the

tendency to develop his energies . . . the means necessary to a harmonious innate development, did not already exist. (1965b, p. 69)

Environment is undoubtedly a secondary factor in the phenomena of life; it can modify in that it can help or hinder, but it can never create . . . [and it] acts more strongly upon the individual life the less fixed and strong this individual life may be. (1964, pp. 105, 106)

Special characteristics in the formative stage. Montessori described three special powers of the child in the period of formation—the absorbent mind, the spiritual embryo, and the sensitive periods.

The absorbent mind is the child's great capacity for learning by observation, taking in and identifying with many images of things, actions, and relationships: "[The child] absorbs knowledge directly into his psychic life. . . . Impressions do not merely enter his mind; they form it. They incarnate themselves in him. . . . We have called this type of mentality, *The Absorbent Mind* (1967, p. 25).

As a physician, Montessori was familiar with the biological concept of *critical periods,* defined by Tanner (1970) as "certain stages of limited duration during which a particular influence, from another area of the developing organism or from the environment, evokes a particular response . . . [They are] frequently times of particular vulnerability of the organism" (p. 79). Montessori extended this concept, which was usually applied only to human fetal development, to include the whole of early childhood: "spiritual embryo" refers to a postnatal sensitivity to environmental influences on psychic and psychological development, which powers the uniquely human ability to create a behavior.

The newborn child should be seen as a 'spiritual embryo'—a spirit enclosed in flesh in order to come into the world. (1970, p. 29)

Just as a physical embryo needs its mother's womb in which to grow, so the spiritual embryo needs to be protected by an external environment that is warm with love and rich in nourishment, where everything is disposed to welcome, and nothing to harm it. (1966, p. 38)

Montessori referred to "sensitive" (rather than "critical") periods, characterized by "transient instincts that furnish impulses toward certain kinds of activity and enable the child to choose from his complex environment what is suitable and necessary for his growth" (1966, pp. 46–51). Compared to a ray of light that focuses the attention, this "sensitivity . . . leads its possessor to perform a certain series of actions" often enough for "the construction of a psychic organ" (1967, p. 51). If a child is unable to act according to its directives, "the opportunity for a natural conquest is lost . . . for good" (1966, p. 46); never again will the child be able to master the particular task as easily. Sensitive periods identified by Montessori include those for language, movement, and refinement of the senses (throughout the preschool period); for order (age 2–4); social skills (age 2¹/₂–6); and writing (age 3¹/₂–4¹/₂).

Practices

How is this developmental theory reflected today in Montessori practices? All Montessori teacher courses devote time to her philosophy and theory. In AMS courses, those I know best, approximately one third of the academic preparation is aimed at helping prospective teachers develop their concept of the child. This content must be at least 100 clock hours (about 7 credits) (Accreditation Council for Childhood Education Specialist Schools [ACCESS], 1989)—more than twice the time typically required of traditional teachers.

In presenting the evolution of her own ideas and intuitions, Montessori discussed other theories (notably those of Itard and Seguin) in a limited way. After all, at the beginning of her career as an educator, there was no field called "child development." Hall had initiated the American child study movement, and such pioneers as Freud and Watson were beginning to build their theories; but the ideas that dominate the field today had not yet been expressed. Montessori's work preceded them; in fact, Piaget made his first formal observations in a Montessori school, and Erikson's only formal educational credential was a Montessori teaching certificate. AMS students of today examine Montessori in the context of contemporary theories, making comparisons and considering the ways in which they support, contradict, or go beyond Montessori; in addition to an outlook congruent with her ideas, the area is enriched and informed by what has happened since.

In Montessori schools, I see teachers who tend to be "students of the child," manifesting concern for the child's nature and needs in both verbal and written communications; for example, almost every school brochure tries to convey a concept of what children are like as a centrally important idea in the Montessori system.

Montessorians still accept the founder's notion that there are certain universals in the nature of childhood. Among those with new, empirical support are (1) the idea of the child's state of initial dependence and long period of postnatal development, (2) the bases and timetable for language acquisition, (3) a sequence of stages in intellectual development and the importance of child-environment interaction, (4) the existence in common of basic emotions, and (5) the importance of educational networks (Loeffler, 1980). We still use Montessori's terms for her basic concepts, although some educators find that using these terms limits their ability to communicate with other educators and so they translate them into more contemporary educational jargon.

CHILD'S RESPONSE TO THE PREPARED ENVIRONMENT

Writings

Child's Process. Montessori wrote that when children first enter the "prepared environment," a certain initial disorder is characteristic (1965b, p. 87). But she postulates a hidden and higher nature in the child that emerges by a process of transformation through work.

> There exist . . . two psychic states in the child: one that is natural and creative, therefore normal and superior, and one that is forced and inferior. (1970, p. 152)

> The Montessori teacher is constantly looking for a child who is not yet there. . . . [she] must have a kind of faith that *the child will reveal himself through work.* (1967, p. 276)

The first step, and the "normal beginning of the inner life of children," is "the polarization of attention," by which Montessori seems to mean that the child's attention organizes to focus on an interesting task. This "mental grasp of the idea," if followed by the kind of repetition that "engages the child's whole personality," refines the powers of observation and leads the child sooner or later to self-correction and observable behavior change (1965a, p. 75).

Montessori likens this process to "the phenomena of a higher consciousness, such as those of conversion" (1965b, pp. 68–69). The result is "a psychic cure, a return to what is normal. Actually the normal child is . . . precociously intelligent, has learned to overcome himself and to live in peace, and prefers a disciplined task to futile idleness" (1966, p. 180). "Normalization" implies the organism's condition of balance or harmony with its environment.

> No sooner has he found his work than his defects disappear. (1967, p. 202)

Experience has shown that normalization causes the disappearance of many childish traits, not only those which are considered to be defects but also others which are generally thought to be virtues. Among the traits that disappear are not only untidiness, disobedience, sloth, greed, egoism, quarrelsomeness, and instability, but also the so-called "creative imagination," delight in stories, attachment to individuals, play, submissiveness, and so forth. They also include traits which have been scientifically studied and identified with childhood, such as imitation, curiosity, inconstancy, and wavering attention. The disappearance of these childish characteristics shows that the true nature of a child has hitherto not been understood. (1966, p. 188)

Cycles of Activity. This evolution of order and self-discipline in the child was associated with a pattern of typical activity, first in individuals and then in the whole class (1965b, pp. 67–124). The beginning of every school day in the first casas was devoted to individual work. Once concentration began to develop, in the first hour of the day the child was observed to move through tasks he found easy or slightly challenging. Then came a brief period of unrest: "He ceases working, walks about the room, and appears less calm; to a superficial observer he would seem to show signs of fatigue" (1965b, p. 97). But the cycle is not yet complete; as if in search of the maximum satisfaction for his interest, the child next chooses a difficult task, becomes completely absorbed in it (his "great work" of the day), and perseveres until it is finished. Afterward, the child appears "rested, satisfied, and uplifted . . . contemplates his handiwork . . . then approaches the teacher [to share it]" (p. 97) Montessori warns against interruption of the peculiar period of unrest, which she called "false fatigue":

> If . . . an inexperienced teacher interprets the phenomenon of suspension or preparation for the culminating work as disorder and intervenes, calling the children to her, making them rest, etc., their restlessness persists, and the subsequent work is not undertaken. The children do not become calm; they remain in an abnormal state . . . Interrupted in their cycle, they lose all the characteristics connected with *an internal process regularly and completely carried out.* (p. 99)

The Explosion into Writing. When the normalized children and their mothers pleaded for instruction in reading and writing, Montessori (1964, pp. 267–68) overcame her prejudice against allowing it before the age of six—with surprising results. Prepared by materials she adapted from Seguin, many of the four- and five-year-olds suddenly "exploded into writing," discovering they could translate spoken language into the alphabetic signs they had learned to associate with the phonetic sounds. And Montessori reports (p. 302) that reading, at least at a mechanical level, was only a few weeks behind. To avoid such excited disruption, Montessori made the materials permanently available, so that the child was led "more *calmly* to this new power . . . He still has the great joy of the first written word, but . . . no longer the overwhelming surprise, since he sees just such wonderful things happening each day, and knows that sooner or later the same gift will come to all" (p. 290).

The Society of Children. Does "individual work" mean children do not socialize with each other? Montessori's descriptions often give an impression of each child involved in a different task, working alone in silent concentration, yet she also reports children working together (1965a, pp. 39, 64; 1964, p. 192).

By grouping in a three- or four-year age range, Montessori intended to create a more natural, familylike setting in which the children help each other. Her teachers were surprised to discover, even in those so young, a spontaneous need for unity, for "cohesion in the social unit" (1967, p. 232–33). The classroom became a "society of children," whose members were caring and supportive of each other and cordial to visitors. The children learned much by watching (1965a, p. 75), and sometimes it was another child, rather than the teacher, who presented the material. The special communication and harmony between peers made these lessons very effective, and the child acting as teacher derived benefits from having to analyze and rearrange knowledge in order to pass it on. Montessori insists:

> In the old type of school, too often, the brighter children became conceited and dominated the others; in our schools the 5-year-old feels himself a protector of the younger one. . . . The class gets to be a group cemented by affection. Finally, the children come to know one another's characters and to have a reciprocal feeling for each other's worth. (1967, pp. 226–27)

Individual Differences. Montessori's theory of development postulated a universal child, and most discussions of individual differences focused on what she referred to as "deviations" in children who had not yet become normalized. Differences of both sex and culture were deemed irrelevant: "There is no sense in talking about differences of procedure for Indian babies, Chinese babies, or European babies; nor for those belonging to different social classes. We can only speak of one method, that which follows the natural unfolding of man . . . Every one of us has to pass through the same phases of growth" (1967, p. 75).

PRACTICES

The Child's Process. Do today's children react to the prepared environment as Montessori described? When a new grouping of children starts the fall term, teachers report a "honeymoon" of about a week, followed by a "testing" period that corresponds more closely to the initial disorder Montessori talked about. Even if many of the children have been in school before, there is still a settling-down phase of about eight weeks, during which the adult expectations are absorbed, familiarity grows, involvement with activity increases, and social relationships stabilize.

Today's Montessorian still observes the "polarization of attention," and some may call it "making the match," a phrase borrowed from Hunt (1964, p. *xxviii*). The opportunity to repeat activities is still a given of the Montessori class, with most activities made available to children throughout the year.

The traditional Montessori educators indicate that normalization is not a steady state, but tends to come and go. Yet Montessori's writings never refer to it as anything but permanent, speaking only of conversion and never of backsliding. Normalization as a recurrent phenomenon is somewhat reminiscent of the "up and down" pattern of developmental plateaus alternating with periods of disequilibrium noted by such observers as Gesell, Piaget, and Spock. This kind of change may be noticed only by someone who sees an individual child regularly, over a long period of time. So it may be appropriate to remind ourselves that Montessori never had that kind of experience with normal children; after the orthophrenic school, she never lived with a class all day long, day after day.

Despite her somewhat brash description of the normalized child, Montessori seems to be talking about the quiet self-assurance of one who accepts his or her own competence. We certainly don't see children lose their capacities for imagination, attachment, play, and curiosity. Most teachers would agree that almost all children do change with their experience in a Montessori setting, but rather than a dramatic, rapid "conversion," change is more visible in retrospect; attention focuses with increasing regularity and intensity, and behavior seems to become more organized. The "sins" of childhood don't completely disappear; the children still seem fully human, capable of the same foibles as before, but they are more aware, and they grow in both social and mental competence.

What Montessori observed was a "natural learning cycle" (see Figure 2–2). Rambusch (1988) outlines it in five steps:

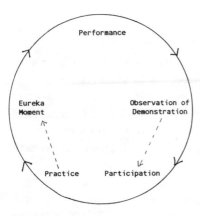

Figure 2–2 Natural Learning Cycle

1 Observation of demonstrations: on more than one occasion, the child watches as a trusted model (such as a family member) performs a task the child is interested in mastering (such as making peanut butter sandwiches).

2 Participation: the child interacts in the model's performance of the task, which becomes a collaborative effort suitable to the child's level of competence.

3 Role-playing practice: in self-regulated repetition, the child assumes responsibility for the action, learns from trial and error, and moves toward refinement.

4 Eureka moment ("Aha!"): the child achieves a sense of accomplishment, an "I know how to do this" feeling.

5 Performance: the child revels in mastery, delights in demonstrating the newly acquired skill for all comers, and begins to use it in a context of social purpose. (pp. 9–13)

The natural learning cycle is observable in almost any family with young children and in those school settings that maintain a true spirit of the Montessori system.

Cycles of Activity. The cycles of activity Montessori described can still be seen in both individuals and the group as a whole. The "commotion" of the false fatigue point comes a little over an hour into the individual activity period and disappears by itself if the class is allowed to continue. But if schools cut off or interrupt this time due to crowded playground schedules or group lessons with specialized staff, the same intensity of involvement and concentration does not seem to develop in the children.

Learning. As Montessori predicted, the "explosion into writing" occurs today as a more gradual process. Considering her scientifically oriented treatises on language mechanisms (1964, pp. 310–25; 1967, pp. 108–26) and on embryonic development and cell growth (pp. 34–50), it is perhaps curious that Montessori makes no such attempt to describe learning. She specifies attentional focus as an important starting place, and she sees sensory education as a primary means of stimulating the growth of intelligence by turning the child into a careful observer. Despite the assumptions of some recent Montessori critics (DeVries & Kohlberg, 1987), Montessori never claims that perceptions themselves exist in any place except consciousness or that her didactic sets are "materialized abstractions." In fact, she says it is "the intelligence, with *its* characteristic orderliness and power of discrimination" that "is capable of distinguishing and extracting the dominant characteristics of objects, and it is upon these that it proceeds to build up *its internal structures*" [italics mine] (1965b, p. 210). Searching to the baseline of Montessori's ideas for explanation of what happens in the intellect itself, we find only her statement that activity "*awakens and sets in motion* the central nervous mechanisms" (p. 200). She apparently felt no need to investigate how "sensing" and "doing" are transformed into "knowing" (DeVries & Kohlberg, 1987, p. 286).

Yet Montessori's discussion on the child's internalization of *culture* connects with some recent discoveries about the process of perception. She explains that the child's "mathematical mind" takes in patterns or forms abstract representations ("the basic or summarized part") of his environment (1967, p. 189). Modern research (Pribram, 1979) has shown that perceptions from at least four body systems enter the brain as wave patterns, which are, in effect, mathematical representations of a whole rather than discrete bits of detail. When Montessori wrote, "It is possible to say that there is a mathematical relationship between the beauty of his surroundings and the activity of the child" (1970, p. 96), she may have been more accurate than she knew.

Society of Children. Although the majority of today's Montessori schools still group children in a three-year age range, some are placing their five-year-olds in either a special "kindergarten" or the early elementary program. I think this changes how the system works; the five-year-olds lose valuable opportunities for peer teaching and a special position of social responsibility as the oldest. Teachers vary greatly in both their problem-solving approaches and allowance of autonomy, but the "community spirit" is always visible in a Montessori class where prosocial and egalitarian behaviors are modeled and encouraged.

Individual Differences. Though Montessori expected teachers to adapt their procedures to individuals, her general view of differences seems to oversimplify and negate their importance to learning. Recent studies of the newborn reveal some striking differences in temperament and behavior among ethnic groups, suggesting that we are *not* all born alike regardless of background, and that culture and biology are perhaps inseparable (Freedman, 1979). Though much of the explosion of research on the brain in the past twenty years supports Montessori's view of the young child's experiential, multisensory learning style, it has also contributed to our understanding of how individual differences can relate to learning and influence learning problems (Williams, 1983). Some researchers (McGuinness, 1979) have presented strong evidence of inherent sex differences that affect learning capabilities and interests. These examples have one point in common: the same environment, because it is experienced differently, is *not* the same for all children.

THE ENVIRONMENT

HISTORY

Until Montessori's time, the essential requirements for a school were considered to be a teacher, some children, (in most cases) a curriculum, and a room to contain them. Pestalozzi had developed a model for curriculum organization in a graded sequence beginning with "real" experience. Itard, Seguin, and Froebel designed special objects to stimulate learning through the child's own activity. But it remained for Montessori to conceive of the educational environment as a wall-to-wall totality in which everything—every object, piece of furniture, even the decor itself—was present by deliberate design and preparation.

WRITINGS

In fact, Montessori's notion of environment included indoors, outdoors, and more: not only the physical surroundings, but the "psychical" or psychological conditions of the place.

Facilities. The first Montessori school, a ground-floor tenement room, was christened by a friend "Casa dei Bambini" or "Children's House" and described as "like a bit of the house itself set apart by a mother's hand for the use and happiness of the children" (Montessori, 1964, pp. 43, 49). Montessori soon expanded the description to "a real house . . . a set of rooms with a garden of which the children are the masters." A central working room was surrounded by smaller bathroom, parlor, gymnasium, and so on, "according to the means and opportunities of the place" (1965a, pp. 37–38). "Larger than the customary classrooms," the working room required more space for the little tables and chairs, the small rugs on which children spread their work, and freedom of movement around the furniture (p. 40; 1965b, p. 143). An ample playground with room for a garden, she says, is not an original idea; what's new is her use of this space, which should adjoin the schoolroom "so the children may be free to go and come as they like, throughout the entire day" (1964, p. 80).

Furnishings are always described as child-size, lightweight, washable, and varied; there are tables, chairs, cupboards for "the didactic material [common property of all the children]," little armchairs, and a chest with a drawer for each child "to put things belonging to him" (1965a, p. 38). The walls are hung with low blackboards and pictures of "simple scenes in which children would naturally be interested" (1964, p. 82). Like a home, the classroom should be "a place of comfort and peace, with full and varied interests. The essential charm . . . is its cleanliness and order, with every-thing in its place, dusted, bright and cheerful" (1967, p. 277).

> But what is essential is that it should be "artistically beautiful" . . . not beauty produced by superfluity or luxury, but by grace and harmony of line and color . . . absolute simplicity. . . . The spiritual school puts no limits to the beauty of its environment, save economical limits. No ornament can distract a child really absorbed in his task; on the contrary, beauty both promotes concentra-tion of thought and offers refreshment to the tired spirit. (1965b, pp. 143–44)

Educational Materials. Montessori does not refer to the content of her educational program as a curriculum, but as a "method." Each didactic material is intended to isolate and embody a motor skill, perceptual quality, or concept. The goal was to attract the child, enable the polarization of at-tention, then motivate spontaneous, self-directed exercise (1965b, p. 154). Montessori makes it clear that not just any materials will do; these external stimuli must be determined in quality and quantity by experimen-tal research, to ensure "the means really necessary for psychical develop-ment" (1964, p. 72).

> In order to expand, the child, left at liberty to exercise his activities, ought to find in his surroundings something *organized* in direct relation to his internal organization which is developing itself by natural laws. (p. 70)

> To make the process one of self-education, it is not enough that the stimulus should call forth activity, it must also direct it. (1965b, p. 74)

This "direction" enabling auto-education was assisted by a design characteristic Montessori called "control of error"—a factor that leads the child to notice and correct himself. These self-correction strategies take several, increasingly abstract forms in the Montessori materials: mechanical (in the design of the material itself), visual (in the eye of the user), and comparative (in a model).

The "Montessori curriculum," then, consists of an array of materials from which the child chooses according to internal directives. The freedom to work is made possible only by thorough organization of the environment and materials, which Montessori (1967, p. 244) approached in two ways: with basic areas that relate traditional content to aspects of development; and, within each area, sequences reflecting levels of difficulty.

Montessori soon compiled her original seven areas into three: motor education, sensory education, and preparation for writing and arithmetic (1965a, p. 50).

Care and management of self and environment were the principal means of muscular education—the "practical life" (PL) area—which also included rhythmic movements with locomotor patterns, gymnastics on innovative outdoor equipment, gardening, and manual work with clay. PL materials are the least specified but can employ any activity typical in the home life of the child's culture, ranging from how to manage fasteners on one's clothing to more complex tasks like cooking or washing dishes. The activities provide opportunities for purposeful activity, concentration, coordination, awareness of order and sequence, independence, successful experience, and a sense of personal and social responsibility. Because materials and tasks look familiar, the area is a "security bridge" from home to school.

Eleven of Montessori's sets of didactic materials (1965a, pp. 50–52) promoted sensory education by isolating specific attributes of objects and a particular sense mode. In addition to the shapes, sizes, and colors important to visual perception, these materials address smell, taste, hearing, and the tactile senses. Basic strategies involve matching and sorting (recognition of identities), naming attributes (recognition of contrasts), and grading (discrimination between objects that are very similar). The purpose of the exercises, Montessori insists, is not to teach a specific content or technique, but rather to "lay the foundations of intelligence by a continual exercise of observation, comparison, and judgment" (p. 34).

With the eight "preparation" materials, Montessori's original intent for language went no further than "preparing the hand" for writing and familiarizing children with the graphic and phonetic alphabets (in Italian, a one-to-one correspondence). She explains that through the sensorial material the child has already experienced mathematical ideas of quantity, identity, and difference (pp. 51, 164).

In determining which materials became part of her method, Montessori claimed selection by trial in schools all over the world: "We may truly say these things have been chosen by the children" (1967, p. 223). Among the changes she noted were the removal of duplicate sets of equipment (1964, p. 201; 1967, p. 223) and the use made of toys. The Children's Houses had "a great many toys," Montessori (p. 297) says, although to her surprise, even when "shown how to play" with them the children did not care to do so, preferring to go "off on their own" (1966, p. 148). The toys stayed, but they were employed primarily as objects to be labelled in Montessori's writing games.

PRACTICES

Facilities. Although teacher education traditions seem in basic harmony with Montessori's vision of the "Children's House," real schools have their problems in pursuing this ideal: building from scratch or modifying to meet state requirements is expensive; leased facilities may appear threadbare or have to be shared. Yet this doesn't mean the concept is a myth. Whatever its physical reality, the "house for children" concept is powerful and consistent; it communicates the spirit of Montessori as a basic position of deep respect for the child.

Educational Materials. Determining the congruence of Montessori's writings with the curriculum and materials of contemporary schools and teacher education is a more complicated proposition. Practice seems broader in some respects, but more narrow in others. For example, most teacher education programs now divide the curriculum into five basic areas, including separate math and cultural subjects (i.e., fine arts, science, and social studies). Materials not discussed in Montessori's writings but included in her training courses are now part of the standard classroom (Kocher, 1973), and most modern courses have done considerable work in expanding the curriculum through additions and extensions. The nurture of creativity requires inclusion of so-called plastic materials to be reconfigured by the child (Barron, 1969; Seefeldt, 1976; Edwards, 1979). Information and materials available today help us to understand the young child's development in art (Lowenfeld, 1947; Kellogg & O'Dell, 1967), design appropriate activities (Barnett, 1981; Turner, 1982), and make use of the connections between art and language (Ashton-Warner, 1963; Lee &

Allen, 1963; Moore & Moore, 1978). Revaluing art, fantasy play, and fairy tales (Bettelheim, 1976), I conclude with Kramer (1976) that these things are part of a good Montessori program:

> Critics accused Montessori of emphasizing the motoric and the realistic at the expense of the creative imagination and dramatic play, [but] what they failed to see was that she had worked out her system in a culture in which . . . less was expected of the school. [Its] function was "instruction" . . . "pedagogy," a matter of intellectual training as distinct from . . . upbringing in general, including what is transmitted outside of school by family, community, and society at large. School was expected to teach one all there was to know about how to read but not necessarily all there was to know about how to live. . . . The games, singing, dancing, and drawing which critics found lacking in her system . . . existed in her schools; she did not dwell on them in her lectures because she couldn't conceive of a system of education without them. (pp. 253, 261)

Now for a list of concerns about things that lack congruence. If we take her writings at face value, Montessori herself had no particular prejudice against play with toys; she simply found the children of her time to be more interested in her educational material (or perhaps subtly influenced by the values of the adults in the school). Yet it may be overlooked that today's children may spend so many hours in day care that there is no time left for play after they get home. The Practical Life materials require some money and a lot of effort to keep clean, attractive, and complete, but under-equipped classrooms deprive children of many opportunities for motor competence. Do all Montessori practitioners allow children to choose freely from the array of materials? I have observed materials arranged on the shelf without much thought for level of difficulty. I've also observed classrooms in which the children's choices were limited to the teacher's ideas of what should come next! If children are allowed to work with materials only in an "approved" sequence, the result is a serious misapplication of Montessori's original intent.

One last issue relates to the balance of activities in the total program of both schools and teacher education. Rambusch (1978) has suggested that Montessori's attempts to standardize her message so it could be "transmitted around the world with minimal distortion" resulted in teacher preparation focused on the didactic material rather than the child (p. 13–14). Two-thirds of the required time in teacher education courses is called out as curriculum, but curriculum encompasses more than just materials, and the abilities to be developed go beyond the "ritualized uses of equipment" deplored by Rambusch. Only four of the thirty-one separate competencies for student teachers require skills with specific materials; the rest relate to broader areas of knowledge, like developmental continuum, environmental design, teaching strategies, assessment, leadership, and parental involvement (ACCESS, 1989, pp. 11–12). But perhaps more than any other component, the materials make Montessori's system *replicable*. And they do work! Using these models, children's capabilities expand and teachers learn to design effective activities for children. Montessori preparation provides a set of guiding principles that enables teachers to function as "self-starters" who are not dependent on a textbook.

Is today's Montessori preprimary in danger of overemphasizing intellectual activities? It does offer access to them, and in a self-pacing way. For parents, the enduring appeal of a Montessori school is probably its reputation for fostering competence in the child—not a negative thing to want, unless it leads to inappropriate expectations and pressures. If schools and teachers are effective in educating parents about their child's real needs, parents may not demand 99th-percentile test scores. (And maybe they will!) Only one of the seven daily hours of the first Casa was devoted to "intellectual exercises"; equal time went to practical life, outdoor periods for free and directed games, clay work, and "collective gymnastics and songs." Montessori (1964) wrote: "The Children's House is a garden of child culture, and we most certainly do not keep the children for so many hours in school with the idea of making students of them!" (p. 121).

The organization of the Montessori classroom is a good example of what Elkind (1987, p. 143) has called "permeable" curriculum—that is, it makes learning a matter of "doing things" rather than of "studying a subject." For young children, who see no boundaries between subjects or between types of knowledge, the Montessori environment can provide just what they need: a social context; an array of purposeful, hands-on activities; the right to choose what appeals to them most; and the freedom to pace themselves.

THE ADULT

Although the most important adults in a child's life are undoubtedly the parents, time and topic limit this section to the classroom adult: the teacher.

HISTORY

The role of today's teacher contains a number of strands dating from ancient times: the model of morality, agent of state or society, seeker of truth, and reservoir of knowledge—in short, the "star" of the classroom. More recent additions cast the teacher *in loco parentis* (Almy, 1975; Katz, 1970) and as a "helping instrument" (Combs et al., 1974).

WRITINGS

Role of the Directress. Montessori saw the teacher as "a *director* of the spontaneous work of the children" (1964, p. 370). Significantly different from other approaches, this concept of the teacher as directress is analogous to the director's role in theater, which entails setting the stage, observing the actors in the context of their dramatic development, providing feedback, and, if necessary, guiding them toward achievement of the desired effects. The performance finds the director in the wings, rather than center stage. Montessori says the teacher is not a *passive* force, but must "*guide* the child without letting him feel her presence too much . . . always ready to supply the desired help, but . . . never the obstacle between the child and his experience (1965a, p. 131).

Through this role, Montessori links the two vital conditions of her system: the organization of work and liberty for children limited only by the collective interest (1964, p. 87). The teacher formulates both the physical and psychological environments to facilitate children's independence of action, thus freeing them to learn through their own efforts (Rambusch, 1965, p. 24).

Montessori describes three stages of development in the teacher's classroom functioning. At first the teacher is the keeper of environment, who warms, enlivens, invites, and observes. In the second stage the teacher may entertain the children with stories and rhymes, games and singing; every action becomes a call and invitation. When finally the children begin to take an interest in something, the teacher becomes the observer and protector of concentration, helping them to act and think for themselves (Montessori, 1967, pp. 276–80). Before concentration occurs, there is no need to fear that the teacher will interrupt some psychic process, because these processes have not yet begun. The teacher refrains from interfering when a child is absorbed in work, to avoid interrupting the cycle or preventing its free expansion, but the right technique at first is just the opposite—to break the flow of disturbing activity.

Instructional strategies. The instructional strategies of the directress are compatible with the child's natural learning cycle and experiential, multisensory mode of operation. To familiarize children with the contents of the room, the teacher gives demonstrations that invite participation. Montessori explains:

> The number of such lessons must be rather high, for the child tends to ignore almost all the things that surround him, and he cannot guess their uses himself. (1970, p. 136)

> The instruction . . . should be so directed as to *lessen his expenditure* of poorly directed effort, converting it instead into the enjoyment of conquest made easy and infinitely broadened. (1964, pp. 108, 237)

> The instructions of the teacher consist merely in a hint, a touch—enough to give a start to the child. The rest develops of itself. (1965a, pp. 58, 75)

> The child, once launched on his attempts, often improves on the examples set him. (1967, p. 159)

> The teacher moves quietly about, goes to any child who calls her, supervising operations in such a way that anyone who needs her finds her at his elbow, and whoever does not need her is not reminded of her existence . . . Such is our duty toward the child: to give a ray of light and to go on our way. (1964, pp. 346, 115)

Montessori's verbal strategies required brevity, simplicity, and objectivity—to avoid confusing the child with too much or irrelevant information (1964, p. 108). Her model for teaching nomenclature was adapted from Seguin's "three-period lesson"; it presents two stimuli at once on the theory that the effort to discriminate between them will assist the memory. If the lesson is well prepared, but the child makes an error, it is simply a sign that he or she does not yet understand and further exercise is encouraged. Montessori reminds us that the *real* sense education *precedes* the naming lesson: refined differential perception is acquired only through auto-education (pp. 177–78).

Leadership. Collective order, Montessori maintained, could be established only after individual self-discipline developed through the child's work, revealing itself in respect for the work of others and consideration for their rights (p. 94; 1965b, p. 93). At that point the teacher could instruct the child in how to be still by introducing the "silence game," an exercise that combined listening and "centering." But not all children "normalized" at the same time, and Montessori addresses deviations of two types, labeled as fugues (flights from reality) and barriers (prolonged defenses) (1966, pp. 188–216). Also discussed are pampered children, overattachment and possessiveness, desire for power, inferiority complex, fear, lies, and repercussions on physical health.

When the teacher encountered deviant behavior, the first step was to interrupt the disorder. If negative behavior persisted, the teacher was advised to remove the child from the situation—by taking the child on a walk in the garden with the assistant, or by using a treatment Montessori called "isolation," in which the child was given favorite games or toys, but restricted to a table from which he or she could observe the activities of the other children. This was done kindly and with special care, as if the child were ill or very little; according to Montessori, the child was calmed, eventually saw advantages to being part of the group, and wished "to go back and do as the others did" (1964, pp. 103–4).

Preparation. "My method is *observation,*" Montessori once stated in discussing preparation of the teacher, although she seems to offer no techniques for learning how to observe save repeated exposure. "You alone can prepare yourselves to observe, as the children must develop themselves by their own experience," she told one training course (Rambusch, 1965, p. 14). Clearly, however, a necessary first step is observation and examination of the self, to find what

> prevents us from seeing the child as he is . . . [and impedes our] relations with children . . . We have need of a special kind of instruction. We must see ourselves as another sees us . . . be initiated, be taught and . . . willing to accept guidance if we wish to become effective teachers. . . . *First remove the beam from your own eye and then you will see clearly how to remove the speck from the eye of a child.* (1966, pp. 15–19, 183)

> Other men of science . . . must always remain extraneous to the object of their study . . . but the object of the [teacher] is humankind itself; the psychical manifestations of children evoke something more than interest in the phenomenon; we obtain from them the revelation of ourselves. (1965b, pp. 130–34)

If the neutrality Montessori advocates with her talk of scientific observation and respect for the child leaves the impression that the teacher is rather a cold fish, let me stress that she has a great deal to say about love. At first, the child needs approval from the teacher; when the child "feels sure of himself, [he] will no longer seek [it] after every step" (1967, p. 274). Somewhat like the materials, teachers are psychic objects, "the objects of his love, the objects by means of which he is organizing his life . . . [We must be] passive in abnegation, yet active as wellsprings of affection" (1965b, p. 333).

The directress must master both observation and technique because they are necessary foundations for intervention, the personal art of the educator; only clear ideas of guiding the child and of the individual exercise permit the teacher to apply the method. But the teacher's preparation should be directed toward the spirit, rather than the mechanism: "We wish to awaken in the mind and heart of the educator an *interest in natural phenomena* to such an extent that, loving nature, he shall understand the anxious and expectant attitude of one who has prepared an experiment and who awaits a revelation from it" (1964, p. 9).

PRACTICES

Role of the Directress. The Montessori teacher of today faces a dilemma: the choice between replicating a model and moving children through a curriculum on the one hand, or creating a responsive environment on the other (Turner, 1980). At some point we have to decide: is Montessori a curriculum or an experiment? This conflict is, of course, a continuum. But the teacher's view of his or her role, the variety and use of material allowed, the kind of record-keeping and assessment developed, and the dozens of daily decisions about intervention—all are determined by the teacher's position on that continuum. My own research on Montessori teachers (Turner, 1978) indicates that attitude, rather than knowledge, is the more important contributor to classroom success. Teacher performance rated most highly by evaluators is associated with a constellation of attributes that includes positive self-concept, self-confidence, openness, tolerance, and sensitivity to others. These dimensions were also found to be predictive of classroom performance.

The learning process of the modern Montessori teacher parallels Montessori's three stages of functioning, but I see it as repeating again and again, in complement to the child's cycle of natural learning (see Fig. 2–3). The adult process still begins with preparation of the self and includes organizing program goals and criteria, as well as environments. Design of the psychological environment includes identifying rules, procedures, schedules, and necessary information and communicating clear expectations to other participating adults. The next step is demonstrating to the child how to operate the environments, through both instruction

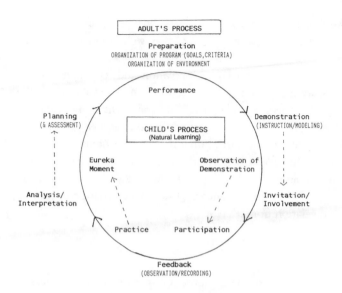

Figure 2–3   The Teaching-Learning Cycle

and modeling, which leads immediately to inviting the child to participate in the activity. At this point in the cycle, observation provides feedback; recording is part of this stage, because it can facilitate observation.

Although such analysis and interpretation become automatic in experienced Montessori teachers, they still need organized and reflective attention every week. Assessment and planning—for individual children and the whole class—often result in revision of goals, criteria, or environment, thereby bringing teachers back to the beginning of the cycle, ready to start it anew.

Instructional Strategies. Verbal strategies seem consistent with Montessori's "brevity, simplicity, and objectivity." I find that schools view the individual work period as the heart of the program, that lessons are fairly frequent, and that most teachers are warm, responsive to the child's need for help, nonjudgmental about errors, and flexible about uses of materials. One study by a member of the AMS Teacher Research Network compared different three-period lesson variables and found that, just as Seguin and Montessori said, two stimuli were more effective than one or three in the child's retention of nomenclature (Smythe, 1987).

Leadership. Leadership is the area most people nowdays call "classroom management." (I refuse to do so on philosophical grounds, because for me "management" connotes manipulation.) Perhaps practices in this area are *too* congruent with Montessori's writings, by which I mean that some practical and philosophical issues are not thoroughly explored. For example, students may leave the academic phase of their preparation with the impression that the child enjoys water only for pouring or washing things. They may never suspect that during their student teaching a child may go deaf when reminded to put work away, fall asleep at school, drop ugly pieces of lunch on the floor and then step on them, go potty somewhere other than the toilet, or explore the body (not always his or her own) as if it were one of the didactic materials. And yet how teachers deal with these nitty-gritty matters may have more influence on the quality of classroom life, the psychological environment, and freedom for the child than how they give lessons or develop new materials. Teachers may fail to give every disciplinary intervention one simple test: they walk away—and don't look back! To miss the message in a child's face and behavior is to lose feedback on the effectiveness or implications of one's teaching philosophy. Montessori's strategy for dealing with the disruptive child by kindly restriction apparently worked well for her. But as Rudolf Dreikurs once said, "What happens if the child won't stay in the chair?" Further, should there even be a chair? What outcomes do we really want from discipline? It is healthy for teachers to examine these questions regularly.

   Preparation. In preparing teachers to observe, Montessori teacher education has moved from admonishment to implementation that is often very well developed. At the least, observation must be documented and must involve discussion with the instructor that explores alternative interpretations. At most, sophisticated frameworks for observing and recording are used that include ethnographic techniques and in-depth case studies. The full-term internship required in AMS courses ensures that the student has contact daily with an in-class supervisor who offers feedback and direction—in contrast with Montessori's short, intensive courses that included no on-site experience, supervision, or follow-up.

CONCLUSIONS

In conclusion, this examination of agreement between Montessori's writings and Montessori practices has considered Montessori as a system with three basic but interactive elements: child, environment, and adult. Writings and practices are found to correspond most highly with regard to the child's nature, diminishing as we consider the child's response to the setting, the prepared environment itself, and the role of the adult. It seems clear that some accommodation has occurred, because of cultural and temporal differences; yet if a basic Montessori principle is response to the child, accommodation is inherent in the system itself.

That system survives because it is relatively well defined and replicable. It promotes initiative in the teacher and holistic development of the child, liberty within limits and a workable balance of inputs from both child and adult. Because it represents a unique and original synthesis based on insightful observations of real children in a naturalistic, reality-oriented, and competence-promoting environment, the Montessori system is different from what came before.

Is the Montessori system still viable? To me, that question really means: does it meet the needs of today's children? The 100,000 parents of children in AMS schools seem to think so, because more than 90 percent of those eligible come back the following year (Turner, 1990).

But perhaps another test can be applied. Abraham Maslow (1943, 1971) saw human needs as a hierarchy of basic motivations proceeding from the physiological level through needs for safety, love and belonging, and esteem to the acme of self-actualization. His theory proposes that fulfillment of "lower" (more basic) needs propels the human organism on to the next level. Ultimately, the realization of our potentials, capacities, and talents will depend on whether we satisfy our other, more basic needs. If Maslow's hierarchy is adapted to the needs of the child in an early education setting (as in Fig. 2–4), the progression of needs will develop from movement through order, social connection, and success to independence and autonomy.

A Montessori class values and encourages movement with many age-appropriate activities and freedom to move and do for most of the day. It provides the security of order, structure, and dependability in both its physical and psychological environments. The love and belonging of social connection is facilitated by warmth and respect of the teachers, vertical grouping, communal ownership and responsibility, and positive approaches to problem solving. The Montessori environments are organized to promote competence, choice, personal acknowledgment, and self-discipline, all of which contribute to feelings of success. In the long run, the goal of growing up is to be able to take care of oneself and the environment; the "manageability" of a Montessori setting and its many opportunities for successful coping, personal and social responsibility,

Figure 2–4   Hierarchy of a Child's Needs

development of practical skills, and access to the culture support the child's sense of independence and autonomy.

Yes, Montessori is a viable system for our future. And lest we forget the importance of our children to that future, Montessori reminds us of our debt to that child each of us used to be:

> We fail to comprehend the toil and labors [our child self] endured . . . We can now use the reason which the child begot in us, the will which he trained, the muscles which he animated for us. If we can orientate ourselves in the world, it is because the child has given us the means of doing so. And if we are conscious of ourselves, it is because the child has made this possible. We are rich because we are the heirs of the child who started with nothing and provided us with the foundation of our future life. (1966, p. 73)

REFERENCES

Accreditation Council for Childhood Education Specialist Schools (ACCESS). (1989). Section 4, Curriculum content and emphasis: Guidelines for development and accreditation of specialized teacher education courses. In *Accreditation handbook*. New York: ACCESS.

Almy, M. (1975). *The early childhood educator at work.* New York: McGraw-Hill.

Ariès, P. (1962). *Centuries of childhood: A social history of family life.* (R. Baldick, Trans.). New York: Knopf. (Original work published 1960)

Ashton-Warner, S. (1963). *Teacher.* New York: Simon & Schuster.

Ausubel, D. P. (1958). *Theories and problems in child development.* New York: Grune & Stratton.

Barnett, R. R. (1981). *Let out the sunshine: A Montessori approach to creative activities.* Dubuque, IA: Wm. C. Brown Co.

Barron, F. (1969). *Creative person and creative process.* New York: Holt, Rinehart & Winston.

Bettelheim, B. (1976). *The uses of enchantment: The meaning and importance of fairy tales.* New York: Knopf.

Combs, A. W., Blume, R. A., Newman, A. J., & Wass, H. L. (1974). *A humanistic approach to teacher preparation.* Boston: Allyn & Bacon.

Crain, W. C. (1980). *Theories of child development: Concepts and applications.* Englewood Cliffs, NJ: Prentice-Hall.

DeMause, L. (Ed.) (1974). *The history of childhood.* New York: Harper & Row.

DeVries, R., & Kohlberg, L. (1987). *Programs of early education: The constructivist view.* New York: Longman.

Edwards, B. (1979). *Drawing on the right side of the brain.* Los Angeles: J. P. Tarcher.

Elkind, D. (1987). *Miseducation: Preschoolers at risk.* New York: Knopf.

Freedman, D. G. (1979). Ethnic differences in babies. *Human Nature, 2* (1), 36–43.

Holdaway, D. (1986). The structure of natural learning as a basis for literacy instruction. In M. Sampson (Ed.), *The pursuit of literacy: Early reading and writing.* Dubuque, IA: Kendall, Hunt.

Hunt, J. M. (1964). Introduction. In M. Montessori, *The Montessori method,* xi–xxxix. New York: Schocken.

Katz, L. G. (1970, September). *Teacher-child relationships in day care centers.* Urbana, IL: ERIC Clearinghouse for Early Childhood Education.

Kellogg, R., & O'Dell, S. (1967). *The psychology of children's art.* New York: Random House.

Kocher, M. (1973). *The Montessori manual of cultural subjects.* Minneapolis, MN: T. S. Denison.

Kramer, R. (1976). *Maria Montessori: A biography.* New York: Putnam's.

Lee, D. M., & Allen, R. V. (1963). *Learning to read through experience.* New York: Appleton, Century, Crofts.

Loeffler, M. (1980, March). *What is a child?* Paper presented at the American Montessori Society Teacher Training Institute, Erlanger, KY.

Lowenfeld, V. (1947). *Creative and mental growth.* New York: Macmillan.

Maslow, A. (1943). A dynamic theory of human motivation. *Psychological Review, 50,* 370–96.

———. (1971). *The farther reaches of human nature.* New York: Viking.

McGuinness, D. (1979). How schools discriminate against boys. *Human Nature, 2* (2), 82–88.

Montessori, M. (1964). *The Montessori method* (Anne E. George, Trans.). New York: Schocken. (Original work published 1912)

———. (1965a). *Dr. Montessori's own handbook.* New York: Schocken. (Original work published 1914)

———. (1965b). *Spontaneous activity in education: The advanced Montessori method* (Florence Simmonds, Trans.). New York: Schocken. (Original work published 1917)

————. (1965c). *The Montessori elementary material, Vol. II* (Arthur Livingstone, Trans.). Cambridge, MA: Robert Bentley. (Original work published 1917)

————. (1966). *The secret of childhood* (M. Joseph Costelloe, Trans.). Notre Dame, IN: Fides. (Original work published 1936)

————. (1967). *The absorbent mind* (Claude Claremont, Trans.). New York: Dell. (Original work published 1949)

————. (1970). *The child in the family.* New York: Avon. (Original work published 1936)

Moore, V., & Moore, J. (1978). Organic reading in a Montessori environment. *The Constructive Triangle, 5* (3), 30–43.

Pribram, K. (1979). Holographic memory. *Psychology Today, 12* (9), 71–76.

Rambusch, N. M. (1978). Montessori teacher training: The calypso paradigm. *The Constructive Triangle, 5* (3), 5–29.

————. (1988). Natural learning. *The Constructive Triangle 15* (3), 9–13.

Seefeldt, C. (1976). Art. In Carol Seefeldt (Ed.), *Curriculum for the preschool-primary child: A review of the research* (pp. 177–200). Columbus, OH: Charles E. Merrill.

Smythe, Catherine (1987). *The effect of the 3-period lesson format on the retention of nomenclature.* Unpublished manuscript, AMS Teachers Research Network.

Standing, E. M. (1984). *Maria Montessori: Her life and work.* New York: New American Library. (Original work published 1957)

Tanner, J. M. (1970). Physical growth. In Paul H. Mussen (Ed.), *Carmichael's manual of child psychology* (pp. 77–155). New York: John Wiley & Sons.

Turner, J. (1978). *The Montessori early childhood teacher inventory.* Unpublished master's thesis, California State University, Long Beach, CA.

————. (1980). How do you teach reading? *The Constructive Triangle, 7*(2), 5–30.

————. (1982). Art and Montessori. *The Constructive Triangle, 9* (2), 4–41.

————. (1990). To stay—or not to stay? *Montessori LIFE, 2* (1), 11–13.

White, B. L., & Watts, J. C. (1973). *Experience and environment: Major influences on the development of the young child.* Englewood Cliffs, NJ: Prentice-Hall.

Williams, L. V. (1983). *Teaching for the two-sided mind.* Englewood Cliffs, NJ: Prentice-Hall.

3

IS THERE AN AMERICAN
MONTESSORI MODEL?

Let me begin by stating that simply to make something American does not, necessarily, mean to make it better! But to make something more relevant to a cultural group, while maintaining its original and essential excellence, may mean to make it "better" in terms of its meaningfulness and effectiveness for that cultural group.

Now that the Montessori method of educating children has been in use for more than thirty years in the United States, we are able to analyze how certified Montessori teachers have implemented it here. For many of us in the field, the Montessori method has a certain studied and internal philosophical basis, as well as a depth and breadth of experiential components. We often pride ourselves on our own belief that we truly know the Montessori method philosophically from both our readings and our studies, and that we know it practically from our wealth of experience in working in Montessori environments. And yet I wonder how consistent our understanding of Dr. Maria Montessori's philosophical approach is with our implementation of it in our Montessori classrooms. Where differences appear, do they reflect the result of our cultural adaptation?

This is obviously a broad and many-faceted area worthy of our consideration. Looking at different aspects of this question will eventually lead to a comprehensive analysis of the whole. In this case, I would propose that the whole be a clear, concise, and objective study of

1 The Montessori method as based on Dr. Montessori's writings
2 The Montessori method as interpreted and philosophically disseminated by certified Montessori professionals in America

3   The observable implementation of the method in American Montessori classrooms, and finally

4   The outcomes of the method based on classroom observational assessments of children's intellectual, creative, physical, social, and emotional behaviors.

Put quite simply, what is the Montessori method and what does it look like in American classrooms today?

Before discussing the data that I have collected, I would like to share some observations about contemporary writing and research on Montessori education. It is with optimism that I observe the increasing number of scholarly articles on the Montessori approach to education—whether they treat the method exclusively or consider it in the context of other educational approaches. These writings authored by both Montessori and non-Montessori professionals give credence to the existence, growth, and acceptance of the Montessori method as a viable philosophy and approach to educating children.

These articles vary in the accuracy of their descriptions of the method and its implementation based on what would appear to be the knowledge and experience of the authors. It seems that some authors have read little on the method and have not observed it extensively in practice. There does, however, seem to be increasing interest on the part of respected non-Montessori professionals in observing the method in operation before they write or comment.

An example of the concern just described is a recent article in the National Association for the Education of Young Children Journal titled "Why Not Academic Preschool?" (Greenberg, 1990). I have chosen this article for the following reasons:

1   Because of its recent publication and therefore relevancy to the present considerations

2   Because it appears in a professional journal for which I have great respect and which has wide circulation

3   Because the author has written an article which deserves attention due to its worthwhile content.

In this article, the Montessori method was classified as a "behavior modification" program and described as follows:

1   The choices are not the child's.

2   Cooperative and collegial planning on the part of the children, pretend play, playing, and conversation are strongly discouraged.

3 Play (spontaneous) and projects (group) are not as important a part of the program as using the special (excellent) Montessori materials.

4 There is a right answer to everything, which does mean that creativity is not central to the program. (For example, children are not usually free to use the materials in their own ways in addition to the correct way.)

In the References and Suggested Readings at the end of this article, I found no author who is considered a Montessori professional, let alone expert, nor any books or articles written specifically on the Montessori method.

If this list were read to me today, after twenty-three years as a teacher, teacher trainer, consultant, and observer in hundreds of Montessori classrooms, I would not recognize even one of these descriptions as accurate.

Although it is disconcerting to find such questionable information in a professional journal, I do, nevertheless, view the inclusion of Montessori in these articles as a positive step in fostering awareness, discussion, clarification, and mainstreaming of the method into American education. I thank the article's author for such an opportunity. I also want to highlight a particular word included in the first phrase to describe the method—*traditional*. The author started by saying, "The traditional Montessori method . . ." and therein may lie the key to understanding the Montessori method as separate from its implementation in the classroom.

We may also be dealing with problems of semantics. Certain words become associated with certain programs, often causing greater confusion, rather than lending clarity to an understanding of the method. For example, "independence" and "individualized" are often used to describe the Montessori method. Those words imply to some that children are strongly encouraged to work alone and without assistance. In reality, those words mean that children are supported in their individualized learning styles and pacing, and that they are encouraged to strive for independent, creative, and spontaneous process learning without feeling the need for adult permission or approval. Many terms such as these may need clarification in order for the Montessori method to be properly understood.

Where research in America on the Montessori method is concerned, we see a similar trend. Both Montessori and non-Montessori professionals are increasingly interested in having reliable research data on the philosophy and method. This attitude was evident to me in the early eighties when I proposed a "within Montessori" research study as my doctoral dissertation at the University of Michigan. My proposal was enthusiastically accepted because it focused on the implementation and outcomes of the method on its own, not in comparison with other methods. I will share some of the results of that study in this paper.

For research data to be generated, there must be a history of the method, providing substantial information on its implementation and effects. A certain historical perspective and longitudinal implementation lend credence to the collection of consistent, recognized, and generalized descriptive norms and data.

It is a prime time to focus on the need for good research within the field. Until recently, much of the research involved comparative studies of the Montessori method. These studies often did not verify the interpretation and efficacy of the particular classrooms being studied in terms of the Montessori philosophy and method; in addition, they analyzed effects and outcomes on children that were not consistent with the implementation of the method or its goals. As a result, many of these studies were ineffective in providing meaningful data pertinent to a better understanding and evaluation of the method.

Probably the greatest weakness in many studies has been the primary (and sometimes sole) reliance on standardized tests to evaluate program implementation and outcomes, rather than on observational assessments of teacher and child behaviors. In research we often isolate children (in order to test them) from the very settings that we are trying to evaluate and from which we are trying to discern correlations between the environmental and program influence and the outcomes. This appears to be a critical oversight in research designs because many program outcomes can be evaluated only through direct observation to determine whether results are consistent with the stated goals of the program. This research approach is certainly necessary for any valid data collection in the Montessori field.

At a 1962 meeting in Connecticut with Mario Montessori and Nancy Rambusch, Ronald Koegler, a California psychiatrist and associate of David Elkind, stated while discussing the Montessori movement world-wide and specifically in this country, "One of the essences of Montessori is observation of the child, not testing." At that same meeting, Mario Montessori stated: "I think that tests are dangerous. Dangerous in this sense—that people come to conclusions that are wrong" (Koegler, 1962).

Interestingly, in one of the most recent publications of the National Association for the Education of Young Children (NAEYC), a book entitled: *Achievement Testing in the Early Grades, The Games Grown-Ups Play* (Kamii, 1990), Vito Perone of Harvard University states: "Teachers and parents have been told that tests have meaning, that they point out what children know and understand, that they can help give important direction to instruction. The tests don't match that promise. Their contribution to the education of young children is virtually nil." Constance Kamii argues further: "Many people say that achievement testing can stop only when better instruments are offered to replace achievement tests. We do not agree with this statement because using a better instrument would be like putting a better cart in front of the horse. As long as educators feel compelled to make themselves look good in short-term evaluations, they will go on with behaviorism and associationism, which produce quick results. The authors of this book are calling for a halt to . . . testing."

How can we know what the method is or how it affects children if we never look at it in action in the classroom? Valid research in the field must be based on collecting data that reflects children's and teachers' classroom behaviors. To understand the Montessori approach is to know that the most important goals for children are not the acquisition of learned skills or information, although children are involved in the learning process and in the acquisition of new skills throughout the program. As will be reflected in the data presented here, however, the goals for the method are primarily of a behavioral nature that cannot be readily assessed or validated within the standardized testing format. Let us now review data that have been collected as part of a teacher survey.

THE QUESTIONNAIRE—DATA COLLECTION

In an attempt to continue my dissertation study, "The Montessori Method, Implementation and Outcomes" (Neubert, 1980), I designed the "Montessori Teacher Questionnaire." This questionnaire was sent nationally in 1986 to two hundred randomly selected, certified Montessori teachers. Eighty-six (43 percent) of these teachers completed and returned the form. Background information on the participants was collected in the following categories: level of Montessori certification, type of Montessori certification (professional organization), and number of years teaching as a Montessori head teacher. The results were as follows:

1   Level of Montessori certification
    3–6 years: 84.9%
    6–12 years: 15.1%

2   Type of Montessori certification
    A.M.S.: 83.1%
    A.M.I.: 13.3%
    St. Nicholas: 3.6%

3 Number of years as a Montessori head teacher
   1–3: 31.3%
   4–6: 24.1%
   7–10: 24.1%
   11–19: 20.5%

The questionnaire elicited information in six categories. Five of these asked for up to nine one-word responses prioritized in lists. (For some responses, more than a one-word response was accepted if needed and appropriate—for example, a hyphenated description such as "self-directed," or a description such as "sense of security," which was then categorized under the term security.) The sixth category allowed the respondents to give a descriptive answer.

1 Five one-word priority list categories:

- What do you see are the roles of the Montessori teacher in the classroom?
- What are your goals for your children in your classroom?
- What do you feel are the overall goals of the Montessori Method for children?
- How would you describe yourself in terms of teacher characteristics/ your manner, in the classroom?
- If asked to give some descriptive terms to explain the Montessori approach to non-Montessori groups, what terms would you use?

2 One descriptive category:

- Briefly describe how you implement your roles in the classroom to accomplish your goals.

All of the questionnaires were mailed out in early fall, 1986, and were returned within a few weeks.

THE RESULTS

In analyzing the responses, each category was surveyed individually. For the five one-word list categories, the first nine responses that met the criteria described above, were recorded. Additional responses and responses that did not meet the criteria were disregarded. Words were grouped together by identical use of the word and by interpretive identification. I used the term *Interpretive identification* to mean that words with similar meanings (for example, "self-esteem" and "self-worth") were grouped together. Associated interpretive identification words are listed in the raw data of the study.

For the one descriptive category, words and simple phrases were highlighted and listed in relation to the areas of implementation and goals. The results in this category are presented in a descriptive, not a statistical, cause and effect and "correlational" type of analysis.

I will present the results in a preliminary format. The data invite further analysis, but even this preliminary presentation gives interesting information about how teachers view themselves, their roles, their goals, and the Montessori method. The questionnaire was subsequently completed by certified Montessori teachers in 1987 in Wilmington, Delaware (approximately thirty teachers), and St. Louis, Missouri (approximately twenty-five teachers), with similar results. Furthermore, in my original dissertation study, teachers had listed goals for their programs that were almost identical to the results of the present survey. This certainly indicates a degree of reliability in the results, since the population consists of teachers in different regions of the United States surveyed over a ten-year period.

For each of the five one-word list categories, the following results will be given:

- *Greatest Number of First Choices:* Rated number one by the highest number of respondents.

- *Second Number of First Choices:* Rated number one by the second highest number of respondents.

- *Third Number of First Choices:* Rated number one by the third highest number of respondents.

- *Highest Second Choice:* Rated number two by the highest number of respondents.

- *Highest Third Choice:* Rated number three by the highest number of respondents.

- *Highest Overall Rating:* Most frequently given to the question regardless of priority ranking.

- *Second Overall Rating:* Second most frequently given to the question regardless of priority ranking.

- *Third Overall Rating:* Third most frequently given to the question regardless of priority ranking.

- *Fourth Overall Rating:* Fourth most frequently given to the question regardless of priority ranking.

- *Fifth Overall Rating:* Fifth most frequently given to the question regardless of priority ranking.

MONTESSORI TEACHER QUESTIONNAIRE: SUMMARY OF RESPONSES

More than one result (response) in a category indicates that they were given with equal frequency.

Words in parentheses are terms that were used frequently and appeared to be interchangeable with the main term. Unlike "interpretive identification" words, which are used less frequently yet are associated with the main term, these terms were associated with and used almost as frequently as the main word.

1. WHAT DO YOU SEE ARE THE ROLES OF THE MONTESSORI TEACHER IN THE CLASSROOM?

Greatest Number of First Choices:	OBSERVER
Second Number of First Choices:	TEACHER (Director)
Third Number of First Choices:	PREPARER of the ENVIRONMENT
Highest Second Choice:	OBSERVER
	FACILITATOR (Encourager)
Highest Third Choice:	AFFIRMER of the INDIVIDUAL
Highest Overall Rating:	FACILITATOR (Encourager)
Second Overall Rating:	OBSERVER
	AFFIRMER of the INDIVIDUAL
Third Overall Rating:	MODEL
Fourth Overall Rating:	PREPARER of the ENVIRONMENT
Fifth Overall Rating:	TEACHER (Director)

2. WHAT ARE YOUR GOALS FOR YOUR CHILDREN IN YOUR CLASSROOM?

Greatest Number of First Choices:	INDEPENDENCE
Second Number of First Choices:	LOVE OF LEARNING (Enjoy School) (Happy)
Third Number of First Choices:	SELF-ESTEEM
Highest Second Choice:	LOVE OF LEARNING (Enjoy School) (Happy)
Highest Third Choice:	LOVE OF LEARNING (Enjoy School) (Happy)
Highest Overall Rating:	LOVE OF LEARNING (Enjoy School) (Happy)
Second Overall Rating:	SOCIALIZATION
	INDEPENDENCE

Third Overall Rating:	SELF-ESTEEM
Fourth Overall Rating:	SELF-CONFIDENCE
Fifth Overall Rating:	RESPECTFUL

3. WHAT DO YOU FEEL ARE THE OVERALL GOALS OF THE MONTESSORI METHOD FOR CHILDREN?

Greatest Number of First Choices:	INDEPENDENCE
Second Number of First Choices:	DEVELOP CHILD'S POTENTIAL
Third Number of First Choices:	SELF-CONFIDENCE
	SELF-RESPECT
	LEARNING AT ONE'S OWN PACE
Highest Second Choice:	INDEPENDENCE
	JOY OF LEARNING
Highest Third Choice:	SELF-CONFIDENCE
	SELF-RESPECT
	RESPECT FOR OTHERS
Highest Overall Rating:	INDEPENDENCE
Second Overall Rating:	SELF-CONFIDENCE
	RESPECT FOR OTHERS
Third Overall Rating:	JOY OF LEARNING
	SELF-RESPECT
Fourth Overall Rating:	CURIOSITY (Creativity)
Fifth Overall Rating:	SELF-CONTROL
	CONCENTRATION
	DEVELOP CHILD'S POTENTIAL

4. HOW WOULD YOU DESCRIBE YOURSELF IN TERMS OF TEACHER CHARACTERISTICS/ YOUR MANNER, IN THE CLASSROOM?

Greatest Number of First Choices:	RELAXED (Calm)
Second Number of First Choices:	FRIENDLY (Loving)
Third Number of First Choices:	SUPPORTIVE
Highest Second Choice:	FRIENDLY (Loving)
Highest Third Choice:	SUPPORTIVE
Highest Overall Rating:	FRIENDLY (Loving)
Second Overall Rating:	SUPPORTIVE
Third Overall Rating:	CONSISTENT
Fourth Overall Rating:	RELAXED (Calm)
Fifth Overall Rating:	ENTHUSIASTIC

5. IF ASKED TO GIVE SOME DESCRIPTIVE TERMS TO EXPLAIN THE MONTESSORI APPROACH TO NON-MONTESSORI GROUPS, WHAT TERMS WOULD YOU USE?

Greatest Number of First Choices:	INDIVIDUALIZED

Second Number of First Choices:	LEARNING AT ONE'S OWN PACE
Third Number of First Choices:	PREPARED ENVIRONMENT
	(Organized) (Scientific)
Highest Second Choice:	LEARNING AT ONE'S OWN PACE
	(Self-Correcting) (Self-Teaching)
Highest Third Choice:	PREPARED ENVIRONMENT
	(Organized) (Scientific)
Highest Overall Rating:	LEARNING AT ONE'S OWN PACE
Second Overall Rating:	PREPARED ENVIRONMENT
	(Organized) (Scientific)
Third Overall Rating:	AIDE TO LIFE
Fourth Overall Rating:	INDIVIDUALIZED
Fifth Overall Rating:	SEQUENTIAL LEARNING
	LEARNING BY DOING (Hands-on)

ANALYSIS OF THE RESULTS

As stated previously, the initial results of this study have not been fully analyzed statistically but are the basis for further research. For the purposes of this presentation, the results are given without specific statistics (for example, without percentages within each category).

The results indicate that certified Montessori teachers see OBSERVER as one of the primary roles of the teacher, if not the most important one. Of similar significance in the classroom are the roles of TEACHER (Director), acting as a FACILITATOR (Encourager) and, what appears to be a closely aligned role, an AFFIRMER of the INDIVIDUAL.

As we may surmise from comparing the first category (Roles) with the fourth category (Teacher Characteristics), although *observer* is seen as an important role of the Montessori teacher, it was not used by Montessori teachers to describe their behavior in the classroom. Perhaps the question, because it used the words *characteristics* and *manner*, did not bring forth terms associated with roles. In the future, the fourth category question could be changed so that it simply asks teachers to describe their manner and roles in the classroom.

The discrepant results may also reflect a simple reality, however; perhaps most teachers in the classroom do not perceive of themselves as primarily observers of the children. It is obvious that teachers perceive themselves as RELAXED, FRIENDLY (Loving) and SUPPORTIVE. It may be that teachers see themselves in the classroom as more involved with the children and their work than as standing back in a noninteractive manner to observe and record. Perhaps this reflects an American (cultural), or more broadly, contemporary, implementation of the Montessori method with less emphasis on observing. American society places a great value on active participation, and less on standing back and assessing a situation. We are reared to strive for acceptance and success, which are often based on demonstrating what we can do. This cultural practice was also an integral part of education for most of us while growing up. And so it may be that it is natural for American teachers to want to take a more active role in the classroom and to feel less valued and less comfortable simply observing or "doing nothing," as it might be misinterpreted by others.

Observation is basic and significant to Dr. Maria Montessori's work and method. She refers to her educational approach as a "scientific pedagogy" (Montessori, M., 1948, pp. 21–41) with its foundation based on observation and experimentation. I believe that Montessori professionals need to determine to what degree observation is actually implemented and consistently used by teachers in the classroom as a basis for the ongoing development and daily functioning of the Montessori method.

We need to determine our commitment to using the observational approach in the classroom. Do we, as American Montessori teachers, practice observation and record keeping, which should be one of the resulting processes, in our classrooms on a consistent and significant basis? Is observation as important a practice to each of us in our teaching today as it was to Montessori?

Another consideration with respect to the responses to the first question is that although teachers do see PREPARER OF THE ENVIRONMENT as an important role, greater significance was placed on what would appear to be more personal teacher characteristics such as being a FACILITATOR and an AFFIRMER. These responses correspond nicely with those for both category two and category four. Let me first place the responses in a paradigm for clarity and then approach the results descriptively.

Category 1: Roles (Teacher)	Category 2: Goals (Children)	Category 4: Manner (Teacher)
FACILITATOR (Encourager)	INDEPENDENCE	RELAXED (Calm)
AFFIRMER OF THE INDIVIDUAL	LOVE OF LEARNING (Enjoy School, Happy) SELF-ESTEEM	FRIENDLY SUPPORTIVE

As we look at the results in these three categories, there appear to be an association and a correlation between them. Certain terms such as FACILITATOR—FRIENDLY and AFFIRMER—SUPPORTIVE appear to be associated. In a correlational sense, there may be a cause and effect relationship that could be expressed in the following format: Role + Manner = Outcome or Goal.

ROLE	+ MANNER	= GOAL
Method	+ Implementation	= Results
AFFIRMER	+ SUPPORTIVE	= SELF-ESTEEM
FACILITATOR	+ RELAXED & SUPPORTIVE	= INDEPENDENCE
AFFIRMER	+ FRIENDLY	= LOVE OF LEARNING

Obviously, the formulas could be rearranged and even certain analogous words might be substituted, but it appears that even though there was no indication on the teacher questionnaire of a relationship between any categories, the responses lend themselves to this type of analysis and might lead to interesting practical implications for the classroom. For example, if a teacher has SELF-ESTEEM as the most important goal, it would be helpful to know that developing an AFFIRMATIVE ROLE and SUPPORTIVE MANNER may encourage greater SELF-ESTEEM in children.

In looking at categories 2 and 3, we see an obvious association between what teachers see as their most important goal in their classrooms—INDE-PENDENCE—and what they see as the most important overall goal of the Montessori method—also INDEPENDENCE. In addition, LOVE OF LEARNING is significantly important to Montessori teachers. Both of these goals fit within Dr. Montessori's philosophical theme.

As we look closer at these two categories, we perceive that the primary goals for Montessori teachers, both within their own classrooms and within the broader philosophy of Montessori education, are all related to behaviorally acquired characteristics and not to learned academic skills. In other words, these Montessori teachers do not place high priority on skills in math and language as the primary goals or outcomes of the Montessori method. Instead, they value the development of the intrinsic nature of the child. One might assume that these teachers believe that the development of these characteristics (independence, joy of learning, self-confidence, self-esteem, etc.) is the foundation for the acquisition of learned skills and that given an opportunity to prioritize a larger number of goals, acquired skills would be found further down on the list, as was evident on my dissertation survey.

Now, let us look to Dr. Montessori's work. Certainly, Maria Montessori placed great emphasis on the intrinsic nature and development of the child. She writes at length about the "psychic life of the child" and the "absorbent nature of the child's mind." (Montessori, M. 1967) She also speaks about the "sensitive periods" of the young child, which child developmentalists today refer to, using slightly different terminology. Just as Jean Piaget believed in the importance of studying the inner nature of the child's thinking, Dr. Montessori also demonstrated the importance of observing and respecting the inner nature of the child's psychic life. It may well be that teachers who have been oriented through their academic training to the Montessori philosophy are "baptized" with the belief in the importance of the inner nature of the child as the basis for all development.

The question now arises: Do these American Montessori teachers, who survive in a society that promotes active participation by teachers and places little value on standing back and observing, really implement the Montessori philosophy and method by observing and respecting children in their own independent creations of themselves? It is difficult to do! Montessori teachers have to undo much of their own early training and cultural experiences, test society's values, and be willing to stand back and respect the child, knowing that they can be available as guide, facilitator, and protector when needed.

It is worth noting that the Montessori method is criticized in this country and the criticisms reflect the age-old dilemma: "It's too free," "It's too structured!" or "Children are given no choices," "Children are given too many choices." Two particular criticisms are expressed in categories 1 and 2. One is the now familiar statement: "In Montessori schools, children are not allowed to socialize; they make children work by themselves." In category 2, we find that teachers rate INDEPENDENCE and LOVE OF LEARNING as the two most prominent goals within their classrooms while SOCIALIZATION received the second highest overall rating.

Now, to take this analysis one step further, SOCIALIZATION was not given a top priority rating in category 3 (perceived goals of the Montessori method), which might indicate an Americanization of the Montessori approach. In other words, certified Montessori teachers did not perceive SOCIALIZATION as a goal of the Montessori method per se, but they did give it a high priority within their own classrooms. This may indicate that contemporary American Montessori teachers have integrated into their classrooms an interactive, socialization goal that has value in this culture.

We might also look back to category 1 and highlight the perceived role of the Montessori teacher as MODEL. There has been an emphasis in the fields of child development and education on the importance of modeling and its effects on the development of young children. It would be interesting to discover through additional data gathering whether the role of MODEL is perceived as generic to the Montessori method as developed by Dr. Montessori, or, as demonstrated on this survey, is seen as a role of the Montessori teacher in American education today.

A second criticism leveled at the Montessori method is as follows: "Children in Montessori classrooms are not allowed to be creative. They have to do things exactly the way they were shown." Interestingly, in category 3, Montessori teachers perceived the overall goals of the Montessori method to include INDEPENDENT, DEVELOP CHILD'S POTENTIAL, SELF-CONFIDENCE, LEARNING AT ONE'S OWN PACE, and, as the fourth highest overall rating, CURIOSITY/CREATIVITY. These characteristics seem in obvious opposition to the criticism that the Montessori method strives to inhibit creative and divergent thinking and the unique individual development of each child.

In fact, two essential components in the lesson plan as it is taught in American Montessori teacher education centers and used by American Montessori teachers are *variations* and *extensions.* Students in training and teachers must give credence to the creative and explorative "work of the child" as he or she manipulates the materials in unique, divergent, and self-initiated activities.

Finally, as we look at the survey data in category 5, we find great consistency across the subareas. Three descriptive terms come out as the top choices for explaining the Montessori method to non-Montessori groups: INDIVIDUALIZED, LEARNING AT ONE'S OWN PACE, and THE PREPARED ENVIRONMENT. Certified Montessori teachers today might therefore describe the Montessori method as "an individualized educational approach that allows the child to learn at his or her own pace within a prepared learning environment."

SELECTED RESULTS FROM THE ORIGINAL STUDY

Before closing, I would like to share a few highlights from my dissertation study, "Implementation and Outcomes of the Montessori Method." This study utilized the following forms of data collection:

1   Specifically designed "teacher behavior observational scales" with regard to program and interactional implementation of the method.

2   Specifically designed "teacher scales" with regard to environment and curriculum implementation of the method.

3   Specifically designed "child behavior observational scales" of outcomes.

4   Standardized tests.

5   "Teacher outcome survey" with background information.

6   "Parent questionnaires."

The purpose of this study was as follows:

1   To examine the implementation of Montessori principles and techniques by certified Montessori teachers within Montessori classrooms in order to describe variations in implementations within the model.

2   To determine the outcomes of the Montessori method.

3   To determine the effects of the Montessori method in relation to expected outcomes.

4   To investigate how variations in implementation influence expected outcomes.

The basic question was: Is there a significant relationship between teacher implementation practices in Montessori programs and the performance of children on expected outcomes?

Ten Montessori classrooms were randomly chosen for the study. Five children in each classroom were randomly picked from those who were in at least their second year of Montessori education with that certified teacher and were at least five years of age.

Each of the ten classrooms was visited on eight separate occasions for the purpose of completing the implementation and observational scales, for a total of approximately 24 hours per classroom, or 240 total hours of data collection. Four of the observation visits focused on the teacher, and four on the children. A ninth visit was made to each classroom in order to involve the children in the set of standardized tests.

Some of the results from that study are as follows:

1   In analyzing the programming data, teachers in these classrooms devoted an average of 63 percent of class time to the "Independent Work Period" (I.W.P.), 23 percent to the total group time, and the remaining 14 percent to transitional activities. It would appear that American Montessori

teachers place a high value on the child-centered I.W.P. rather than on the teacher-directed group routines. This programming schedule may be the result of teachers listing their primary goals/outcomes as self-direction, independence, self-discipline, and, interestingly, social skills. It may be that the I.W.P. offers children more opportunity to develop social interactional skills that do not take place spontaneously during the teacher-structured group time.

2 In analyzing the interactional data, children in these classrooms spent an average of 41 percent of their time during the I.W.P. (and as high as 77 percent in certain classrooms) in independent, individualized activities. In these cases, children often sat together at tables working on different materials. The next highest activity involvement was children working together on the same activity—an average of 28 percent of the time, and as high as 50 percent in some classrooms, during the I.W.P. These data are rather significant in respect to the notion stated earlier that Montessori classrooms do not encourage children to work together.

3 In further analyzing the interactional data, we observed that teachers directed or were involved in an average of only 11 percent of activity during the I.W.P. The majority of teachers' behavior seems to center on short-term assistance and guidance of the child's self-initiated and directed activities. These data seem to support the survey information in which teachers described their manner in the classroom as nondirective and facilitating.

4 As suggested earlier, teachers associate observation with the Montessori model, but do not use it to describe their own manner in the classroom. In this study, we found that an average of only 3 percent of the I.W.P. was devoted to teacher observation. Again, this may be a more American approach.

5 Looking further at teacher behaviors, we found that the teachers' interactions with children (whether demonstrations, assistance, or social) were usually one-on-one. Eighty-three percent of interactions observed were with one child, 12.5 percent with two children, and 4.5 percent with three or more children. These data certainly support the teachers' highest first choice for describing the Montessori approach as individualized.

6 Looking at the data on child observation, we found that when comparing the percentage of activities that are child initiated, rather than teacher directed, the following results appeared:

	Child Initiated	Teacher Initiated
Child working alone	65.9%	34.1%
Children working in pairs	79.5%	20.5%
Children working in group(3+)	56.4%	43.6%

Overall, 71.6 percent of all activity choices on average were child initiated, and 28.4 percent teacher initiated or teacher assisted. These data would seem to refute the notion that "choices are not the child's."

7   Finally, and I almost hesitate to share these data since they deserve further investigation and could be misinterpreted, our research design gathered data on the materials in the classrooms most frequently used by the children. Materials were classified as Montessori and non-Montessori. Further subclassifications by area and teacher-made materials were also done.

One area of implementation of the Montessori method that may be susceptible to cultural adaptation is the curriculum. Certainly subject matter is made appropriate to the participants' culture.

However, there may be further adaptation here in America involving a more open and ecumenical inclusion of a variety of non-Montessori materials, whether culturally specific or not, to enhance the Montessori curriculum. It would seem to be a more American notion and trend to adapt programs and products to include innovative ideas and concepts.

And thus most American Montessori classrooms offer a wide variety of supplemental, non-Montessori materials. In our study, we found that 30.8 percent of teacher- and child-initiated activities involved Montessori materials, whereas 69.2 percent involved non-Montessori materials. It is important to keep in mind that the curriculum includes all areas—art, practical life, senses, science, math, geography, cultural subjects, language, and so on.

Interestingly, when directors of American Montessori Society teacher-training programs were asked to give ideal and realistic estimates of percentages of the use of Montessori materials and non-Montessori materials in the classroom, the following results appeared: for Montessori materials, 65.5 percent of choices would ideally be for these materials, whereas 49.5 percent would be what they would expect to observe (actual data: 30.8 percent); and for non-Montessori materials, 34.5 percent of choices would ideally be for non-Montessori materials, whereas 50.5 percent would be what they would expect to observe (actual data: 69.2 percent).

These data obviously run counter to the notion that the most impor-tant aspect of the Montessori program is the use of the Montessori materials. In future studies, we may need to focus on several factors affecting the development and implementation of the curriculum that seem potentially indicative of an Americanization of the Montessori method.

We finally return to the original question: "Is There an American Montessori Model?" We might wish for a simple answer, a yes or a no. But as educators, we realize that even simple answers tug at us for greater explanation and qualification. If we take the responses of the certified teachers who participated in the survey and try to summarize their descrip-tions of the Montessori approach to education, we might come up with the following: "The Montessori method is an individualized, educational approach which aids the child to learn by doing at his or her own pace within a sequentially prepared, socially enriching environment that encourages creative process learning."

Within this definition are descriptions of the approach that don't fit certain of the more traditional views of the method. If we look at some of the descriptions of the Montessori method as presented in American literature and see an observable difference between those perceived notions about Montessori and the perceptions of the certified teachers on the one hand, and the observable practices and behaviors in the classrooms on the other, then it is possible to give credence to both positions by answering our question with yes. We can view the perceived notions as representing a more traditional and orthodox view of Dr. Montessori's method, whereas the descriptions given by certified Montessori teachers reflect the actual implementation of that method in contemporary Amer-ican culture.

Certain aspects of the curriculum have been Americanized out of necessity. But there would appear to be additional modification in their implementation. As we celebrate the thirtieth anniversary of the Ameri-can Montessori Society, this may be the time to look back at the original goals of the American Montessori movement and organization. From read-ings of the minutes of meetings, letters, and conversations with those leaders of the early movement, it would seem that the goal was to establish Montessori teacher-training standards that were reflective of U.S. teacher-training standards and to establish the teaching of Montessori's insights in an American cultural setting, as opposed to a dogmatic presentation of Montessori's principles in a culture-free manner. The intent seemed to be to integrate Montessori's ideas into the American culture rather than to introduce a distinct Montessori phenomenon parallel to the American educational scene.

In summary, these initial goals seem to form the basis for the answer already suggested to the question. But, as Dr. Montessori believed, the learning is in the process and not in the product or answer. In our present case, our learning may be in the question itself as it catalyzes greater interest and effort to research the Montessori method as it is practiced in our culture today.

REFERENCES

Greenberg, P. (1990). Why not academic preschool?, Part I, *Young Children 45* (2), 70–80.

Koegler, R. (1962). American Montessori Society National Conference Report. American Montessori Society Archives.

Neubert, A. B. (1980). *Is there an American Montessori model?* Unpublished dissertation manuscript, University of Michigan.

Montessori, M. (1962). *Discovery of the child.* Adyar, Madras 20. Vasanta Press, The Philosophical Society (First published in 1948).

———. (1967). *The absorbent mind.* New York: Dell Publishing Company. (First published in English in 1958, Claude A. Claremont, translator. Holt, Rinehart, and Winston, Inc.)

Perone, V. (1990) In Constance Kamii, ed., *Achievement testing in the early grades: games grownups play.* Washington, D.C.: National Association for the Education of Young Children.

4

WHAT DOES RESEARCH SAY ABOUT MONTESSORI?

The Montessori method of education continues to grow in importance in American education, both in private settings and in public schools. The Montessori Public Schools Consortium estimates that more than fifty school districts now operate Montessori programs, most of which are magnet programs for desegregation purposes (Kahn, 1988). Despite this, there is widespread lack of knowledge about this method among traditional early childhood educators and others in the mainstream of American education. Montessori supporters have typically not strongly supported research efforts or the communication of the results of research on Montessori to those outside the Montessori community. Thus, despite the existence of more than two hundred studies on Montessori, neither Montessori adherents nor mainstream educators are aware of these findings. This problem is made more difficult by virtue of the inaccessibility of many of the articles, since many of them are "fugitive" documents: publications (such as AMI [Association Montessori Internationale] *Communications* or the *Bulletin* of the American Montessori Society [AMS]) that are not indexed in ERIC or other abstracting services, conference papers, or unpublished dissertations.

This paper will attempt to review critically the most important research, both process research and outcome research on the Montessori method. (See also Chattin-McNichols, 1981; Boehnlein, 1985 and 1988—important sources for this paper.)

PROCESS RESEARCH

MILLER AND DYER STUDY

The single most important recent research study of the effects of the Montessori preschools is Miller and Dyer (1975). The study took place in several phases. First, the sample ($N = 248$) was randomly assigned to one of four preschool treatments.

The sample was composed of approximately 98 percent Black children, with mean family incomes of approximately $3,000 (in 1968). There were four school sites, and four replications of each program (Bereiter-Engelmann, traditional, DARCEE, and Montessori) except the Montessori program, for which there were only two replications.

The Bereiter-Engelmann (BE) program is heavily didactic with a behavioral orientation; it is the antecedent of the DISTAR program, a behaviorist program in wide use today. The DARCEE program is new (in contrast to Montessori [MONT] and traditional [TRAD]), with some direct teaching and some time for children to use cognitively oriented materials.

Two of the programs (Bereiter-Engelmann and DARCEE) were small-group programs that used didactic methods (direct instruction) to develop foundational skills necessary for school. The content was academic; for DARCEE, it involved association, classification, and sequencing in the processing of information along with the development of motivation to achieve, persistence in tasks, resistance to distraction, and delay of gratification. In BE, the instructional materials were primarily visual and auditory. In DARCEE, there were also games and many materials to manipulate. The TRAD program was based on the usual nursery school practices and represents a typical Headstart program.

One of the very few flaws of the Miller and Dyer study was that only two Montessori classrooms were studied. This was because "none of the 22 Headstart teachers available was qualified for Montessori training" (p. 17); two individuals, therefore, were recruited. These teachers substantially differed from the other teachers in age, experience, educational background, race, IQ, and personality variables. Perhaps more importantly, these women, with less experience than the other teachers, were in a summer eight-week training program. The year of Montessori teaching on which the study is based was their internship year, but they were without an experienced head teacher in the classroom contrary to the usual practice.

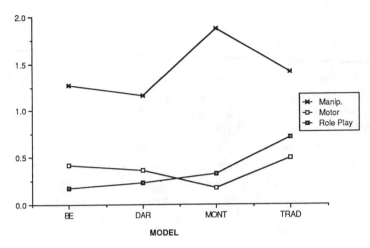

Data from Miller and Dyer, 1975

Figure 4–1   Child Activity Variables in Four Preschool Programs

In addition to the relative inexperience of the Montessori teachers, it must be remembered that the Montessori program is designed as a three-year program, for the child from age three to six, not for a single year, as was the case in this study. For these reasons, the results of this study must be interpreted as representing the lower bounds of the effects of Montessori preschool experience.

Miller and Dyer first conducted an examination of the different philosophies of the four models by having the teachers report their agreement with a list of statements derived from each model. This part of their study showed that teachers from the four models did have differing views of the goals and means of preschool education. Next, consultants rated the classrooms on a variety of measures to determine the extent to which the classrooms could be judged to represent the models. Finally, both live and videotaped observations were conducted. This thorough job of assessing the programs, rather than assuming that a program labeled "Montessori" would be an adequate model, is one of the exemplary features of this study.[1] (See Figure 4–1.)

The four programs are shown on child activity variables in Figure 4–1. The Montessori program, as might have been predicted from Montessori's

---

[1] See, e.g., Carta and Greenwood (1989) on the vagueness of the independent variable in studies in early childhood education.

writings, shows the highest incidence of manipulation of materials. Large motor activities are, however, the least frequent in MONT classrooms. Somewhat surprisingly, MONT is second-ranked (after TRAD) in the amount of role play. Perhaps because Montessori preschools are usually compared to traditional nursery schools, researchers have generalized that Montessori classrooms are low in role playing. (Another source would be the common confusion on Montessori's own thoughts on this area.) In comparison with academic preschools, Montessori children are, at least in this study, engaging in more role playing. (This area—the frequency of role play—is addressed below in summarizing Torrence's (1988) work.)

In other data from Miller and Dyer, there are clear program differences predictable from the models. The BE program has large amounts of verbal recitation, the MONT program moderately large amounts, and low amounts of recitation were recorded for DAR and TRAD. Despite the perception of little social behavior in the Montessori classroom, in fact MONT students are the highest (virtually tied with TRAD) on the amount of conversation recorded. This finding is made more clear in the light of Black's (1977) findings, discussed below.

Figure 4–2 shows that BE has by far the most group time, and MONT the least. DAR and MONT share first place in the amount of time alone. In examining teacher behavior, BE has by far the highest amount of asking behaviors, and MONT the least, whereas MONT is the highest in giving information. MONT is the only group in which more giving than asking

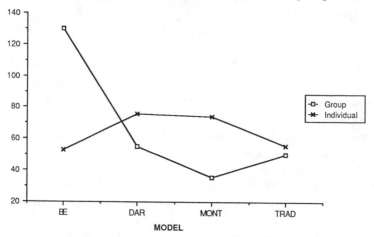

Based on ten hours of observation; data from Miller and Dyer, 1975.

Figure 4–2   Group vs. Individual Time

occurs. The behaviorally oriented BE program had large amounts of positive and negative reinforcement occurring. Surprisingly, at least in terms of common perceptions of Montessori, MONT teachers were providing more, not less, positive reinforcement than TRAD teachers, and less negative reinforcement. In other findings, TRAD was found to be the highest on conduct control, and MONT dramatically lower than other programs in the amount of language imitation requested (BE was the highest).

Overall, the observation data from the Miller and Dyer study paint a complex picture. In most areas, Montessori classrooms are as Dr. Montessori described them decades ago: the children work with materials, often individually. The teachers very seldom give large group lessons. Little conduct control is needed from the teachers. But in two areas, these findings contradict the common view of Montessori: role play is not absent, but exists at a moderate level, in comparison with the other three programs; in addition, conversations are going on at a fairly high rate. This second area, social interactions, was studied in more detail by Black (1977), Reuter and Yunik (1973), by Wirtz (1976), and by Baines and Snortum (1973).[2]

SOCIAL INTERACTIONS IN MONTESSORI CLASSROOMS

Black (1977) compared classrooms at each of three schools representing British Infant School and at three more representing Montessori. Her findings in the areas of outcome are presented later; her observational measures shed some light on social behaviors:

> British infant subjects were more likely to engage in Social Activity (i.e. Game Playing, Conversation, and Social Interaction) than Montessori subjects ($p <$ .025). (p. 83)

> Of all the variables in the study, the one that best discriminated the two groups was Prepare and/or Clean Up[3] . . . [Also differentiating the groups were] Requests Cognitive Information, Seeks Proximity to Adults, and Offers Cognitive Information to Peer. These behaviors characterized the Montessori Ss . . . These categories [Seeks Attention and Seeks Attention from Adult] were more characteristic of the British Infant group. . . . The finding that Montessori Ss were high on Ratio of Peer to Adult Interactions appears to be in contradiction

---

[2] Related studies of interest include Berger (1970), Karlson (1972), and Reuter (1974).
[3] This variable was higher for the Montessori group.

with the ANOVA result that the British Infant Ss were more likely to engage in social activity. It should be noted, however, that Social Activity refers to types of activities, while the Ratio of Peer to Adult category refers to persons with whom the child interacts. *Thus, Montessori children had a high ratio of peer interaction even though their activity was less play-oriented.* [My emphasis] Apparently, they were more likely to work together in non-social situations. The criticisms cited by Miezitis (1972) that Montessori education isolates children from each other was not supported by the findings of this study. Rather, the results tend to support Montessori's (1967) view that work with materials leads to increased self-confidence which eventually results in mature social interaction with children. (pp. 122–23)

These findings are interesting to compare with those from Reuter and Yunik's study (1973). These researchers compared a Montessori preschool with a token economy laboratory preschool and a parent cooperative preschool using traditional nursery school methods. Contrary to their hypotheses, Reuter and Yunik found that it was the token economy classroom that spent the least time in social interaction (16.5 percent), with the Montessori children spending 25 percent. The parent cooperative group was not significantly different from either of the other two groups. Also, social interaction increased with age. This finding is confirmed, with some interesting twists, by Wirtz (1976).

Wirtz's study used time-sampling observations to see if there were differences in the amounts of social interaction occurring in the four curricular areas in the Montessori classroom. Sex and age differences were also examined. There were both age and area differences in the uses of the materials. The use of the language area and especially the math area decreased with age, and the use of the practical life area increased. The only sex difference was that boys interacted significantly more in the math area than girls. Keep this finding in mind in relation to the long-term sex differences in math achievement by Miller and her colleagues, which are reported below under "Outcome Research."

Baines and Snortum (1973) examined the behavior of children in a traditional public elementary school and a Montessori elementary classroom, using time-sampling methods similar to those of Wirtz. Montessori children ($N = 8$) spent the largest percentage of time (44 percent) in self-directed study. The traditional school children spent over 90 percent of their time under direct supervision of the teacher. One of the most interesting findings from Baines and Snortum is that the Montessori children spent sizable amounts of time teaching each other (and being taught).

FANTASY AND ROLE PLAY

A second important finding from Miller and Dyer was in the area of role play, as was discussed above. One of the most important studies on role or fantasy play in Montessori schools remains unpublished. In a study in conjunction with the Teachers' Research Network, undertaken in 1987 and 1988, Torrence (1988) studied 123 teachers in AMS-affiliated Montessori preschools with a questionnaire on fantasy play. This study has limitations in its generalizability because it was restricted to AMS schools and because there was no attempt to see if the responding schools differed in any way from those who did not choose to respond. Finally, these are questionnaire data, which have not been verified by on-site observations. Social desirability may have influenced the responses. Despite these limitations, this study remains our only glimpse into the issues around fantasy in Montessori schools today.

The most important finding is that the majority of the 97 schools responding did report that they had fantasy play occurring. It appears to happen much more frequently in the practical life and sensorial areas than elsewhere.

Figure 4–3 shows how common various non-Montessori items (frequently used for fantasy play in traditional nursery schools) are in the sample. In another interesting aspect of the study, Torrence compared the presence of these sorts of materials in schools that were half-day only versus those that were full-day programs. In almost every area, activities such as

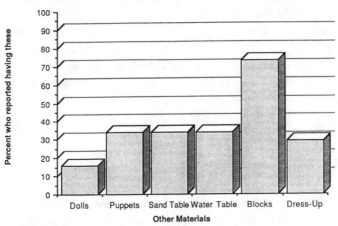

N = 97. Data from Torrence, 1985.

Figure 4–3   Presence of non-Montessori Materials in Classrooms

use of blocks or fantasy play with clay were related to the length of day. So, at least in this sample, the programs with children in them for longer periods of time are more likely to have the more traditional materials used for role play and fantasy play.

Finally, Torrence assessed whether the teachers felt that their training programs had prepared them well enough for the issues of fantasy they faced in Montessori schools. Over 64 percent said that they felt they had not been well prepared: a strong message that training program directors need to respond to.

TEACHER INTERVENTION IN FANTASY

In the intervention study that I conducted, several questions dealt with teacher's intervention in fantasy situations. This study, still in progress, used questionnaires to ask Montessori teachers about how likely they would be to intervene in a child's actions in a variety of situations. Data were collected from Trinidad, Haiti, the United States, and Canada, from every major Montessori teacher education tradition.

In general, there is a tendency to let most fantasy behaviors go on; the frequencies of the responses are averaging in the 2s and 3s on a scale in which 1 means "never intervene" and 7 means "always intervene". The intermediate score of "sometimes" may mean that the teacher takes individual differences into account in deciding when to intervene or that teachers vary in their ideas. This could be due to poor or inconsistent training or an ambiguity in the model.

In one case, the use of counters preparing to "attack" another group, however, it was quite a different story. This item had one of the highest likelihoods of intervention of any, almost as high as questions concerning danger to the children. It's not clear whether the teachers felt that this would lead to noise or disruption, or even danger, or whether this was seen as a gross misuse of materials. In any case, this warlike fantasy would be stopped by almost all teachers.

OTHER WORK ON CLASSROOM PROCESSES

Feldman's (1983) work examined physical movement in the 3–6 and 12–15 Montessori classrooms in Ohio, finding very similar rates of movement. Feltin (1987) documented what occurred in four elementary classes. All four classrooms were in private, tuition-charging schools in the Seattle area, thus limiting the generalizability of the study. All four classrooms had experienced teachers with AMS elementary certificates. The observation data were based on six morning observations in each of the four classes during October and November. The age ranges for the four classes were 5–8, 5–10, 8–10, and 9–11. Years of previous Montessori for the total sample ranged from zero to eight years. In the observation of students, the following breakdown of time was observed. (Percentage of total behaviors shown as decimals, from Feltin, 1983.)

Working Alone   (68 percent)

Visual evidence of checklist	.04
with pencil/paper	.34
with manipulatives	.28
aimless	.02

Other Activity Alone   (21 percent)

organizing desk/work space	.03
choosing/gathering material	.07
correcting work	.02
misusing materials	.00
being distracted	.03
cleaning up, putting away	.04
leaving the room	.02

Working with Peers   (13 percent)

interactive	.04
parallel	.03
verbal	.02
nonverbal	.04

Talking with Peers   (21 percent)

student initiated	.04
peer initiated	.03
sharing ideas/activities	.02
seeking help	.00
assisting another	.01
disagreeing	.00
conversing	.03

With Teacher   (32 Percent)

teacher initiated	.04
student initiated	.06
with assistant	.03

verbal	.07
nonverbal	.02
management	.04
instructional	.05
personal	.01

(146 per cent of total time)

The total individual student observed behaviors is more than 100 percent since some activities were occurring simultaneously, such as verbal, student-initiated, instructional interaction with the teacher. Again, the pattern seen here is the familiar one: Montessori children appear to be spending their time as Montessori predicted, moving independently, doing work, talking with each other about both work and social topics, and requiring relatively little conduct control.

SUMMARY

First, it is clear that more and better research into the processes of Montessori environments is needed. This will become even clearer when the effectiveness of these environments is discussed in the following section.

Second, the Montessori environments studied so far have revealed that students are spending relatively little time in whole group instruction. Rather, they move about the classroom, choose their work, work individually, and talk with each other. They do spend significant amounts of time conversing, but a relatively high portion of this is either related to school work or actual peer teaching. Lack of similarity in observation instruments obscures the extent to which this is true at different age levels.

Lastly, some of the ideas about what goes on in Montessori classrooms—such as little social interaction and role play—must be carefully reexamined. More research is needed here in particular, to examine the extent and depth of role play at various age levels, and to examine social interactions in even greater detail.

OUTCOME RESEARCH

In an attempt to clarify and organize a large number of studies, the results are presented in several sections: (1) general verbal intelligence; (2) perceptual, motor, and performance IQ development; (3) academic achievement and school readiness; (4) attention, concentration, resistance to distraction, and impulsiveness; (5) Piagetian conceptual development; and

(6) creativity and motivational factors. A section on methodology and suggestions for future research concludes this chapter.

DESCRIPTION OF THE MAJOR STUDIES

Di Lorenzo (1969) studied the effects of a year prekindergarten school experience on 1,807 low-income children. Again, the majority of the children studied were Black. The study was a truly experimental design, with stratified random assignment, in eight school districts in New York. Four of the programs were described as early childhood oriented, four as cognitively oriented. Of the four cognitively oriented programs, one (Mt. Vernon) was a Montessori program. The type of training of the teacher and the orientation of the Montessori program were not specified; talking typewriters were used as a supplement to the traditional Montessori curriculum. Three waves of children were tested on measures including the Stanford-Binet IQ test, the Peabody Picture Vocabulary Test, the Illinois Test of Psycholinguistic Abilities, the Learner Self-Concept Test, and the Metropolitan Readiness Test, at the beginning and end of prekindergarten, kindergarten, and first-grade years.

The Sands School Project (Banta, 1969) was conducted in Cincinnati with seventy-five Black children from lower-middle and lower socioeconomic status (SES) families. These children were placed into four groups: Montessori preschool/Montessori primary school, Montessori preschool/ open-classroom primary school, Headstart/conventional public school, and a no-preschool/conventional school group. Banta (1969) evaluated these children between the ages of five to six on the Cincinnati Autonomy Battery, which includes tests of cognitive style, performance IQ, curiosity, and impulse control. Follow-up studies (Gross, Green, and Clapp 1973; Sciarra and Dorsey 1974) examined thirteen similar measures at the end of the second year, interviews with the parents on their feelings about the project at the end of the third year, and achievement test results for the next three years.

Karnes (1969; Karnes, Shwedel, & Williams, 1983) compared the effects of five different nine-month nursery school programs (including one Montessori program) for four-year-old Black and White children from low-income homes. The follow-up study done in 1989 presents some interesting summary data on the overall effectiveness of various models of preschool education in helping low-income children succeed in public schools.

GENERAL VERBAL INTELLIGENCE

Kohlberg (1968) has reported finding no significant overall changes using alternate forms of the Stanford-Binet intelligence test among children in a Montessori summer Headstart program enrolling Black low-income and White middle-income children. In a year-long Montessori program, however, ten low-income Black children studied showed a mean Stanford-Binet IQ increase of 17 points between October and January. The children of average IQ on the first testing increased as much as the children of low IQ. A group of middle-income children in the same class showed a mean increase of 10 IQ points.

Using fourteen matched pairs of middle-income children of above-average IQ, Dreyer and Rigler (1969) found that those in a traditional nursery school obtained higher scores on the Peabody Picture Vocabulary Test than those in a Montessori nursery school.

Pendergast (1969) administered the Peabody Picture Vocabulary Test twice seven months apart, to three groups of upper-middle–income children attending (1) a Montessori nursery school, (2) a conventional nursery school, and (3) no preschool. There were approximately forty children in each group. There were no significant differences among the groups on Peabody Picture Vocabulary Test performance. The author concluded that the enriched upper-middle–income environment tended to outweigh any effects of special training, and therefore the school programs may have contributed little to the children's developmental needs.

Di Lorenzo (1969) compared the effects of eight year-long prekindergarten programs longitudinally, as described previously. Post-tests at the end of one year and follow-up testing at the end of kindergarten indicated that pupils in the four cognitively oriented programs, one of which was a Montessori program, surpassed those in the four traditional nursery school programs on Stanford-Binet and Peabody Picture Vocabulary Test scores. The Montessori program (N = 177) was found to be associated with modest but significant gains in Stanford-Binet IQ.

Karnes (1969; Karnes, Shwedel, & Williams, 1983) reported that the Montessori program produced lower gains in Stanford-Binet IQ scores than in the Karnes Ameliorative Program, which included development of perceptual, attentional, conceptual, and language skills; self-concept; and achievement motivation. There were no significant differences among the five groups in Peabody Picture Vocabulary Test gain scores. In a follow-up investigation with the five groups at the end of one year of public school attendance, Karnes found that the Montessori children, particularly those on the low IQ range, made continuing IQ gains, suggesting that the program was relatively effective in establishing improved intellectual functioning with children who had initially indicated limited potential. This finding takes on more significance in the light of the long-term effects of Montessori preschool experience reported in the follow-up studies of the Miller and Dyer research (Miller and Bizzell, 1983, 1985). The long-term follow-up by Karnes et. al. (1983) is also important here.

Stodolsky and Karlson (1972) investigated changes in performance on the Stanford-Binet intelligence test over an eight-month span among twenty-nine low-income and twenty-nine middle-income preschool children who were in their first, second, and third years of attendance in a private Montessori school. They found that all the children in their first year of preschool showed a statistically significant gain in Stanford-Binet IQ from pretest to post-test. Children in their second and third years of preschool, however, did not show significant IQ gains.

Stodolsky and Karlson present several possible explanations for these findings. One is that gains after first school exposure are due more to rapport and test practice effects than to cognitive growth. Alternatively, the curriculum may not be sufficiently powerful to do more than has been accomplished in the first year of schooling to boost test performance. Additionally, the failure to see change in subsequent years of preschooling on a measure like the Stanford-Binet also may be a function of its gross quality; measures sensitive to specific areas emphasized in the curriculum might be necessary to gauge the effects of the program.

Fleege, Black, and Rackauskas (1967) matched a group of twenty-one children from a Montessori classroom with another twenty-one from a non-Montessori preschool on variables including age, sex, IQ, birth order, SES, and parental education. The two groups were compared on standardized tests (Peabody Picture Vocabulary Test, SRA Primary Mental Abilities) and on ratings by the teacher in eight areas of competence. A second phase compared achievement test scores and teacher ratings of children in elementary grades who had had Montessori, other preschool, or no-preschool experience. In the comparison between the two matched groups, a complex analysis showed superiority of Montessori children on a verbal ability factor. The comparison of teacher ratings showed "no particular adjustment problems peculiar to Montessori trained children" (Fleege, Black, & Rackauskas, 1967, p. 54).

Miller and Dyer (1975) also studied changes on several measures of general verbal intelligence after one year of Montessori preschool. Stanford-Binet scores averaged across the whole group rose from two to ten points. The average of the two Montessori classes was a larger gain than the DARCEE or control groups' average gain and slightly less than the gains for the Bereiter-Engelmann or traditional nursery school groups at the end of the preschool year.

Changes from fall to spring on the Peabody Picture Vocabulary Test favored the Montessori group over the traditional nursery school group slightly, and were significantly higher than the control group. Bereiter-Engelmann and DARCEE classrooms gained slightly more than the Montessori classrooms.

The Parallel Sentence Production and Expressive Vocabulary Inventory tests (Stern, 1968) were administered to provide a more direct assessment of language skills, especially the mastery of standard English, by this sample. Bereiter-Engelmann classes scored highest, followed by DARCEE, Montessori, traditional, and controls, in that order.

A most interesting finding are the results of Stanford-Binet testing at the end of kindergarten and first and second grades. *The Montessori classrooms, one in Work Spend (a behavior-analysis Follow Through program) and one in a regular Louisville elementary school, showed the least decline in IQ scores and had the highest IQ scores at the end of the project.* The high score of the control group was explained by Miller and Dyer as a possible artifact of the background characteristics of the control group, in particular a higher likelihood of family intactness than the experimental groups.

Follow-up studies by Miller and Bizzell (1983, 1985) and Karnes (Karnes, Shwedel, & Williams, 1983) indicate that this trend continues, at least until the children are in tenth grade. The Montessori group retained their superiority over the other programs on Stanford-Binet test scores at a follow-up testing. The most significant effects are on math scores for males. Differential drop-out rates or other artifacts do not account for this difference. This raises a most interesting question: What aspects of the one-year Montessori program could be affecting math scores in tenth graders? Clearly, content taught to the four-year-olds is not relevant. Among the most likely mediating variables are self-esteem, self-confidence, or attitudinal changes.

The Sands School Project (Banta, 1969) tested Black, lower-SES children on a subtest of the Wechsler Preschool Skills inventory that required them to repeat sentences back to the examiner. Nonsignificant differences favored the Montessori preschool and primary group followed by the Montessori preschool/ open-classroom group next; the no-preschool group had the lowest scores.

In conclusion, these findings suggest that Montessori preschool, over a period of approximately one year, has positive short-term effects upon general intelligence, as measured by tests that are heavily based on verbal performance, such as the Stanford-Binet. The Montessori program compares favorably with traditional preschools, but it is less effective (in short-term effects) than academic programs such as Bereiter-Engelmann or the Karnes Ameliorative Program. Gains, however, appear to be more resistant to decline over time; this may be due to changes in distractibility, or other attitudinal or motivational characteristics.

PERCEPTUAL, MOTOR, AND PERFORMANCE IQ DEVELOPMENT

Pendergast (1969) administered the Frostig Developmental Tests of Visual Perception twice, seven months apart, to upper-middle–income children (1) who attended a Montessori nursery school, (2) who attended a conventional nursery school, and (3) who did not attend preschool. This study evaluated eye-hand coordination and visual perception skills. Pendergast found that the Montessori children showed significantly greater gains in eye-hand coordination than those who attended the conventional nursery school. In figure-ground perception and position in space skills, there were nonsignificant gains in favor of the Montessori children.

Berger (Berger, 1970) conducted a longitudinal comparative assessment of ninety-three Black and Puerto Rican three- and four-year olds enrolled in Head Start Montessori programs and conventional preschool programs. On an experimental test battery of perceptual-conceptual functioning, significant differences in favor of the Montessori children were found only on the perceptual measures, and the pro-Montessori trend was most salient for the poor perceptual achievers.

Stodolsky and Karlson (1972) examined changes in scores on selected performance scales of both the Wechsler Preschool and Primary Scale of intelligence and the Merrill-Palmer Scale of Mental Tests, among twenty-nine low-income and twenty-nine middle-income preschool children. These children were in their first, second, and third years of attendance in a private Montessori nursery school. Results indicated that, in general, the Montessori curriculum appeared to be effective over a period of two years in nurturing continuing development in children in the areas of visual-motor integration, matching and sorting skills, and psychomotor skills.

The Sands School Project (Banta, 1969) tested children with preschool and primary Montessori experience against control groups with and without a non-Montessori preschool year. The Montessori/Montessori group, Montessori/open classroom group, control with preschool group, and the no-preschool group finished in this order on all tests. The difference in the scores was significant at $p < .01$ for a test that involved matching two appropriate objects out of three objects. Scores on Banta's (1970) Early Childhood Embedded Figures Test (ECEFT) were significantly different in the order given above at $p < .01$.

No significant program or experimental versus control group differences on the ECEFT (Banta, 1970) were found by Miller and Dyer (1975).

In conclusion, the evidence suggests that the Montessori method is effective in nurturing development in the areas of visual-motor coordination and integration, matching appropriate objects, and visual-perceptual ability, but of uncertain effectiveness in developing in the ability to disembed figures from their contexts. This cognitive style may not be affected by the Montessori school experience, or only some Montessori children's experience may have an impact on figure-ground perception. This is an area for future research, as is the whole question of the relationship of Montessori school experience and cognitive styles.

ACADEMIC ACHIEVEMENT AND SCHOOL READINESS

Bereiter (1967) conducted an experimental comparison of the effects of the Montessori method ($N = 17$) and of the Bereiter-Engelmann method of direct verbal instruction ($N = 18$) on upper-middle–income children ranging in age from three years ten months to four years ten months. The children given the Bereiter-Engelmann training were drawn from the waiting list of the Montessori school and thus were assumed to be similar to the Montessori group in SES and other home background factors. The Montessori group had attended school one full year whereas the direct verbal instruction group had not. Montessori "instruction," in Bereiter's terms, was for two hours daily and included training in verbal reasoning, reading, arithmetic, printing, and experimental science. The measure of academic achievement employed was the Wide Range Achievement Test, administered six weeks after the beginning of instruction and again at the end of the school year. Results showed that the direct verbal instruction group performed significantly better than the Montessori-trained group in reading, spelling, and arithmetic. This echoes the short-term effectiveness of the Bereiter-Engelmann program found in Miller and Dyer (1975). It's unfortunate that Bereiter did not follow up this study to see if long-term results would also favor his program.

In Di Lorenzo's (1969) study it was found that children attending highly structured, cognitively oriented, language prekindergarten programs—including one Montessori classroom—performed better on the Metropolitan Readiness Test at the end of kindergarten than children in traditional nursery school programs. The children in the cognitive programs also performed better on the Metropolitan Achievement Test at the end of first grade.

Karnes (1969) found that four-year-olds attending a Karnes Ameliorative Program (development of perceptual, attentional, conceptual, and language skills, self-concept, and achievement motivation) or a Direct Verbal Instruction program (Bereiter-Engelmann) showed higher gains on the Metropolitan Number Readiness Test than a group of children attending a Montessori program.

The more recently published long-term follow-up of Karnes's research (1985) is very important, since it is, along with the Miller and Dyer study, one of the few long-term studies of the effects of Montessori. The results show a similar pattern to those found by Miller, with the exception of a delayed decrease in the scores of the Bereiter-Engelmann and Karnes programs in the early school years. This difference from the Miller findings reflects an important difference in the studies: the Karnes and Bereiter preschool groups (but not others) were given special "booster" classes during two additional years. Karnes comments on the "sleeper" effect that the Montessori program seems to have, and she offers attentional differences as a possible reason. Overall, in a composite measure of the effects of four preschool programs on a wide range of measures, the *Montessori program was rated as the most effective in producing long-term school success, ahead of the Karnes and behaviorally oriented programs.*

Fleege, Black, and Rackauskas (1967) compared children (N = 124) in public and private school with Montessori preschool, non-Montessori preschool, and no-preschool backgrounds. Teachers rated the children in several areas on an experimental questionnaire. Montessori children were rated significantly superior on interest in learning, independence, interpersonal relations, leadership, and learning ability.

In the results of the program versus control group comparisons in the Miller and Dyer (1975) study for scores on subtests of the Metropolitan Readiness Test, the Montessori children appeared superior to the other groups in tests of numbers and alphabet knowledge, similar to controls in a test of copying, and intermediate in a test of word meanings. On the California Achievement Test administered at the end of grades one and two, an interesting pattern emerged. The preschool versus control difference was the only significant one at the end of grade one. But by grade two, the Montessori and control groups had risen dramatically, in relation to the others' scores. Montessori children, particularly males, had higher reading scores at the end of grade two. Montessori theorized that there are sensitive periods for several areas of development, among them reading. Elliott (1967) reviewed a series of research studies on reading and concluded that "Current research has substantiated the value of an earlier start in reading (earlier than grade 1), placing it between the age of 4 and 5, which is within sensitive period theorized by Montessori. Thus, most reading principles involving the sensitive period are similar and consistent with current research findings of contemporary reading specialists" (p. 165).

The follow-up (Miller and Bizzell, 1983, 1985) showed that the Montessori group maintained statistically significant differences in reading and math, and nonsignificant superiority on all other tests. Miller and Bizzell elaborately analyzed the drop-out patterns among the groups and other possible spurious causes of this result, but concluded that the Montessori program itself was responsible for the achievement test superiority.

Sciarra and Dorsey (1974) followed up the children in the Sands School Project on the Montessori Achievement Test. This important study represents one of the few reported empirical studies on the effects of Montessori elementary school experience. Because the children ranged in age from eight to almost ten years, age was used as a covariate to adjust the scores. The use of analysis of covariance (see Cronbach et al., 1977), the small number of subjects, and the possibility of differential attrition by groups all suggest caution in the interpretation of the results. The authors conclude that continued experience in this Montessori system increases the benefits of preschool exposure—an interesting point in the context of the Miller and Dyer (1975) findings. Perhaps the most important conclusion from this area is that the effects of Montessori elementary school should be investigated in more detail.

Dawson, in an unpublished master's thesis (1988), examined the academic performance of public elementary Montessori school students by race. This revealing study showed that the Montessori magnet schools in Houston were extremely effective for children of all races, but especially for Hispanics. In all cases, class means for achievement were above district norms. This was the case even though another magnet program for gifted students "siphoned off" some of the brightest students.

Duax (1989) examined the performance of children in a Milwaukee public Montessori program. His findings were very similar to Dawson's: 84 percent of the graduates were above the fiftieth percentile on achievement as measured by standardized tests. More importantly, to my mind, only one student did not score at or above the average score. In addition, Duax's teacher survey data showed that Montessori graduates in middle school had higher scores on the following:

- Use basic skills necessary to survive in middle school.
- Be responsible and can be counted on.
- Show enthusiasm for class topics.
- Be individualistic and not afraid to be different.
- Exhibit multicultural awareness.

Takacs and Clifford (1988) report on a sample of graduates from the Cleveland public Montessori program. In the Reading subtest of the California Achievement Test, the Montessori group had higher scores: sixty-second percentile versus forty-eighth percentile for a matched comparison group. On a teacher survey form, several significant differences were again found in areas such as "pursuit of a task beyond the minimum."

In an intriguing study (Glenn, 1989), graduates of the Franciscan Earth school in Portland, Oregon, were asked about their occupational choice: Montessori graduates preferred investigative jobs (such as botanist or computer programmer) rather than social jobs (teacher, social worker). This study also reported that Montessori graduates were "more guarded in response, more critical of others, and less freely expressive" (p. 64) on the Children's Personality Questionnaire. All results were in the normal range.

A most important final area of research that needs continued investigation is whether the Montessori environment has any impact on the understanding of math concepts, such as subtraction. Working from Kamii's efforts in this area (1985), Baker (1988) and a variety of Teachers' Research Network members have attacked this problem, with some findings indicating a difference, and others not. Instrumentation is clearly an issue here. The entire nature of the Montessori math curriculum and the role of manipulatives in general can be investigated here (see also Bauch and Hsu, 1988).

In conclusion, studies that have focused on the effects of Montessori training upon measures of academic achievement and school readiness suggest that preschool programs that emphasize direct training in academic areas and in language skills produce greater gains on these types of measures than Montessori programs. Montessori training, in turn, appears to produce greater gains on these types of measures than traditional nursery schools. The gains produced by Montessori preschools are less likely to deteriorate over time than those of other programs, and they may not fade out at all if the Montessori program is continued beyond preschool.

ATTENTION, CONCENTRATION, DISTRACTIBILITY, AND IMPULSIVITY

In summarizing his observations on Montessori, Gardner (1966) has noted that the development of attentional controls seems to be particularly encouraged in the Montessori environment, and he has called for research in this area.

Judge (1974) compared four Montessori classrooms, four classrooms using the Science-A-Process Approach method, and two classrooms described as non-Montessori/non–Science-A-Process Approach, on the Science Process Instrument, which tests competence in observation. Montessori children did not differ from the Science-A-Process Approach group, although both differed from the two control classrooms. The Montessori classrooms showed large variability because of the teacher factor. The Montessori school experience, then, was found to be as effective as a program specifically designed to increase observational skills.

Kohlberg (1968) has reported finding an increase in ratings of distractibility, in the test situation in a permissive classroom, as compared to students receiving Montessori experience during summer-long preschool intervention programs. A drop in IQ was found to be correlated with increased distractibility; behavioral observations in the classroom supported the distractibility rating data. In the year-long programs, he found that an IQ increase shown by low-income children receiving Montessori preschool training was matched by an increase in ability to attend.

McCormick and Schnobrich (1971) administered, as an addition to the regular Montessori training, a seven-month program of perceptual-motor training that stressed control of impulsiveness and development of attentional skills to twenty-five children ranging in age from three to five years attending a morning Montessori preschool. The children in the afternoon Montessori preschool class, not receiving the special training program, were the controls. Measures of attention, administered before and after preschool, were the auditory-vocal sequencing and the visual-motor sequencing subtests of the Illinois Test of Psycholinguistic Ability. Results showed greater gains on both measures for the group receiving the training. The authors concluded that perceptual-motor training can improve the ability to concentrate visually and auditorily and that this training would be a useful addition to the present Montessori curriculum because "Montessori training itself does not seem to result in such improvement" (McCormick and Schnobrich, 1971, p. 77).

In a series of studies, Miezitis (1971) found that middle- and upper-income children attending either a child-centered, play-oriented nursery school or a regular public kindergarten were more impulsive, as measured by Kagan's Matching Familiar Figures Test, than a matched group of children attending a Montessori nursery school. The children (N = 80) in the study, ranging in age from five to six years, were matched for age, sex, and SES and were of at least average intelligence.

Berger (1970), in a longitudinal assessment of ninety-three Black and Puerto Rican three- and four-year olds enrolled in Head Start Montessori programs and conventional preschool programs, found that motor impulse control scores from the Cincinnati Autonomy Test Battery consistently favored the Montessori children.

Banta (1969) found nonsignificant differences that favored control groups over the Montessori preschool groups on the Draw a Line Slowly Test of impulse control, the only negative finding in the original assessment of the Sands School Project.

Miller and Dyer (1975) made use of Banta's (1970) Replacement Puzzle Test, in which each child is rated on items that can be summed to produce scores on aggression, verbal-social participation, timidity, independence, and achievement motivation. Also, the face sheets of the Stanford-Binet and the Preschool Inventory were used. In these, the tester rates the child on factors that may influence performance, such as motivation, confidence, and the like.

On the aggression and verbal-social participation ratings of the Behavior Inventory administered after one year, the Montessori program (along with the Bereiter-Engelmann program) produced lower gains than DARCEE. Bereiter-Engelmann, DARCEE, and Montessori programs reduced the aggression rating more than the traditional program. Comparison to the control groups during this first year were not made. DARCEE and, to a lesser extent, the traditional program were favored over Montessori on verbal-social participation. For both of these variables, differences favored all groups over controls.

Montessori classrooms were consistently first or second highest in aggression ratings, with a high score representing low aggression. Overall, Montessori children were less distractible, more persistent, more verbal-social, but not consistently less aggressive than controls. Montessori programs did not differ significantly from the other preschool programs in fostering persistence or resistance to distraction, but Montessori programs were less successful than traditional and DARCEE at fostering verbal-social participation. This finding offers partial support for my hypothesized explanation for the lower Peabody Picture Vocabulary Test scores of Montessori children. Bereiter-Engelmann and Montessori programs are more successful, however, than DARCEE and traditional at reducing aggression (Miller and Dyer, 1975).

The Face Sheet ratings for preschool indicate that Montessori children were rated intermediate between Bereiter-Engelmann and DARCEE children on achievement motivation and other factors affecting their ability to score at their potential.

In summary, the limited amount of research to date suggests that Montessori preschool experience is effective in increasing children's ability to pay prolonged attention to school-related tasks. This increase in attention may be a major factor accounting for the observed positive effects of Montessori preschool training on performance on intelligence tests of the Stanford-Binet type. There is also evidence (McCormick and Schnobrich, 1971) suggesting that perceptual-motor training, stressing control of impulsiveness and development of attentional skills, added to the regular Montessori preschool curriculum can increase the effects of Montessori experience on the ability to concentrate visually and auditorily.

Resistance to distraction and persistence, as measured by Banta's (1970) Replacement Puzzle Test, is increased more by the other preschool programs studied, although Montessori children perform better than controls. Montessori children are less able to inhibit a motor response, such as drawing a line slowly, than control groups with Head Start or no preschool experience. Similar results were obtained for Behavior Inventory scores on ambition and verbal-social participation, with Montessori faring slightly better than DARCEE and traditional programs in reducing rated aggression.

PIAGETIAN TASKS

In his contrastive analysis of the concepts and methods of Montessori and Piaget's theories of development, Gardner (1966) has raised the questions of (1) whether the sensorimotor approach of early Montessori training affects the ages at which children move from one Piagetian stage of development to another, and (2) whether the attentional controls developed with Montessori training accelerate the process of decentration. Testing for Piagetian development has its own set of problems, in addition to the general problems associated with research on Montessori. (See Kuhn [1974] for relevant comments on the training for, and testing of, conservation.)

Kohlberg (1968) reported finding little change on performance on Piagetian tasks of conservation of length and mass, and of transitivity, involving ordering and measuring, among a group of racially integrated low-income and middle-income children participating in a Montessori preschool classroom for one summer. Results of a series of studies by Miezitis (1971) confirmed Kohlberg's (1968) findings, using as subjects preschool children of at least normal intelligence from middle- and upper-middle–income families. This series of studies found no significant differences in performance on Piagetian conservation tasks (number, length, and substance) in three groups of children attending (1) an "orthodox" Montessori preschool; (2) a private university–affiliated preschool featuring a child-directed, play-oriented, nursery school program; and (3) a regular public kindergarten, with no previous nursery school experience.

In two important new studies in this area, Yussen, at the University of Wisconsin at Madison, investigated the effects of Montessori school experience on areas of Piagetian cognitive development, social cognition, and memory. In his first study (White, Yussen, & Docherty, 1976), he examined seriation, classification, and conservation skills in Montessori and traditional schools. The groups were further divided into first-year and second-year students. There were twenty students in each group. The Montessori children were superior in seriation and classification skills, but not in conservation tasks, and there were no differences between the first- and second-year students. The lack of differences in the classification tests was hypothesized to be due to the relatively advanced level of the skills required and the less direct work on this area in the Montessori classroom.

In their 1980 study, Yussen, Matthews, and Knight studied three social cognition tasks: referential communication, speech differentiation, and identification of emotions. There were no differences between the Montessori and traditional nursery school children on any of these tasks. On two tests of memory, there were no differences between the groups on free recall, but the Montessori children were superior on tests in recognition memory. This makes sense in the light of the structure of the three-period lesson, in which recognition memory is much more often called for than free recall.

Kohlberg (1968) speculated that the Piaget-based focus on testing conservation and transitivity might be too narrow for tapping operations of classification and ordering. In addition, he noted that his findings also put in question the adequacy of Montessori's view of cognitive operations as resting directly on sensory experience, a view shared by his protégé DeVries. Kohlberg suggested that some additional ordering experiences might be used to supplement the Montessori activities for the development of systems of ordering, number, and conservation.

In new research, DeVries and Goncu (1988) state that when Montessori children and children from a constructivist preschool play a board game without supervision, the Montessori children show significantly more conflict and less conflict resolution.

In informal research conducted as a part of the Teachers' Research Network, several teacher researchers have examined children's understanding of numbers and place value with a simple test. A child is shown a set of 17 objects or dots on a paper. After counting, the child and the researcher agree that there are 17 dots and the child writes down the numeral 17. Underlining the 7 digit, the researcher asks the child to circle the number of dots or objects that that numeral stands for. Almost all children succeed easily at this task. Then, the 1 (in the tens place) is indicated, and the child is asked to show the dots or objects that this stands for. Despite having agreed that that numeral stands for that many, most children fail this task and circle only 1 dot. Furthermore, when asked about the 9 remaining (uncircled) objects, most are unconcerned: "Those are leftover." Kamii (1985) has found that many children as late as second grade fail this test. Teacher researchers found significant differences favoring Montessori children when the test was given to children in Montessori and public school programs. The other differences that may exist between the Montessori and public school children, such as socioeconomic status, limit the generalizability of these findings. Here is an excellent, important, but simple research project for someone with access to the children in a public Montessori school setting.

In conclusion, research evidence thus far suggests that the general sensory experience and training in Montessori preschools do not affect the acquisition of Piagetian conservation and transitivity, but are more effective than traditional nursery schools for fostering development of seriation and classification skills.

CREATIVITY AND MOTIVATIONAL FACTORS

One area of controversy surrounding the Montessori method is the extent to which it might affect the young child's creativity. The concern is based on the observation that the method requires the teacher to demonstrate the correct way to use classroom materials.

In a series of studies by Miezitis (1971), performance on measures of divergent thinking (Torrance Toy Dog and Kangas Action-Agent tasks) was compared among five- to six-year-old middle- and upper-income children attending three different types of nursery school: (1) an "orthodox" Montessori program; (2) a child-directed, play-oriented, nursery school; and (3) a regular public kindergarten. The children (N = 80) were matched for age, sex, and SES and were at least normal in intelligence. No significant differences were found among the three groups on divergent thinking.

Dreyer and Rigler (1969) compared fourteen matched pairs of five-year-old middle-income children of above average IQ attending a Montessori and a traditional nursery school. As a measure of creativity they employed the Torrance Picture Construction Test, a nonverbal task of the Minnesota Test of Creative Thinking. In this task the child is presented with a blank sheet of paper, a piece of red gummed paper, and a pencil, and asked to draw a picture in which the colored paper is an integral part. Performance is assessed by a summed score which takes into account degree of originality, elaboration, activity, and title accuracy. Dreyer and Rigler (1969) found that the traditional nursery school children performed significantly better than the Montessori children on this nonverbal measure of creativity.

Brophy and Choquette (1973) conducted a study with Montessori children to test the hypothesis that teacher instruction in the correct use of classroom equipment inhibits children's ability to generate other uses for that same equipment. Subjects were thirty-one matched pairs of four- and five-year-old suburban, upper-middle–income White children from two Montessori preschools and two traditional nursery schools. Measures of creativity were four adaptations of the Unusual Uses Test from Torrance's Minnesota Tests of Creative Thinking and Writing. Children were given a stuffed toy dog, a fork, a triangular wooden shape used to fit into the Montessori geometric cabinet apparatus, and a Montessori button frame, and asked to tell as many different uses of these items as they could.

Responses were scored for fluency, flexibility, originality, and elaboration, following Yamamoto's (1964) scoring guidelines. The analyses revealed no signs of reduced ability on the part of Montessori children to produce verbal responses regarding divergent uses for objects: a majority of the significant comparisons favored Montessori children.

Banta (1969) found significant differences favoring a Montessori preschool/Montessori primary group and a Montessori preschool/open classroom group over two control groups on a measure of task initiation, on manipulation of the curiosity box, and on verbalizations made while exploring the box. Dog and Bone test scores are designed to measure divergent production, a variable often assessed as an important aspect of creativity. Banta (1969) reports significant differences on this test favoring the two Montessori groups over the no-preschool control group.

Both Curiosity Box and Dog and Bone test scores were also reported by Miller and Dyer (1975) for preschool through second grade. DARCEE and Montessori were significantly higher than the Bereiter-Engelmann and traditional programs on the Dog and Bone test of divergent production after one year of preschool. Over all four testing periods, DARCEE children had, on the average, higher scores than Montessori; Bereiter-Engelmann children had the lowest. On the Curiosity Box measure, Montessori children had the highest score at the end of grade two.

This area is difficult to summarize because of the wide variability in the methods used to assess creativity, in addition to the usual problems encountered in trying to make generalizations from several studies. Montessori children do less well than traditional nursery school children on the Torrance Tests of Creative Thinking, which test originality, elaboration, activity, and title accuracy in a drawing. On several tests of divergent production, across several samples, Montessori children are superior to control groups and most other preschool programs. Verbal creativity, while not as widely assessed, seems to be developed to the same or greater extent in Montessori children as in children attending other preschool programs.

TEACHERS' RESEARCH NETWORK

Before summarizing this article, the Teacher's Research Network should be mentioned; it has already been referred to as an ongoing source of new research about Montessori. For a more detailed look at the TRN, see Chattin-McNichols and Loeffler (1989). Out of a long-time desire to make research more relevant to teachers, especially Montessori teachers, and to empower teachers, Loeffler began the TRN in 1986 with a grant from the American Montessori Society. The program has been based on the campus of the University of Oklahoma since its inception. Teachers from across the country were recruited for the program and twenty-eight teachers were on hand for the first session in April, 1986. For one week, the teachers worked long hours learning about the research on Montessori to date, research design (both qualitative and quantitative), and other topics. Then teachers in groups or as individuals chose a research question and, with support of research "mentors," including Loeffler and Chattin-McNichols, reviewed the literature on their topic and came up with a research design. Teachers and mentors alike shared critiques of the designs and later of measurement instruments, human subjects concerns, and so on. At the end of the week, each teacher left with a completed research design and a timetable for completion of data collection.

At a second five-day session one year later, almost 100 percent of these teachers returned to analyze and write up their work. The high point for many teachers was the sharing sessions in which they presented their findings. Many of the teachers left this session with plans to continue their own research for another year or to cross-replicate another teacher's study. Furthermore, the teachers thought that the experience had challenged them, improved their observation skills, and made them better teachers. Some TRN members have engaged in leadership activities in their areas, returned to graduate school for doctoral study, published their findings, and so on. Overall, more than fifty new studies on Montessori have been conducted.

SUMMARY AND CONCLUSIONS

In this chapter I have reviewed the process research and research on the effects of Montessori school experience on children in several areas. The Montessori method cannot be considered to have received a complete or detailed evaluation by the research undertaken to this point. In general, however, it was found that the Montessori program performs as well as most preschool programs in most areas, such as school readiness and intelligence. Direct-instruction programs produce faster gains in academic subjects; Montessori program gains, however, appear to be longer lasting.

Special programs, with a focus in one area such as language, Piagetian development, or perceptual development, can produce better scores in these areas in most cases. This is not surprising, given the wide range of learning that should be going on and the close match between content and test in these studies.

In vocabulary recognition and ratings of verbal-social participation, other programs produce higher gains than Montessori ones do.

In the development of attentional strategies, general intelligence, achievement in academic areas—and especially in maintaining these gains—the Montessori method performs better than most programs studied. Evidence also indicates that a continuation of Montessori experience beyond preschool would consolidate the gains made; the need of research to examine this possibility is seen as the strongest conclusion to be drawn from the research evidence presently available.

Limitations of the research on Montessori are of two kinds: those shared with other research on early childhood education programs, and those unique to Montessori. In the first group are problems such as small sample size, short-term rather than longitudinal designs, confounding of teacher and method by using a single teacher to represent a model, confounding of the effects of a model with the effects of parent selection, and so on. The selection of inappropriate measures and the use of only part of an instrument (thus invalidating any information on the reliability and validity of the instrument) are also problems. Although other research may also suffer from problems relating to the relationship between programs and the model they supposedly represent, these have been a major source of confusion in the research on Montessori. What is needed is a clear and objective way to assess whether a given classroom is within the bounds of typical Montessori practices. At the very least, researchers must specify in more detail the teacher and environment of the Montessori classrooms they study.

Unique to Montessori research are the problems of designing research studies that address the goals of Montessori education. Much more work needs to be done in this area.

REFERENCES

Baines, M., and Snortum, J. (1973). A time-sampling analysis of Montessori versus traditional classroom interaction. *Journal of Educational Research*, 66, 313–316.

Baker, K. (1988). *The interpretation of subtraction held by children in the Association Montessori Internationale curriculum.* Unpublished master's thesis, University of Maryland.

Banta, T. J. (1969). Research on Montessori and the Disadvantaged. In R. C. Orem (Ed.), *Montessori and the Special Child.* New York: Putnam.

———. (1970). Tests for the evaluation of early childhood education: The Cincinnati Autonomy Test Battery (CATB). In J. Hellmuth (Ed.) *Cognitive Studies*, New York: Brunner/Mazel.

Bauch, J., and Hsu, H. (1988). Montessori: Right or wrong about number concepts? *Arithmetic Teacher.* 35, 6, 8–11.

Bereiter, C. (1967). *Acceleration of intellectual development in early childhood.* Washington, D.C.: Department of Health, Education and Welfare, U.S. Office of Education, Bureau of Research.

Berger, B. (1970). A comparative investigation of Montessori and traditional pre-kindergarten practices. *American Montessori Society Bulletin, 8 (2).*

Black, S. (1977). *A comparison of cognitive and social development in British Infant and Montessori preschools.* Unpublished doctoral dissertation, Temple University.

Boehnlein, M. (1988, Summer). Montessori research: analysis in retrospect. Special Edition of the *North American Montessori Teachers' Association Journal, 13, (3)*, (entire issue).

———. (1985, Summer). The NAMTA Montessori bibliography. Special Edition of the *North American Montessori Teachers' Association Journal, 10, (2)*, (entire issue).

Brophy, J., and Choquette, J. (1973, March). *Divergent production in Montessori children.* Paper presented at the biennial meeting of the Society for Research in Child Development, Philadelphia. ED 080 212.

Carta, J., and Greenwood, C. (1989). Establishing the integrity of the independent variable in early intervention programs. *Early Education and Development. 1 (2).*

Cazden, C. (1972). Some questions for research in early childhood education. In J. C. Stanley (Ed.), *Preschool programs for the disadvantaged.* Baltimore: Johns Hopkins University Press.

Chattin-McNichols, J. (1981). The effects of Montessori school experience. *Young Children, 36.*

———. (in press). *The Montessori controversy.* Albany, NY: Delmar.

Chattin-McNichols, J., and Loeffler, M. (1989). Teachers as researchers: The first cycle of the teachers' research network. *Young Children, 44 (5).*

Cronbach, L., Ragosa, D., Floden, R., and Price, G. (1977, September). *Analysis of covariance in non-randomized experiments: Parameters affecting bias.* Unpublished manuscript, Stanford Evaluation Consortium.

Dawson, M. (1988). A comparative analysis of the standardized test scores of students enrolled in HISD Montessori magnet and traditional elementary classrooms. Unpublished master's thesis, Texas Southern University.

DeVries, R., and Goncu, C. (1988). Interpersonal relations in four-year-old dyads from constructivist and Montessori classrooms.

Di Lorenzo, L. (1969). Pre-kindergarten programs for educationally disadvantaged children. New York State Education Department.

Dreyer, A. S., and Rigler, D. (1969). Cognitive performance in Montessori and nursery school children. Journal of Educational Research, 67.

Duax, T. (1989). Preliminary report on the educational effectiveness of a Montessori school in the public sector. North American Montessori Teachers' Quarterly, 14, No. 2.

Elliot, L. (1967). Montessori's reading principles involving sensitive period methods compared to reading principles of contemporary reading specialists. Reading Teacher, 21.

Feldman, D. (1983). . . . And bodies must move. Unpublished research paper, Xavier University (Ohio).

Feltin, P. (1987). Independent learning in four Montessori elementary classrooms. Unpublished doctoral dissertation, Seattle University.

Fleege, U., Black, M., and Rackauskas, J. (1967). Montessori preschool education project 5-1061. Grant No. OE3-10-127. Washington, D.C.: Office of Education. ED 017 320.

Gardner, R. (1966). A psychologist looks at Montessori. Elementary School Journal, 677, 72–83.

Glenn, C. (1989). A comparison of lower and upper elementary Montessori students with a public school sample. North American Montessori Teachers' Quarterly, 14, (2), 63–68.

Gross, R., Green, B., and Clapp, D. (1973). The Sands School Project. American Montessori Society Bulletin, 11, (1).

Judge, J. (1974). A comparison of preschool children in observational tasks from two programs: Montessori and science-a-process approach. Unpublished doctoral dissertation, University of Texas at Austin.

Kahn, D. (1988). Montessori Public School Consortium Special Report 1988. Available from the Consortium, 2859 Scarborough Road, Cleveland Heights, OH 44118.

Kamii, C. (1985). Young children reinvent arithmetic. New York: Teachers College Press.

Kamii, C., and Radin, N. (1970). A framework for preschool curriculum based on some Piagetian concepts. In I. Athey and D. Rubadeau (Eds.), Educational Implications of Piaget's Theory, Waltham, Mass.: Ginn-Blaisdell.

Karlson, A. (1972) A naturalistic method for identifying behavioral aspects of cognitive acquisition in young children participating in preschool programs. Unpublished doctoral dissertation, University of Chicago.

Karnes, M. (1969). Research and development project on preschool disadvantaged children. Washington, D.C.: U. S. Office of Education. ED 036 663.

Karnes, M., Shwedel, A., and Williams, M. (1983) *A comparison of five approaches for educating young children from low-income homes*, pp. 133–169 in *As the Twig is Bent*. The Consortium for Longitudinal Studies (Ed.) Hillsdale, N.J.: Lawrence Erlbaum, Associates.

Kohlberg, L. (1968). Montessori with the culturally disadvantaged: A cognitive-developmental interpretation and some research findings, p. 105–118 in R. Hess and R. Baer (Eds.), *Early Education*, Chicago: Aldine.

Kuhn, D. (1974). Inducing development experimentally: Comments on a research paradigm. *Development Psychology 10, (5)*. 590–600

McCormick, C., and Schnobrich, J. (1971). Perceptual-motor training and improvement in concentration in a Montessori preschool. *Perceptual and Motor Skills, 32,* 71–77.

Miezitis, S. (1971). Cognitive style, exploratory behavior, and verbal fluency in Montessori and non-Montessori trained preschoolers. Ontario Institute for Studies in Education.

———. (1972). The Montessori method: Some recent research. *Interchange. 2,* 17, 41–59.

Miller, L., and Dyer, L. (1975). Four preschool programs: Their dimensions and effects. *Monographs of the Society for Research in Child Development,* (162).

Miller, L. and Bizzell, R. (1983). Long-term effects of four preschool programs: Sixth, seventh, and eighth grades. *Child Development, 54, (3).* 1570–1587.

Miller, L. and Bizzell, R. Long-term effects of four preschool programs: Ninth- and tenth-grade results. *Child Development, 55, (4).* 727–741.

Montessori, M. (1967). The absorbent mind. New York: Dell.

Pendergast, R. (1969). Pre-reading skills developed in Montessori and conventional nursery schools. *Elementary School Journal, 70* 3, 135–141.

Rudominer, R. (1970). *Self-reliance, initiative, and mastery of Montessori and non-Montessori trained preschool children.* Unpublished master's thesis, University of Toronto.

Reuter, J. (1974). A comparative study of social interaction in a Montessori preschool. *American Montessori Society Bulletin, 12,.* (1). (entire issue)

Reuter, J. and Yunik, G. (1973). Social interaction in nursery schools. *Developmental Psychology 9,* (3) 319–325

Schmid, J., and Black, K. (1977). An observational study of the choice and use of toys by Montessori and non-Montessori preschoolers. p. 79–92 in S. Mallick and J. Hennes (Eds.) *Evaluations of Educational Outcomes, Proceedings of the National Conference on the Evaluation of Montessori and Open Classrooms,* American Montessori Society.

Sciarra, D., and Dorsey, A. (1974). Six year follow up study of Montessori education. *American Montessori Society Bulletin 12, (4)* 1–11

Starr, R., and Banta, T. (1966). Manual for the uses of didactic materials schedule. University of Cincinnati.

Stern, C. (1968). Evaluating language curricula for preschool children. *Monographs of the Society for Research in Child Development, 33,* (8).

Stodolsky, S. and Jensen, J. (1969). *Final report: Ancona Montessori research project for culturally disadvantaged children.* Submitted to the Office of Economic Opportunity. Ed 044 166

Stodolsky, S., and Karlson, A. (1972) Differential Outcomes of a Montessori Curriculum. *Elementary School Journal, 72,* 8, 419–433

Takacs, C., and Clifford, A. (1988). Performance of Montessori graduates in public school classrooms. *North American Montessori Teachers' Quarterly, 14,* (1). 2–9.

Torrance, E. P. (1962). *Guiding Creative Talent.* Englewood Cliffs, N.J.: Prentice-Hall.

Torrence, M. (1988). *Fantasy in American Montessori schools.* Unpublished research project of the Teachers Research Network.

Villegas, A., and Biwer, P. (1987). Parent involvement in a Montessori program: The Denver public school experience. *North American Montessori Teachers' Quarterly, 13,* (1), 13–24

White, J., Yussen, S., and Docherty, E. (1976). Performance of Montessori and traditionally schooled nursery children on tasks of seriation, classification, and conservation. *Contemporary Educational Psychology, 1.* 356–368

Wirtz, P. (1976). *Social behavior related to material settings in the Montessori preschool environment* Unpublished doctoral dissertation, George Peabody College for Teachers.

Yamamoto, K. (1964). *Experimental scoring manuals for Minnesota Test of Creative Thinking and Writing.* Kent, Ohio: Kent State University Bureau of Educational Research.

Yussen, S., Matthews, S., and Knight, J. (1980). Performance of Montessori and traditionally schooled nursery children on social cognitive tasks and memory problems. *Contemporary Educational Psychology, 5.* 124–137.

5

MONTESSORI AND CONSTRUCTIVISM

THE CONSTRUCTIVIST VIEW

There has been a great deal of recent discussion about "constructivism"—a label used by educators who base their methods on the philosophy and work of Jean Piaget. Constance Kamii (1985) and Rheta DeVries and the late Lawrence Kohlberg (DeVries and Kohlberg, 1990) argue for a specific type of educational implementation termed constructivism that they believe most nearly translates Piaget's views into educational practice.

But just what is meant by this term and how does it relate to education? If we are to take Piaget as mentor, and most current constructivists certainly would acknowledge their debt to Piaget, we would say that constructivists believe that humans construct their own knowledge. This view implies that knowledge isn't something external that needs to be internalized by the learner, nor is it something innate that unfolds as the organism matures. Instead, constructivists contend that the developing learner constructs knowledge through ongoing interactions with the environment. The role of education is therefore to provide an environment that stimulates and supports the learner in this process.

MONTESSORI AS A CONSTRUCTIVIST

I would like to suggest that there already is a set of well-defined and implemented educational practices that also can wear the constructivist label—the ones developed by Dr. Maria Montessori and based on more than eighty years of successful classroom practice in both Eastern and Western cultures. When I say that Montessori was a constructivist, I mean that she saw the task of the child as being the construction of the developing adult, including, of course, the construction of knowledge. This construction process can be seen in all areas of development, and it provides the inherent motivation for all true learning, according to Montessori. But let's hear her own words on this subject:

> The known establishes itself in the child as a complex system of ideas constructed by the child himself during a series of psychical processes representing an internal formation, a psychical growth. (1965, p. 163)

And later, in the same book:

> The paths the child follows in the active construction of his individuality are indeed identical with those followed by the genius. His characteristics are absorbed attention, a profound concentration which isolates him from all the stimuli of his environment and corresponds in intensity and duration to the development of spiritual activities. As in genius, this concentration is not without results but is the source of intellectual crisis, of rapid internal developments, and, above all of an external activity which expresses itself in work. (p. 218–19)

Montessori also compares the difference between self-constructed knowledge and information given by another verbally as the difference between an impression made in soft wax, soon to be replaced by other impressions, and the form chiselled in marble as an artist's own creation.

Montessori's prepared learning environment—with self-selection and free choice for the child as its major components, coupled with interesting manipulable objects as stimulation for activity, and a three-year age span for social and intellectual collaboration and challenge—provides an ideal setting for the child's self-construction process.

Kamii, a student and colleague of Piaget, has stressed the view derived from him that autonomy should be the primary aim of education (Kamii, 1985). She believes that it is only as children become autonomous learners and actors, both intellectually and morally, that they can be independent, self-directed thinkers.

Kamii suggests that most schools reinforce heteronomy rather than autonomy—that is, being "other directed" rather than "inner directed." She reminds us that we can't have it both ways: we can't encourage children to be heteronomous in the school setting and then expect them to be autonomous or inner directed and able to withstand the pressure of peers or others in the moral area. It simply doesn't work.

Montessori's prepared learning environment, with its focus on self-selection and independence within a community of learners, is designed to foster autonomy rather than heteronomy. Many, however, have not understood this fundamental notion.

Piaget was an early admirer of Montessori's work. He praised her understanding of the use of concrete materials as an essential element in fostering children's intellectual development. Later, Piaget criticized how her followers used the didactic materials in prescribed ways. He believed that the child must be free to experiment with the materials.

Montessori certainly believed that an adult who understood the relationships inherent in the materials should initially demonstrate their use to prompt children to discover these relationships for themselves. It is obvious to any observer, however, that actual American classroom practices encourage experimentation with the materials. Current American Montessori teacher education also emphasizes flexibility and extended uses of the materials.

Piaget's understanding of how the materials were actually used, at least in American classrooms, seems to have been based upon second-hand information; there is no evidence that he ever directly observed these classrooms. Piaget was also incorrectly informed regarding Montessori's early mathematical exercises, as indicated in a 1968 interview with Richard Evans, believing that there was no recognition of the importance of discrete quantities in the young child's number development. Three traditional Montessori exercises (the spindle box, the numbers and counters, and the memory game) all directly address the child's necessary experience with discrete quantities as do the more informal uses of counting things for practical purposes in the daily life of a Montessori environment. There is therefore some doubt about the accuracy of Piaget's information about Montessori's materials and practices.

To understand the Montessori model we need look not only at Montessori's writings but also at the ongoing, successful classroom practices spanning more than eight decades in a variety of cultural settings. These experiences cannot be ignored if we are to judge the viability of this educational model.

When many non-Montessori educators think of Montessori education, they think of colorful and expensive didactic apparatus presided over by a specially trained teacher espousing a nontraditional philosophy. Then, depending on their own personal biases and their information sources, they may conclude that the method either allows children complete freedom, leading to chaos and lack of socialization, or is rigid and inhibiting, thus not permitting children a chance to use their imaginations and creativity.

What they fail to understand is the essential Montessori concept of the prepared learning environment—with its focus upon a social and psychological environment for children as well as a cognitive and physical one. Persons unfamiliar with Montessori's basic principles are sometimes astounded to discover that people have created Montessori environments without a single piece of traditional didactic apparatus and yet consider them to be perfectly functional and within the Montessori tradition. In villages in South America (T. End, personal communication, 1983), Mexico (V. Varga, personal communication, 1985), and Samoa (C. Trudeau, personal communication, 1984) teachers used native materials to create their prepared environments.

THE MONTESSORI ESSENTIALS

But if not the didactic apparatus, what is then essential to a Montessori environment? Several things seem to be essential ingredients. The belief that children are natural learners and are in a better position to make appropriate learning choices than their adult mentors. This doesn't mean, however, that teachers don't have an important role to play.

The teacher's role in a Montessori environment is twofold: to be an astute observer of children with a firm grasp of children's natural development and then to plan a prepared learning environment that meets the developmental and cultural needs of the children. The teacher is the architect of the environment, the resource person, and she or he plans the varied array from which the child will choose. But the choices are not static, nor are they identical from one culture to another, particularly in that aspect of the environment called the exercises of daily living or practical life.

Montessori wanted children to become independent and responsible, and to have a feeling of confidence based on competence. By helping them master the tasks and skills needed to function well in their own environments, she believed that they would develop self-confidence and a sense of responsibility to others. This sense of responsibility and community would begin, in their own small community, the school or Children's House, and later would expand to a responsibility and interest in the larger world.

The notion that Montessori children must work alone on individual activities at all times is one of the most persistent and erroneous of the misconceptions about Montessori. In fact, children from the beginning in Montessori environments and continuing to the present are encouraged to work together on many activities, including caring for the environment, preparing food, role playing, playing games, and working together in the academic areas.

The importance of individual work in the Montessori environment simply reflects the view that children are unique individuals with different strengths, interests, and rates of growth. Different activities are offered to meet their particular needs. But children also are seen as social beings, part of a community of adults and children; consequently, many activities are done together for a common purpose or interest.

In addition, children who are at the same level of cognitive development often are engaged in common intellectual pursuits and this type of collaboration is encouraged. Since there is a three-year age span in most Montessori environments, children are able to learn informally from others and also find appropriate peer groups offering intellectual challenge and support.

Montessori believed that independence must come before interdependence and that the child must construct cooperation and interdependence through the child's own experiences—these cannot be taught or imposed from without. Therefore, the prepared environment offers many opportunities for both independence and collaboration to occur and to develop.

CONTROL OF ERROR

A second misunderstanding about Montessori's ideas concerns her notion of control of error or auto-education. As a long-time child observer who has found that children's errors provide wonderful glimpses into their development and thinking, I decided a few years ago to do some research on Montessori's views on error and its control or correction.

I found that Montessori wrote quite extensively on the subject. Her thoughts may clear up misunderstandings regarding the view that Montessori believed that error should be stamped out at all costs. Of course it is impossible, in this brief space, to present all that she said on the subject; however, I would like to mention several important points in order to clarify the issue.

In her writings, Montessori described at least three levels of error control. Only the first was a mechanical or external control, exemplified best by the cylinder blocks, although this is the only one ever mentioned by her critics.

> As the hollows in the blocks correspond exactly to the cylinders deposited in them, it is not possible to place them all wrongly since at the last there would remain one without a place. Hence a mistake is an obstacle only to be overcome for without it the exercise cannot be completed. On the other hand, the correction is so easy that the child makes it himself. The little problem suddenly presenting itself to the child like the unexpected jack-in-the-box has interested him. (1965, p. 75)

One has only to observe a two-and-a-half-year-old child happily immersed in solving this puzzle of the cylinder blocks in order to appreciate what an astute observer of young children's interests Montessori really was.

After this early interest in solving problems has been awakened, Montessori suggests, the young child arrives at a second level of error control based upon the construction and recognition of certain internalized standards. These standards lead the child finally, after much uncorrected experimentation, to perceive the wholeness of things, for instance, of a series of pink cubes graduated from large to small. These standards pertain to the relationships of the parts to the whole.

A later form of error control, used by elementary children, offers further evidence of the movement of the locus of control to the thought of the child. Montessori cites as an example the teacher who transposes two words in a sentence that the child has composed with word cards, thus allowing the child to discover the change in meaning. In this situation the teacher should not suggest answers (in this case the function of the words) but must instead bring out the full potentiality of the child (in this case the child's implicit knowledge of his or her own language). However, Montessori cautions that the teacher must understand the child's readiness for this problem before it is offered.

And, finally, Montessori (1962) reminds us that errors are a part of life and that even in science, which is seen as exact and certain, error is openly acknowledged. In fact, she notes that in scientific research no figure is ever given or accepted without an indication of its probable error; this acknowledgment contributes to the data's value.

Montessori seems to be implying here that things worth doing always entail the risk and the probability of error, and we should acknowledge this while seeking to understand and to learn.

TYPES OF LEARNING

Piaget has suggested that there are two kinds of learning in which humans are involved: learning in the broad sense, which he equates with development; and learning in the narrow sense, as in specific school-type learning.

The Montessori prepared learning environment offers opportunities for both types of learning to occur at all levels. The open-ended curriculum and the three-year time span for sampling and exploring offer an optimal setting for development and learning.

Specific lessons are given at appropriate times, depending upon the child's development and interest, in order to introduce new exercises or ideas. Contrary to a common but erroneous belief that materials can be used in only one "right" way, once an exercise has been introduced, children are free to explore the parameters of the materials involved within the same general guidelines that exist in most well-managed classrooms. For instance, blocks are not made for throwing, nor is clay to be ground underfoot into the carpet!

THE DIDACTIC MATERIALS

Contemporary constructivists are particularly critical of Montessori's didactic materials which she saw as efficient experiences (not her term but her meaning) created to support children's cognitive development. Based on her experimentation and her observations of children's spontaneous behaviors, Montessori incorporated into these materials what she had determined to be children's aesthetic and sensory preferences in color, dimension, and texture. By providing these materials (blocks, puzzles, beads, etc.) which held and still hold great appeal for children and incorporate precise mathematical relationships; Montessori thought that children would begin to assimilate these relationships through their own activities involving them.

Montessori may have been overly optimistic in her assumption that young children could and would assimilate the specific relationships that she so carefully built into the didactic apparatus through their own activities with them. The truth is that we don't really know how the brain stores and translates this experiential knowledge into abstract relationships and concepts, although some studies do suggest the possibility that spatial knowledge especially may be derived in just this way.

Juan Pascal-Leone (1976, p. 110–25), who studied with Piaget and terms himself a neo-piagetian, offers one possible explanation regarding the transition from concrete activity to abstract thought. He suggests that humans may create models of the world, what he terms mereological representations, as an interim step before using abstract symbols such as language and number. Pascal-Leone also suggests that these more iconic representations might be primarily right-brain activities, referring to the studies indicating the contrasting primary functions of the two hemispheres of the brain.

Whether Montessori's didactic apparatus activities assist children in creating such interim iconic models certainly is not proven. The only thing that is clear is that young children enjoy using the didactic apparatus and have done so for more than eight decades.

DURABILITY OF THE MONTESSORI MODEL

We are now at the most important point to be made in this paper—eighty years of successful Montessori practice.

In her recent book on constructivism (1990), coauthored with the late Lawrence Kohlberg, Rheta DeVries explains why she devotes a chapter to Montessori. After citing Montessori's seminal contributions to the constructivist approach and giving her own criticisms of Montessori's ideas, DeVries concludes that Montessori's educational practices seem sure to continue on into the twenty-first century—a statement she doesn't make about any other educational practices. To quote DeVries:

> Started in the first decades of the twentieth century, it will almost certainly be with us in the first decades of the twenty-first, something that cannot be said with assurance of all the other programs discussed in this volume. (1990, p. 261)

If DeVries is accurate in her predictions, just what is it that makes Montessori's ideas so enduring that they have survived wars, changes of government, and translations into different cultures?

I do not believe that Montessori's didactic apparatus accounts for this durability, for much of the present array of materials wasn't even available in the first Children's Houses in Rome, which were certainly successful. Also, as mentioned previously, Montessori schools have been successfully established in Third World countries without using even a piece of the conventional array.

Certainly, Montessori's concept of efficient experiences, which the activities with the didactic apparatus represent, seems valuable and receives confirmation in Lev Vygotsky's (1978) notions of scaffolding and the zone of proximal development. Vygotsky suggests that children are more intellectually competent (the zone of proximal development) than they can demonstrate when asked to solve a problem or perform a task alone. If, however, they are supported by an adult or a slightly more advanced peer (scaffolding), they will be able to perform at a higher level and move forward in their development more quickly.

By assisting children in solving problems and evaluating their own successes, Montessori's didactic apparatus provides a unique form of scaffolding and, especially in the mathematics and language materials for early elementary children, is designed to help children construct a higher level of abstraction while building upon present understandings and skills. Efficient experiences, however, can be provided through many kinds of materials and activities if the purposes and goals are clearly understood and are not dependent upon special materials.

I contend that the secret of Montessori's successful practices lies not in the physical artifacts of her method, but rather in the creation of a unique social and psychological milieu that supports the child and the child's developing autonomy and independence.

THE PSYCHOLOGICAL ENVIRONMENT

A successful Montessori environment is identifiably different from most other early childhood environments precisely because the children in it are engaged in self-initiated activities with a degree of autonomy and independence that is unique in an educational setting.

The psychological and social ambience created permits children to expand their competencies in ways that are meaningful and functional to them as well as to the larger culture of which they are a part. This success, which children feel and teachers and parents perceive, has been the foundation of Montessori's durability and successful integration into a variety of settings. Of course, the physical environment also plays an important supportive role, but the Montessori prepared environment is more a unique psychological setting than a physical one. This fact is not understood by many who think that the essence of Montessori is found in the sandpaper letters or the cylinder blocks. Unique characteristics of the Montessori environment that contribute to its positive atmosphere for constructive development include the following:

- An unusual respect for children as competent individuals who can be trusted to act in the best interests of the community of which they are a part.

- A small number of well-defined ground rules for acceptable behavior, understood by all.

- A belief that children construct their own knowledge through exploration and discovery assisted by the introduction of efficient experiences planned by the teacher. In accordance with Montessori's admonition to "follow the child," the primary initiator of all learning activities is the child. Direct intervention by the teacher is limited and facilitating rather than didactic.

- Appealing activities for children at various levels of difficulty that match the children's developmental needs, have sensorial and aesthetic attraction, and have cultural value.

The last characteristic has been, no doubt, an important factor in the Montessori model's ability to be integrated into many cultures, but it is often overlooked in planning activities for children. Culturally relevant activities motivate children to learn by connecting the child's developing competence to the perceived technology of the culture. Examples of activities include making leis from native flowers in an Hawaiian preschool, learning origami paper folding in an Asian school, and writing or drawing letter symbols in any culture with a written language. Many of the activities in a Montessori classroom directly connect the activity of the child to the child's culture.

Erik Erikson (1977) who was trained as a Montessori teacher in Vienna, has stressed that it is important for children to perceive themselves as successful in mastering the technologies of their culture. This perception of success relates to the fourth stage of his eight stages of psychosocial development, which involves the development of a sense of industry rather than a sense of inferiority.

THE DIVERSITY OF MONTESSORI CLASSROOMS

Montessori's contemporary critics have said that they must base their evaluations of her work solely on her writings, because Montessori schools are so diverse and varied that critics don't know which schools to use as models. In saying this they reveal that they have missed an essential point of Montessori's work. Although Montessori schools do differ both within and between countries, they are different precisely because Montessori respected the uniqueness as well as the universals in each child's development. These varied environments include activities that speak to the universal needs of young children as well as to the particular needs and interests of individual children and of their cultures. But these schools are more alike than different if one looks beneath the specifics and recognizes the essential elements of the prepared learning environment.

Montessori laid the groundwork for an ongoing research process in the prepared environment. She challenged teachers to become scientific pedagogues who would learn and add to the general knowledge about child development while supporting individual children's growth.

Surely more than eighty years of successful practice based on this process deserves a closer look from scholars and educators. This doesn't mean the initiation of a new round of comparative studies (although in the past Montessori has fared well in these) nor does it mean advocacy for the wholesale adoption of Montessori as a quick fix for children who are failing in the public schools (although, again, Montessori continues to be highly successful in many magnet school programs). Instead, it means that the time has come to put aside differences and begin a meaningful and respectful dialogue between thoughtful and open-minded educators in order to learn and profit from each other's experiences and insights.

Montessori certainly didn't have all the answers, but she did provide extremely perceptive insights about children's development and learning. She also provided useful suggestions for practices that create a stable yet flexible framework for successful early childhood programs.

Contemporary American Montessori classrooms are not static environments, frozen in the early 1900s. They are environments designed by contemporary American teachers to meet the needs of contemporary American children, which means they include materials and methods to meet these changing needs. For instance, dress-up corners and other types of pretend activities now are a part of many Montessori environments, although they were not found in earlier ones. Because children often spend most of the day in these settings, activities that once took place at home and in the neighborhood now are seen as necessary components of the school environment. Computers also have found their way into many Montessori classrooms. Some critics contend that such changes mean that these classrooms are no longer pure Montessori settings, that they represent counterfeit versions of Montessori's original ideas and methods. This recognition of changing needs is completely consistent with Montessori's original insights, however, and with her admonition to "follow the child."

A LOOK TO THE FUTURE

Perhaps we now have reached the necessary distance from Montessori and the force of her personality so that we can begin to understand and appreciate more objectively the importance of her ideas. Although charismatic, Montessori was at times a difficult person, as a reading of her early history in the United States attests. Some of the antipathy to her ideas among American educators, who have been schooled in the traditions of the early nursery school and kindergarten movements, stems perhaps more from this legacy than from any objective evaluation of her work.

The aspects of her thinking that have not been fully understood, I contend, are the importance she attached to the child's developing autonomy as well as her rare understanding of the self-constructive nature of the child's learning and the psychological and social matrix necessary to support it. These essential elements of her method—which she preferred to call a way of looking at the child—place Montessori squarely in the constructivist camp.

Montessori educators owe a debt to Piaget and his American colleagues for articulating so well the constructivist approach. Certainly, there remain differences between Montessori's and Piaget's views, but Piaget lived thirty years longer than Montessori and had time for more study, observation, and reflection. Just as modern Montessori educators would not accept Montessori's 1907 nutrition advice because they now have better information, they also have learned a great deal from Piaget's insights and have integrated this knowledge into their understanding of children.

It often seems that in spite of decades of research confirming the child's inherent motivation for learning, the world is filled with people who lack faith in the child's desire to learn. Many current educational methods, rather than building on this inner resource, seem to be designed to blunt the child's natural curiosity and hunger to learn. For this reason, if for no other, it seems important that those who support the constructivist approach to learning should join forces and, instead of quarreling over differences, should recognize their kinship, applaud their common goals, and get on with the task of public enlightenment. We hope that Montessori educators and others who believe in a constructivist approach will join forces for the benefit of all children.

REFERENCES

Devries, R. and Kohlberg, L. (1990). *Constructivist early education: Overview and comparison with other programs.* Washington, D.C. National Association for the Education of Young Children.

Erikson, E. (1977). *Toys and reasons.* New York: Norton.

Kamii, C. (1985). *Young children reinvent arithmetic.* New York: Teachers College Press.

Montessori, M. (1962). *Discovery of the child.* Adyar, Madras, India: Vasanta Press, The Theosophical Society. Original work published 1948.

———— (1965). *Spontaneous activity in education.* New York: Schocken.

Pascal-Leone, J. (1986, April). Metasubjective problems of constructive cognition: Forms of knowing and their psychological mechanism. *Canadian Psychological Review,* 17, 2.

Piaget, J. (1963). *The origins of intelligence in children.* New York: Norton.

————. (1973). *To understand is to invent.* New York: Grossman.

Vygotsky, L. (1978). *Mind in society.* Cambridge, MA: Harvard University Press.

PART TWO

VIEWS

FROM

OUTSIDE

THE

MONTESSORI

FIELD

INTRODUCTION

In part 2, five professionals from diverse disciplines examine the influence of Maria Montessori's thinking on their own fields.

David Elkind's chapter relates the idea of cultural frames to the Montessori prepared environment. Elkind, who has adapted Erving Goffman's concept of frames to his work with teenagers, now applies the notion of cultural frames to the younger child. He suggests that the Montessori prepared learning environment offers four important types of frames to support the child's emotional and social development: classroom frames, activity frames, teacher/child frames, and child/child frames. These frames (which Goffman described as repetitive social situations with their own rules, expectancies, understandings, and emotional rhythms) assist the child in moving into the broader and more complex social milieu of a group environment. Elkind offers a contemporary explanation for Montessori's often misunderstood concept of normalization.

Linguist Carol Chomsky focuses on Montessori's remarkable insight that writing naturally precedes reading in young children's development. She compares Montessori's early observations to current interest in young children's so-called invented spellings, exploring the similarities and differences. Chomsky begins with her own observations in 1950, continues through the work of Charles Read in the 1960s, and moves on to consider the growing recognition today of the developmental importance of this early writing for the child.

Sylvia Richardson, M.D., who has spent much of her professional life as a pediatrician studying, diagnosing, and developing programs for children with learning disabilities, credits Montessori in her chapter with developing an educational methodology that includes the necessary components to assist children with learning disabilities. She advocates the use of this methodology for young at-risk preschoolers—particularly those with attentional disorders—in order to minimize the problems that they will encounter later. Richardson enumerates how the components of the prepared environment also support the young child's development in perception and in language, both spoken and written, thus preventing the development of many problems.

Psychologist William Crain, from City College of New York, points out an often overlooked characteristic of young children's thinking, richly described by Montessori—the inherently emotional nature of the process. Crain suggests that the trend in recent years to look to computer models for an understanding of human cognition misses the vital role that emotion plays.

Montessori believed that the child's spontaneous cognitive work so directly affects the development of the whole personality that adult interference creates emotional problems. Crain points out that Montessori's descriptions of these problems have anticipated central themes in the psychoanalytic self-psychology of D. W. Winnicott. Both theorists, according to Crain, have been concerned with the ways in which people lose faith in themselves and become slaves to social approval. Montessori's methods offer children opportunities to build a firm sense of themselves based on independent, intrinsically meaningful work rather than on a shallow dependence on social approval.

The final chapter in part 2 is by Lilian Katz, who plays various roles in American early childhood education and represents an important and critical outside voice in this discussion. Katz argues that researchers in early childhood education have a weak data base because of the transient characteristics of their immature subjects and the moral dilemmas posed by carrying out research on children. The field is therefore open to doctrinaire arguments based on competing ideologies. A possible solution is to provide opportunities to examine and debate competing ideas. She challenges Montessorians to address issues relating to Montessori's educational approach as well as to correct misunderstandings held by the broader educational community about Montessori's concepts and practices.

Answers to many of Katz's questions are included in earlier chapters of the book. A follow-up section addresses specific responses to six major questions:

- What are the essentials of a Montessori classroom?
- What is meant by a prepared environment in Montessori's educational framework?
- What is Montessori's concept of multisensory learning and how is it applied?
- Is autonomy an important goal for young children?
- Do Montessori practices fit the developmentally appropriate guidelines delineated by the National Association for the Education of Young Children or are there differences?
- What is the current state of American Montessori practices?

Several representatives of contemporary Montessori thought and practices furnish responses: Beth Bronsil, Xavier University; Marlene Barron, New York University (representing programs affiliated with the American Montessori Society); and David Kahn, North American Montessori Teachers' Association (NAMTA) (an invited participant at the symposium). Their answers may not encompass the views of all American Montessori educators, but they do represent the views of persons actively involved in Montessori classrooms. Katz's questions and the answers must continue to be formulated as an ongoing dialogue among early childhood educators. The need for such a dialogue becomes clear as we continue to seek solutions to the many social and educational challenges that face us as we approach the beginning of a new century.

6

MONTESSORI: SOCIAL-EMOTIONAL PERSPECTIVES

The Montessori method and materials are commonly thought to encourage the development of the child's intellect and the skills of reading, math, and writing. Much less common is the appreciation that the Montessori method and materials also foster emotional and social development and skills. In this chapter I will describe how the Montessori method and materials facilitate social and emotional growth. I believe that this can best be done by discussing the role of frames in a child's development.

FRAMES

The late Erving Goffman, perhaps our most gifted sociologist and anthropologist, described an important structure of social life in his book *Frame Analysis* (1974). Frames are repetitive social situations with their own rules, expectancies, and understandings. Frames also have an emotional rhythm that can be completed, broken, or spoiled. Frames are part of what Goffman liked to call the "dust" of human existence—those aspects of our everyday lives that we tend to neglect or ignore as unimportant and insignificant.

A few examples of frames may help to clarify this concept. A common adult frame is the waiting room situation. Waiting rooms, whether at an airport, doctor's office, bank, or wherever, have some implicit rules, expectancies, and understandings that most people in these situations comprehend and follow often unconsciously. Waiting room rules include taking one's turn and not going out of line, not intruding into other people's space or conversations, not bothering other people with strange behavior such as singing, talking loudly to neighbors, and so on.

Waiting room frames also have an emotional rhythm that can be interrupted or spoiled. If there is a long line of people waiting to get on an airplane and someone walks to the head of the line and cuts in nonchalantly, there is a lot of resentment among the other people waiting in line. The person who cut in effectively spoiled the frame and produced an emotional reaction that needs to be dissipated. The effect can be dissipated by someone saying something to the person who cut in and getting an apology in return. If some remedial work is not performed, those who experienced the spoiled frame may discharge the emotional reaction in other situations and in response to others who have broken frame rules. Unexpectedly harsh reactions to the breaking of a particular frame rule can occur when the person is responding to an accumulation of past spoiled frame experiences.

Spoiled frames are a commonplace in contemporary society. When, for example, we open the door for someone and they do not say "Thank you," we experience a spoiled frame. Good manners are essentially a set of frame rules regarding how to behave in repetitive social situations. Because good manners are less common today, those who do practice them often experience spoiled frames. Likewise, when people behave badly in public places we again have examples of broken frame rules. In a supermarket where we are supposed to pick up bakery items with a set of tongs, the person who uses fingers is breaking the frame rules. So too is the person who eats from the bunch of grapes or bag of candy in the shopping cart while doing the rest of their shopping. The mundaneness and all pervasiveness of the frame rules are reasons we take them for granted. Yet, as Goffman points out, they take up a large proportion of our social consciousness and energies.

FRAME ACQUISITION

Goffman was concerned mainly with the behavior of adults operating in frames. He did not deal with how children attain frames nor with the developmental limitations of such acquisitions. Yet the idea of frames provides an all important insight to the socialization of children. Indeed, I would argue that learning frames *is* the way in which children become socialized. Nonetheless, as we would expect from the work of Piaget, the child's ability to acquire and utilize frames varies with the level of intellectual development.

Here again, a few examples may help. Consider the thank-you frame. To understand this frame the child must know the general rule: "Every time someone gives me something, I must say, 'Thank you.'" They must also be able to deduce from that general rule the conclusion: "This person has given me something, therefore I must say, 'Thank you.'" Clearly learning the frame rule having to do with thank-you requires syllogistic reasoning. To employ the rule, the child must go from the general rule to the particular example. Such syllogistic reasoning, and correspondingly such applications of frame rules, however, depend upon the attainment of what Piaget (1950) has called "concrete operations," which do not usually appear until the age of six or seven.

Some frame rules are sufficiently complex that they cannot be fully understood and utilized until the young person reaches adolescence and has acquired the higher level of mental operations that Piaget describes as "formal operations." Consider the set of social rules involved, say, in asking someone for a date. The rules are complicated, because in addition to asking the person out, it is also necessary to protect oneself in case of rejection. This set of rules, then, involves the ideas of possibility and contingency, which can only be constructed with the aid of formal operations.

When asking for a date and in order to avoid rejection, the person first inquires whether the other person is busy on the evening in question. In this way, the person asking does not have to make a premature commitment. Such an approach also allows the person who is being asked out to avoid the encounter without seeming to reject the other person. This higher order of frame interaction is characteristic of adolescents and adults.

The acquisition of frames, then, has a developmental dimension. Some frames cannot be learned until the young person has attained concrete operations, others cannot be learned until the young person has reached adolescence and attained formal operations. The emotional dynamics associated with these frames also become more complex and will not be fully experienced until the young person has reached the requisite level of mental development.

FRAMES IN MONTESSORI EDUCATION

From the perspective of frames, it is reasonable to propose that Montessori education involves children learning frames at several different levels. At the broadest level there are what might be called *classroom frames*, which operate for all children in the classroom at all times. In addition there are *activity frames* associated with one or another material or activity. There are also *teacher-child frames*, in which the teacher and child interact. And finally there are *child-child frames* that govern the interaction of children with one another. These frames, like all the others we have talked about, have their own system of rules, understandings, and emotional rhythms. We need now to look at these Montessori frames in a little more detail to explore how they operate to further the child's social and emotional development.

CLASSROOM FRAMES

In a Montessori school, the child learns early on the classroom frame rules of Montessori education. One of these rules is *responsibility.* The child is expected to take responsibility for the materials he or she takes out and uses. Teachers instruct the children in this rule both verbally and by example. Very quickly, children come to realize that if they remove materials, they must put them back in their place and in their original configuration.

Another classroom frame rule that children learn early on is *independence.* Again through teacher and pupil example, children learn that they are to work by themselves with the materials and that they are not to disturb other children. Another classroom rule is *cooperation.* If a child wishes to use materials that another child is already using, the first child must wait until the other child has finished working. Children learn other cooperative frame rules at snack time, when they help set the table or serve snacks to the other children.

It is reasonable to ask at this point how it is possible for young children to learn rules that seem to require concrete operations and syllogistic deduction, as in the description earlier of learning to say, "thank you." These classroom rules are essentially action or motoric, rather than verbal. Such rules can be learned by observation and imitation and with little in the way of verbal instruction. The syllogistic rules involved in learning to say "thank you," in contrast, are verbal; that is why their effective utilization depends on the attainment of concrete operations.

What happens when classroom frames are broken or spoiled? In general, a child breaking a classroom frame rule upsets the other children, who will attempt to correct the problem themselves. If a child fails to put away materials, another child will help or remind the first child of what needs to be done. Montessori recognized how much young children come to depend upon frame rules to provide the order and consistency they need to feel secure. Children experience violation of frame rules as a threat to the order in their world and move immediately to put the frame rules back into effect.

ACTIVITY FRAMES

One of the major strengths of Montessori education is the explicit frame rules for using materials. Montessori recognized that a set of frame rules allows children to get the most from working with manipulative materials. This is not intuitively obvious. It might seem that children playing with blocks, for example, in a completely free and spontaneous manner would nonetheless learn a great deal about size, balance, before, behind, and so on. Although that may in fact occur, putting block play within a system of frame rules insures that the child will derive the most knowledge from this activity.

Piaget also recognized the importance of frame rules when introducing children to manipulative materials. He once visited in the 1930s the Malting House School in London where renowned child psychologist Susan Isaacs worked. The school was run on "progressive" principles and children were given a great deal of freedom in choosing the materials they wanted to work with and the way in which they employed them. Piaget was impressed with the school but also remarked that he thought the children might well benefit from a little more adult direction.

Montessori recognized the necessity of structure when children are first starting out with an activity and the importance of free experimentation with the materials once they had mastered the initial procedures. Consider a child who is working with the pink tower (a set of size-graded, square pink blocks that can be built into a tower with the largest block on the bottom and the smallest one on top with a steady progression of smaller size and higher position). Once he or she has learned to order the blocks according to size in the vertical direction, it is quite natural for the child to then arrange them horizontally or to construct other figures with them.

Montessori realized that frames were not meant to imprison us into fixed routines but rather to free us by making the fixed routines automatic and unconscious. Structures or frames are not the enemy of freedom—as some extreme advocates of progressive education argued—but rather an essential condition of healthy freedom. Activity frames, then, are not meant to bind children into fixed routines from which they must not deviate but rather to give them the foundation skills necessary for innovative and creative work.

Montessori gave many examples of children who, after having mastered the initial structure or frame, moved on to creative utilization of these operations. She describes one boy who did mathematical calculations in his head that a visiting teacher had to do with pencil and paper. When the child made a mental correction, Montessori observed, "This subsequent mental correction in quite a complicated calculation caused greater astonishment than the fact that he had been able to carry out the operation itself. The mind of the child possessed a peculiar faculty for retaining these successive phases" (1975, p. 57).

Montessori gave many other examples of children who went beyond the initial frames. "There was a child who had learned the extraction of the square root according to the procedure indicated by our apparatus. He was intensely interested in extracting square roots by himself but he did so in a different way invented by himself, which however he could not explain" (1975, p. 57).

Montessori described her method of education not as a confinement, but as a prelude to freedom: "Our conception of education may be figuratively described by saying that the educator stands behind the child and allows him to go forward as far as he can, whereas the other method is to stand in front of the child and prevent him from going further than limits imposed upon him by the teacher" (1961, p. 65). Montessori education, then, is not aimed at binding children into rigid routines. Quite the contrary—the routines are a path to spontaneous activity and creativity.

This important point is frequently misunderstood by critics of Montessori education. Yet in any discipline—be it art, science, or the professions—freedom and innovation always follow from a solid grounding in structure. Leonardo, for example, could hardly have created his *David* without a solid knowledge of human anatomy. Likewise, Shakespeare could hardly have achieved what he did without a thorough understanding of the structure of language and of the dramatic arts.

To be sure, genius is more than structure, but even geniuses must know the structures of their disciplines to realize their genius fully. And even those creative workers who break the rules of the discipline, such as the French Impressionists did, have to know the rules first. The same is true in science. Creative discoveries are always built upon the work of others. As Darwin said, "If I have seen further it is because I have had such broad shoulders to stand upon." Far from being the enemy of freedom, frames are its closest ally. And freedom is a social and emotional as well as a cognitive experience and orientation.

Activity frames, like all frames, also have an emotional rhythm that further contributes to their social-emotional value. Montessori gives many different examples of the emotional rhythm inherent in frames and the emotional satisfaction that children experience when they are allowed to bring these frames to completion. Again, some of the frames may be constructed by the children themselves. Montessori gave this example:

> Another time I saw a boy who had resolved to work out a gigantic multiplication of numbers consisting of 30 figures by another 25 figures. The partial products accumulated to such an extent that the boy was surprised. He had to have recourse to the help of two friends, who had to find sheets of paper and stick them together to contain this monstrous operation and its enormous development. After two consecutive days of work the multiplication was not finished. It was completed only the next day, yet without the boys showing any sign of being tired of it. They too, seemed proud and satisfied with their great achievement. (1975, p. 56)

If these children had been interrupted and forced to engage in some other activity before the multiplication project was complete, the frame would have been spoiled. Instead of emotional satisfaction and intellectual closure, the children would have experienced emotional and intellectual frustration. Although Montessori did not use the term *frame* she clearly understood the concept and the fact that frames are emotional and social as well as intellectual. In the above example, a single child expanded his frame to include his friends who helped him to complete it.

In a real sense, activity frames are at the heart of Montessori education. And as we have seen, these frames are social and emotional as well as intellectual. Just as intellectual structure is a necessary prerequisite to intellectual freedom, so too are social-emotional structures a prerequisite to social-emotional freedoms. True social freedom only appears with the acceptance of social responsibility, and true emotional freedom will only be present when there is a sense of empathy for others. Social responsibility and empathy are by-products of the acquisition of structures inherent in activity frames.

TEACHER-CHILD FRAMES

I recently met with a group of educators who were deeply concerned about the teaching of values and relativism. They were concerned that they might indoctrinate their students if they took a strong position on certain issues that they believed in. Moreover, they believed that an assertion of values would be an abuse of their power in the sense that the students might feel coerced into accepting those values. This recurrent issue in education needs to be raised in any discussion of teacher-child frames.

Montessori's position on this issue is complex. On the one hand, she herself held certain values that she did not question. She believed in respecting children as individuals with their own ways of thinking and knowing. She believed that children should be given responsibilities in keeping with their abilities. She believed that adults should encourage and support children's spontaneous efforts toward growth rather than restrict and bind them. But she also believed strongly that adults should not place their desire to teach ahead of the child's desire to learn.

Although these values are embodied in the techniques of Montessori instruction, Montessori did not see herself or her teachers as imposing these values on the child. Instead, she saw these values as inherent in the processes of growth and development. She contended that she was espousing the values that were fundamental to the nature of the child. Like the founding fathers in their preamble to the Bill of Rights, she took these values to be "self-evident." Accordingly, Montessori felt no hesitation in communicating these values to children:

> We are not trying to overthrow the great sentiment and veneration which we owe to our parents. But we wish to secure for the child the sense of gratitude and affection similar to that which we bear towards our parents so that we may not consider the child as the product of the adult, but rather the producer of the adult. It is only a cycle in which both adults and children take their places and it is necessary to recognize the parts both play and the relative importance of each. (1961, p. 17)

In many ways, Montessori's criticism of the adult-child and teacher-child frames of her day have been given a modern expression in the voice of psychiatrist Alice Miller (1981). Miller speaks of "poisonous" pedagogy and of narcissistic parents who fail to respect the child as an individual and who as a result destroy the child's budding sense of self-esteem and authenticity. Like Montessori, Miller has no hesitation about espousing her values because she sees them as inherent in the nature of the child rather than as her own personal beliefs.

There is a danger here, of course. Who is to say that Montessori, or Miller, or Piaget, for that matter, is reading nature correctly? Perhaps these individuals, like the rest of us, are merely propounding personal values that we grandiosely and self-importantly pass off as nature's laws. Who is the final arbiter as to what nature's laws really are?

The only answer, or so it seems to me, is the scientific one—the rules of evidence. If Montessori has read nature correctly, then the practices she identifies as deriving from nature should work better than those that do not reflect the child's nature. And, of course, the principles have worked. Otherwise Montessori schools and Montessori education would not have survived and flourished as they have. The proof, in the end, is in the pudding.

There is, then, some empirical justification for employing those child-teacher frames that embody respect for the child, recognition of the child's powers and abilities, and encouragement of the child's independence and spontaneous growth. These values are present in all of the teacher-child frames in the Montessori classroom.

Nonetheless we still have to ask whether Montessori teachers abuse their power position by espousing these values. I don't think so. I believe children appreciate adults who demonstrate a clear set of values. The child is, after all, not an automaton. We show respect for the child when we display our own values because we recognize that the child has the choice to accept or reject those values. To be sure, if we punish a child for rejecting our values and reward him or her for accepting them, then indeed we have abused our powers. But if we put our values into practice and recognize the child's right to accept or reject them, we are teachers in the best and fullest sense of that term.

I have dwelt on values because, like structure and freedom, they are fundamental to the educational enterprise. And not surprisingly, all of the renowned writers on early childhood—from Pestalozzi, Froebel, Montessori, Dewey, to Piaget—have taken the same position, both with respect to structure and freedom and with respect to the teacher's role vis-a-vis the child. With regard to the latter, each of those writers has recognized that we teach children values by who and what we are as people, not through curricular materials. If we respect children, if we appreciate their special talents and abilities, and if we value their energy and forthrightness, these values will be evident in everything we do.

From a Montessori perspective, therefore, teacher-child frames should reflect the teacher's knowledge of child development. How we speak to children, what demands we make of them, and what activities we model must all reflect a sensitive understanding of their abilities and energies.

When we do this, as Montessori recognized, children feel secure and positively challenged—secure because they know that they are in the presence of an adult who respects and understands their worldviews and challenged because the tasks the teachers set are appropriate to their developmental level.

CHILD-CHILD FRAMES

Once, while visiting a Montessori school, I inadvertently stepped upon a child's mat, her personal space. I apologized and she quite comfortably asked me whether I would like to share her mat with her. In this instance, as in the one described above where other boys helped the child who was working on the multiplication project, the essential child-child frame in Montessori classrooms is cooperation. To be sure, there is competition as well, but children compete with themselves, cooperate with others.

These child-child frames are taught primarily by modeling. The teachers model cooperation with the children and the children extend this to one another. Of course there are failures at times; children are children after all. But children immediately work to redress the spoiled child-child frames. A child who does not cooperate will be asked to do so by another youngster or told that he or she should have done so. In Montessori classrooms children themselves feel comfortable about repairing frame lapses and spoiled frames.

CONCLUSIONS

In this paper I have tried to describe some of the social-emotional components of Montessori education. By emphasizing the central role of frames in Montessori education, I hope to have illustrated how this education speaks to the child's social emotional development as well as to the intellect. Frames are at once social and emotional as well as intellectual. Indeed the idea that any system of education could be solely academic or intellectual is in a way absurd. We are social, emotional as well as intellectual beings, and a system of education that ignores a side of our being loses much of its effectiveness and value.

As I have tried to illustrate, Montessori education not only teaches children academic skills, but also works to enhance the child's self-esteem, personal freedom grounded on social responsibility, emotional freedom grounded on social empathy, self-selected values, and cooperation. In a real sense, therefore, Montessori education addresses the child's humanity in all of its mystery and complexity.

This is the ideal of course, and in practice we never reach the ideal. What is important is that the ideal is there, and that we strive to attain it.

REFERENCES

Goffman, E. (1974). *Frame analysis.* New York: Harper & Row.

Miller, A. (1981). *Prisoners of childhood.* New York: Basic Books.

Montessori, M. (1961). *What you should know about your child.* Adyar, Madras, India: Vasanta Press.

———. (1975). *Childhood education.* New York: Signet.

Piaget, J. (1950). *The psychology of intelligence.* London: Routledge and Kegan Paul.

7

WRITING BEFORE READING: EIGHTY YEARS LATER

Writing before reading? The usual order in which we teach reading and writing is the other way around. Schools expect children to read first and to move on to writing only afterwards, when the model has been established. Writing is derivative, based on the standards we learn from reading. There is, after all, an accepted spelling system. First we learn to recognize it, then to produce it. This would seem to be only natural.

We know better than that now, of course. Back at the turn of the century, Montessori recognized that writing precedes reading in young children and developed her methods of instruction accordingly. She explains it all with painstaking care and outstanding clarity in *The Montessori Method* (TMM) (1967). It didn't "take" in the schools, however, and the tradition of starting with reading has remained dominant, certainly in this country.

And in the last few decades, we have seen the growth in the United States of something called *invented spelling*. Invented spelling is the name given to children's early writing systems, created on their own to represent words as they hear them. Before learning to read, or early on in learning to read, children don't yet know conventional spellings and therefore don't use them. In order to write, they invent their own spellings based on how words sound. This kind of prereading and early reading activity also hasn't "taken" in the schools. But at least the phenomenon is recognized and debated in reading circles, and, increasingly, teachers are coming to know about it and even try it out in varying degrees with their young students.

It is interesting to consider how invented spelling relates to the early writing that Montessori described and to trace the development of this phenomenon. What is it, and how does it compare to what Montessori documented and advocated in her *Case dei Bambini* in Rome?

In the spirit of a retrospective on writing before reading, this paper takes up these questions:

- What is writing before reading?

- What is the chronology of the invented spelling "movement" (if its current status warrants this label) in the United States, or, more conservatively, what are the origins of present-day renewed interest in this remarkable ability that young children display?

- What are the differences between the approach and methods that Montessori describes in TMM and those in use today?

- What different aspects of literacy acquisition and children's linguistic development are clarified by Montessori on the one hand, and by recent research in the United States on the other?

I will deal with these questions separately in what follows.

WHAT IS WRITING BEFORE READING?

Young children are able, often before they learn to read, to compose words letter by letter according to the way the words sound. Four- or five-year-olds who know a few letters of the alphabet are in a position to figure out how to represent a word. Knowing just M and E, for example, is enough to construct the word ME. To do this, they need to be aware that the word is made up of separate sounds, in this case a *mmm* (or "muh") sound and an *eee* sound. To represent *mmm*, they need the letter that sounds like it, M. And to represent *eee*, they choose the one that sounds like it, E.

Children with this degree of awareness can compose the word ME, choosing first the M and then the E. They may write it if they know how to form letters, or they may construct it using wooden or plastic letters, alphabet blocks, or letter cards. They might even type it by finding the keys on a typewriter or computer keyboard. The particular implementation doesn't matter. What is important is the cognitive activity: analyzing a word into its separate sounds (sometimes called "hearing" the sounds) and choosing the letters needed to represent them, each one in turn.

This simplified description covers the basis of early writing, whether of the sort Montessori elicited from her children through specific instruction, or the invented spelling encouraged now in some lower schools. The principle the children use to compose words is to figure out how a word sounds and represent it that way. It is a true construction, not a match to a model they have seen. Sometimes they can read it back and sometimes not. It depends how far along they are in reading, a separate matter.

In practice, this kind of writing is not isolated from children's reading, of course. As they learn to read, early writers begin to use conventional spellings in their writing for words they know, alongside invented spellings for words they don't know. Also, many children start writing as they start to learn reading, and conventional spellings appear in their writing from the start.

Here is a typical sample of invented spelling:

WUNS A LITL BUNE HOPT A CROS MY LON
Once a little bunny hopped across my lawn

AND THAT BUNE HOPT RUYT IN MI HAWS
and that bunny hopped right in my house

AND I GAV THT BUNE SUM MILK
and I gave that bunny some milk

(girl, age 5 years, 2 months)

Thorough discussion of invented spelling has appeared in the literature (see Chomsky 1971, 1972, 1975, 1976, 1979; Read 1970, 1971, 1975a, 1975b; Bissex 1980; Paul 1976).

CHRONOLOGY OF INVENTED SPELLING

It is interesting to think back to my own introduction to invented spelling. I first encountered a child who wrote without knowing how to read in the early 1950s. He was the $3^1/2$-year-old son of some friends. They mentioned that he was producing writing that looked very strange, full of misspellings. They were surprised and amused, not sure what to make of it. "It's a riot," they told me, describing this interesting quirk of his. "He sits there and writes letters to his aunt, and little stories, and it's all nonsense. You can't read any of it. It's gibberish."

Of course I was intrigued. I asked to see some of the writing, and they obliged. To the eye of a linguist and phonetician, it was anything but nonsense. It took a while to figure it out, but there was clearly a system at work. The spelling was startlingly regular, a principled rendering of the way English sounds. It was "unreadable" because it was not like conventional spelling. One didn't read it, one deciphered it. What I had stumbled onto was a remarkable construction of a private spelling system, apparently the idiosyncratic invention of a highly creative and unusual child. He had worked it all out in his own way, this child who could not yet read.

This was my first glimpse of what later came to be called invented spelling. For as it turned out, this child was not unique, nor were his abilities rare. His spellings were neither idiosyncratic nor unusually creative. We were to learn later that children can quite commonly write, in their own spellings, before they can read, creating spellings that are surprisingly uniform from child to child. Thus it was not my friends' son who was so unusual. Rather what was unusual, in retrospect, was the lack of recognition on the part of developmentalists and educators of this interesting and important ability that young children command. The ability was not acknowledged, much less exploited in the service of teaching children to read.

It wasn't until some ten years later, in the mid-1960s, that a student at the Harvard Graduate School of Education became interested in children's early writing and decided to investigate it for his doctoral dissertation. Charles Read started with the preserved early writings of this same child, by then a teenager, and searched for examples of other children who were writing on their own in naturalistic situations. He found some twenty young children, in various stages of learning to read, who were producing writings in their own invented spellings. Their spelling systems exhibited common features, different from conventional spelling and based on the way English sounds. They each worked according to principles that were strikingly similar, though devised independently.

What was exciting about this discovery was twofold: that writing before reading (or early on in learning to read) was not an individual quirk but was practiced by larger numbers of children, and that the specific spelling features invented by these children were not idiosyncratic, but shared by all of them. They all made up their spellings in the same way! This was clearly a robust phenomenon, very much worth studying, and Charles Read and others proceeded to do just that in the years that followed.

How does Montessori fit into all of this? Interestingly, she knew it all along. She recognized that the ability to compose words according to their sounds develops in children earlier than their ability to recognize words, and she developed her methods for reading instruction accordingly. At the turn of the century in Rome she expressed it this way: "Experience has taught me to distinguish clearly between *writing and reading,* and has shown me that the two acts *are not absolutely contemporaneous.* Contrary to the usually accepted idea, writing *precedes reading"* (1967, p. 296).

Her account in TMM describes starting with writing in her work with what she calls "deficients" (feeble-minded children) at the State Orthophrenic School in Rome, and later adapting the methods for use with normal children in newly established tenement schools in Rome. The Case dei Bambini, or Children's Houses, were located in the tenement houses themselves, for the education of children of preschool age. Montessori vividly describes the wretched slum quarter of San Lorenzo in Rome, where she directed her schools, and its miserable conditions of poverty, unemployment, and vice. Each Casa dei Bambini was intended to provide sorely needed education in many cognitive domains, attending as well to hygiene, moral and social development, physical development and exercise. The Children's Houses assumed responsibility for virtually all developmental needs of those children ages three to six who were living under conditions of severe poverty and neglect. I mention all this to give some picture of the setting in which our particular interest, writing before reading, was instituted and able to flourish so successfully.

What is interesting here is that Montessori used writing first as the natural way to teach reading—an instructional approach suitable for all children. It was not a method devised for especially talented children. It was entirely effective for children with special needs and for children living and raised in circumstances of poverty, whom we would today describe as severely disadvantaged.

This was of particular significance in light of our own temptation to view the ability to write first as out of the ordinary. The early work that Read did (Read, 1970) was with children who wrote on their own in naturalistic situations. We had no information about how general this ability might be. Read himself was clearly of the view that the children in his sample were not unusual or especially creative. He points out (Read, 1970) that the children he found were normal children. What they shared was not unusual intelligence or talent, but an environment that encouraged their efforts and tolerated their apparent errors. What they wrote was valued. They were never led to believe that there was a right or wrong way to do it, or that they should keep their hands off and depend on outside standards. They believed that writing was something you work out for yourself.

The educational world was not impressed with Read's findings. The reaction was that early writing must certainly be the domain of only a very few children, not available to all and not worth pursuing. I remember a reading conference in the 1970s at which my recommendation for starting reading instruction with word composition was dismissed as utopian, targeted for too few children, and not "cost-effective."

So it was with great interest that I discovered Montessori using writing first as the natural order, designed for and successful with children at an extreme educational disadvantage—children of poverty, even "deficients." My students and I were the Johnny-come-latelies, stumbling onto something real, but without knowing how generally applicable it might be for instruction. We only knew it was great for children who picked up on it on their own. But could it be useful for children more generally, including those who didn't do it by themselves? Montessori already had that answer. She documented the benefits of using writing—even when introduced artificially, as it were—as the introduction to literacy for children of varying backgrounds and abilities. They could all do it and pursued it with zeal.

By now in the United States there is greater acceptance of the idea that writing can be expected of children early on in learning to read. It's hardly the case that teachers routinely begin reading instruction by introducing writing, but more and more teachers accept and encourage early writing in invented spelling. Teachers are more familiar now with the invented features to be expected, such as *JR* for *dr*—*JRAGN* (*dragon*)—and omission of nasals—*DOT* (*don't*). Kindergarten and first-grade teachers know to acquaint parents with the role of invented spelling and warn them about "misspellings" coming home on papers.

The encouragement of early writing fits with the general growing emphasis on the *process* of writing and not just on the product. It is no longer unusual to find reports such as this one, from the Shipley School in Bryn Mawr, Pennsylvania:

I CN RT ThS F U WL RD UT: Unlocking the Mysteries of the Written Word[1]

Every single day in the Lower School, children in grades K–4 *write*. Shipley, like most schools in the country today, begins to teach writing in kindergarten, employing what is known as the "process writing approach."

---

[1]Excerpted from an article by Ann E. Kolakowski in the *Shipley Bulletin*, Spring 1989. Information contributed by Rosalie Lake, head of the Lower School at Shipley.

Children begin writing in invented spelling—the very best guess they can make of how to represent a word in writing. If you slipped into a kindergarten or first grade classroom when everyone was writing, you would hear the effort of sounding out—the *mmm*s, the *b*s, the *rrr*s—the whole room quietly abuzz with children straining to hear and write the sounds inside themselves.

In the first grade Writing Workshop, students work with what they hear (apona= upon a, dr=j, n=and) as well as employ learned skill in the representation of vowels and in the spelling of some words:

ONES APONA TOM A JAGN SHT FIRE AT ME N I SCMD N MY MOM CAME RENIEG TWO SAV ME

So we have come a long way, and now we can often find a healthy mix of writing and reading in the very early grades.

DIFFERENCES IN APPROACH AND METHODS

There are several interesting differences between the approach to early writing that Montessori describes in TMM and our own methods with invented spelling.

HANDWRITING

One such difference is Montessori's emphasis on the physical activity involved in word composition and our own emphasis on the mental activity. In TMM, Montessori gives the handwriting itself a larger and earlier role than we do. She starts with letter formation and focuses heavily on having children learn to write the letters before proceeding to word composition. The methods are ingenious, and the handwriting that results is spectacular. Letter identification and production strengthen each other and the children become completely familiar with the letters as objects to be handled, traced, named, and drawn. Afterward, the children move on to figuring out how to compose words with these letters. Montessori separates her instruction and exercises into three distinct periods: first, holding and using the writing instrument; next, writing the letters and learning to recognize their shapes and sounds; and last, composition of words (1967, pp. 271–85).

Nowadays we don't give precedence to handwriting. Our emphasis instead is on paying attention to the sounds of the words and deciding what letters are needed to represent them. We work later on the mechanics of printing and script. A preschool child may use wooden letters on the tabletop or floor, a kindergarten or first-grade child may print with a mixture of upper- and lowercase letters, and script will be used whenever it is eventually taught. Our children sometimes use a keyboard, either typewriter or computer. Children produce their invented spellings in whatever representation is currently available to them, the particular means of transcription being of secondary importance.

Thus in our scheme the mechanics of early writing are subordinated to the child's decision-making ability, whereas for Montessori these two aspects of the early writing are more closely coordinated and go hand-in-hand, with the mechanics emphasized far earlier. In this regard, I think our present-day approach is preferable. We should recognize, of course, that Montessori's more structured methods were part of a general effort to instill neatness and discipline in children whose lives had been characterized by gross neglect and disorganization. Her approach to the writing should not be considered in isolation.

TARGET POPULATION

Another interesting difference is the children with whom early writing is used—what we might call our views of the appropriate "target population." As we have said, Montessori developed and refined her methods with "deficient" children at the Orthophrenic School and went on to use them in her Case dei Bambini with children of severe poverty in the slums of Rome. She found the early writing entirely appropriate for children at an educational disadvantage. In contrast, the tendency of the educational establishment here is to assume that the children who will be able to write early are the privileged ones who come from highly literate homes. It's easier to persuade teachers in private schools and middle-class suburban schools to try writing first than it is to make headway with teachers in the more difficult conditions of urban schools that service poor children. It's somehow assumed, unfortunately, that the children who can do it are those whose homes have provided models of literacy. What Montessori viewed as effective for children at a disadvantage, we treat as the province of the privileged few.

It is Montessori, I believe, who is the more advanced in her thinking on this score. Those of us who lobby for early writing argue that it ought to be part of the curriculum available to all children, not just those with literate backgrounds. I'm not sure we're having too much success in this regard, regrettably.

TRANSITION TO CONVENTIONAL SPELLING

Another difference that arises in the writing as described by Montessori and as we treat it with our children has to do with differences between Italian and English. This is not a matter of viewpoint and approach, but rather depends on the differing characteristics of the conventional spelling systems of the two languages.

The relations of letters to sounds in Italian is closer than in English. This is sometimes expressed by saying that Italian is written more "phonetically" than English. The letter A, for example, in Italian is pronounced "ah" as in "mama." A child who wishes to represent the sound "ah" in Italian and who chooses the letter A will produce a correct spelling. This letter-sound correspondence works in both directions, as it were, for both writing and reading. In reading/pronouncing an Italian word with the letter A, pronounce it "ah" and you come out right (with some variation in length, minor as compared with variations in English). In English, the situation is far less regular. To represent the sound "ah" in correct spelling, you need not only A ("father"), but you must resort also to O ("bother"), or I ("ride").[2] And when it comes to reading/pronouncing an English word that contains the letter A, you are faced with extensive variation (some dialectal): "cat," "cake," "father," "call," "war," "car," "sofa," "bath"; and then the combinations: "said," "bead," "head," "earth," "aunt," "gaunt," "tail," and so on.

What this means is that Italian children's invented spellings are much closer to the conventional spelling they must eventually master. The way a word sounds in Italian is a fairly reliable guide to its conventional spelling. In English the way a word sounds is often a poor guide to its conventional spelling. There are numerous rules to be learned, and then there are the exceptions to the rules. Invented spellings in English are a far cry from conventional spellings.

It is fair to say that in English there are two writing systems for the inventive speller: (I), invented spelling, and (C), conventional spelling. The principles are different, and children who start with (I) eventually make the shift to (C) in a variety of ways. I have discussed this in some detail elsewhere (Chomsky, 1979) and need not repeat the details here. What is important for this discussion is that English-speaking children

---

[2]The vowel sound in "ride" is made up of two parts—an "ah" sound followed by a "y" sound. Its first part, "ah," is similar in pronunciation to the first vowel of "bother" or "father."

have to adopt a new principle to move from (I) to (C): don't *make up* the spelling, but rather *remember* what it's supposed to be and reproduce that. Italian-speaking children, on the other hand, aren't confronted with two writing systems and don't have to change principles. For Italian-speaking children, adopting conventional spelling means learning certain adjustments to their invented spellings. They can use their made-up spellings as a guide, as long as they remember where and when to finesse them and adjust them.

So the transition to conventional spelling is quite different in the two cases. Montessori doesn't deal with the transition, understandably, because it doesn't arise as an issue. In our case, we do need to understand the principles of (I) and (C), how children make the transition, and what guidance and help they need in doing so (see Chomsky, 1975, 1979).

Perhaps we should discuss this point somewhat further. Since invented spelling in English is so different from conventional spelling, it makes sense to ask why we want to bother with it at all. Why should we ask English-speaking children to struggle to represent some forty–fifty sounds with only twenty-six letters, particularly when they're only going to have to abandon their invented system quite soon? Why should they learn something they just have to unlearn so quickly?

One answer is that it helps them learn to read. It gets them started in working with letters and sounds in many cases before they are ready to read. It makes them active participants in becoming literate. And it's not a struggle. English-speaking children have no trouble making up what they need and filling in for sounds where letters aren't available. They don't have a problem with (I), nor do they have a problem recognizing that there are the two different systems, (I) and (C), mentioned above. The transition from (I) to (C) is accomplished easily and readily, when appropriate. This transition consists of recognizing a new principle of spelling and replacing the old one with the new.

When using (I), children are composing words as they sound. It is their creation, their construction. In (C), they are reproducing a learned sequence according to a model, producing a replica of something experienced and memorized. They are matching their spelling to a pattern that they've been exposed to, that they have a picture of in their mind.

This is not to say that learning conventional spelling is a matter of memorizing every word as a separate item. It's more systematic and structured than that. You build a system and fit the individual words into it where they belong. But there is a fixed domain whose properties you need to discover and master.

So writing in (I) and in (C) are very different activities. There's room for both in children's learning to read and write. They need to get to (C)—that's the destination. No one disputes that. The argument is over the route to take to get there: whether there's a point to going through (I). I believe that yes, there's a point to (I), for the active participation it fosters on the part of the child, the phonetic practice it provides, and its contribution to *reading*. (I) will serve its purpose and be abandoned after it's done its job.

INSIGHTS OF MONTESSORI AND INVENTED-SPELLING RESEARCH INTO WRITING BEFORE READING

The final point I'd like to make concerns the theoretical discussion of writing before reading in the literature. Montessori's writings and recent invented-spelling work focus on somewhat different aspects of children's linguistic development and literacy acquisition, and the contributions of both are fundamental to understanding early writing. Montessori's particular contribution, it seems to me, is her clarification of the intellectual differences between writing and reading. I find her analysis of writing and reading in TMM and her characterization of the differences unique in insight and clarity. They are a gem. More recent work on psycholinguistic development, on the other hand, has paid attention to children's ability to deal with the sounds of words. Study of the growth of this metalinguistic ability, crucial to mastering an alphabetic writing system, is a separate focus that has added considerably to our understanding of early writing. I will close this paper with a brief consideration of each of these areas of concern.

DIFFERENCES BETWEEN WRITING AND READING

In TMM, Montessori discusses beginning reading and writing at the word level, and she brings out clearly why writing precedes reading for a child. In both cases the child translates between sounds and letters, but reading is not the reverse of writing. In writing the word is already known, whereas in reading it must be discovered. This discovery requires an extra step of the intellect.

In writing, sound is converted into letters. Once you have converted the sounds into letters and written them onto paper, you're done.

The reverse of this process, converting the letters to sound, is not reading, however. This sounding out what the letters say is only a first step in reading.

You can figure out the sounds that the letters stand for, and you can even pronounce them (making some decision about where to place the accent), but that is not reading. That's a form of declaiming, perhaps. You can do this in a language you don't even know, if you have learned some simple pronunciation rules. Or even if you haven't learned any rules for the language, as long as the alphabet is the same as your own (in our case the Latin alphabet), you can pronounce according to your own language's rules. But to count as reading, you have to *recognize* the word, not just pronounce it. You have to recognize what Montessori calls the sense of the word, or the idea the word represents. You have to recognize *which* word it is in your language. In present-day terminology, you have to access the right item in your memory store.

Here is Montessori's description in TMM. This is a continuation of the passage quoted earlier, pointing out that writing and reading are not contemporaneous, but that writing precedes reading.

> I do not consider as *reading* the test which the child makes *when he verifies* the word that he has written. He is translating signs into sounds, as he first translated sounds into signs. In this verification he already knows the word and has repeated it to himself while writing it. What I understand by reading is the *interpretation* of an idea from the written signs. The child who has not heard the word pronounced, and who recognises it when he sees it composed upon the table with the cardboard letters, and who can tell what it means; this child *reads*. The word which he reads has the same relation to written language that the word which he hears bears to articulate language. Both serve to *receive the language* transmitted to us *by others*. So, until the child reads a transmission of ideas from the written word, *he does not read. . . .*
>
> The child who *knows how to write*, when placed before a word which he must interpret by reading, is silent for a long time, and generally reads the component sounds with the same slowness with which he would have written them. But *the sense of the word* becomes evident only when it is pronounced clearly and with the phonetic accent. Now, in order to place the phonetic accent the child must recognise the word; that is, he must recognise the idea which the word represents. The intervention of a superior work of the intellect is necessary if he is to read. (1967, p. 296–297)

The step of accessing the correct item in memory, the *recognition*, is what is absent from the writing act.

How important to the recognition process is pronouncing the word? Not very, for the experienced reader. Translating the letters into sounds as the first step in reading a word is a characteristic of the beginning reader. This translation to sound plays a diminishing role as the reader becomes more experienced. Skilled readers can access the correct item in their memory store without pronouncing. They can go straight to the meaning, because the *sound* of the word isn't what counts. It's the way a word *looks*, not the way it *sounds*, that matters.

To clarify this point, consider this sentence:

> The none tolled hymn that she had scene and herd a pear of bear feat in the haul.

On the basis of the sounds of the words, it's meaningful. Read it aloud and your listener has no trouble. When you look at it, however, you're in trouble. You are misled because you access the wrong items. You access by the *look* of the word, not the sound. At least that's what the experienced reader does. But to understand this sentence, you have to override your well-practiced mechanism of access and substitute an artificial one of working according to the sounds. The difficulty involved shows how far this deciphering method is from actual reading.

The beginning reader, however, doesn't recognize anything yet by its looks. Beginners have to work through pronouncing the sounds to be able to link to the right word in their memory store, that is, to identify the word. Learning to read means, among other things, building up the number of recognizable words, so you can locate the right item in your store without stopping to work through the actual pronunciation. You come to locate the correct item directly.

It is this aspect of word recognition that Montessori puts her finger on so adroitly. Beyond the translation between letters and sounds, reading is more complex than writing, because in reading "the intervention of a superior work of the intellect is necessary" (1967, p. 297). In light of this formulation, it is quite natural to expect children to start with the simpler task.

PHONEMIC SEGMENTATION

We have said that in order to create spellings, a child must be aware of the separate sounds that make up a word. This kind of awareness has received considerable attention in recent research.

Recent research in this country has dealt in some detail with the question of phonemic segmentation, the separating of continuous speech into the separate sounds, or phonemes, of which it is composed. In terms of its physical properties, the speech signal is a continuum. There are no pauses or clear boundaries in the signal itself to mark the separation between adjoining sounds, syllables, or even words. We know where the word boundaries come because we know what the words are, not because of pauses or acoustic cues that occur in the speech that we hear.

And even when individual words are identified, additional skill is needed to divide a word into syllables and into its separate sounds. Literate adults ordinarily have no trouble subdividing speech in this way, and they can identify the separate sounds of words if asked to do so. Children, on the other hand, need to develop this ability. They need sufficient metalinguistic awareness to enable them to pay attention to the sounds of words as distinct from their meanings. Once they can attend to the way words sound, they have a basis for recognizing words that rhyme, for example, or begin alike, or are long or short. Further, they can undertake thinking about the separate sounds that make up a word. This kind of metalinguistic awareness can be fostered through discussion, reflection, and even instruction.

Young children need to progress to the point where such metalinguistic discussion is fruitful, however. Some children are ready to engage in such metalinguistic reflection by age three, others not until four or five. At some point they become able to attend to the sounds of words as separate from their meanings, and a consideration of how words are composed becomes possible.

There has been considerable work on children's developing abilities in this area and on the relation of phonemic segmentation ability to beginning reading (Liberman, 1973; Liberman et al., 1974; Rozin and Gleitman, 1977). Learning to read an alphabetic writing system such as English both depends on and contributes to the ability to segment words into their phonemes. Segmentation ability among readers of nonalphabetic writing systems or illiterate adults may be less facile than among people who have learned to use alphabets.

Being able to divide a word into its separate sounds is a sine qua non of writing before reading. You can't invent spellings if you can't identify the sequence of sounds. And you get better at identifying the sound sequences as you work at creating the spellings. The interaction works so that each ability contributes to the other. Children become more able as they go along.

In summary, our own understanding also improves as we go along. Our view of writing before reading has developed and sharpened in response to the contributions over time of the many people working in the field. I look forward to a continuation of this work.

REFERENCES

Bissex, G. (1980). *GNYS AT WRK: A child learns to write and read.* Cambridge, Mass.: Harvard University Press.

Chomsky, C. (1971). Write first, read later. *Childhood Education, 47:* 296–99.

———. (1972). Write now, read later. In C. Cazden (Ed.), *Language in early childhood education,* Washington, D.C.: National Association for the Education of Young Children. 119–126.

———. (1975). How sister got into the grog. *Early Years, 6:* 36–39.

———. (1976). Invented spelling in the open classroom. In W. von Raffler-Engel (Ed.), *Child language—1975,* Milford, Conn.: International Linguistics Association. (Originally published in *Word, 27* [1971], 499–518)

———. (1979). Approaching reading through invented spelling. In L. B. Resnick and P. A. Weaver (Eds.), *Theory and practice of early reading,* vol 2. Hillsdale, N.J.: Lawrence Erlbaum. 43–65.

Kolakowski, A. E. (1989). I CN RT ThS F U WL RD UT: Unlocking the mysteries of the written word. *Shipley Bulletin* Spring: 7.

Liberman, I. Y. (1973). Segmentation of the spoken word and reading acquisition. *Bulletin of the Orton Society, 23:* 65–77.

Liberman, I. Y., Shankweiler, D., Fischer, F. W., & Carter, B. (1974). Explicit syllable and phoneme segmentation in the young child. *Journal of Experimental Child Psychology, 18:* 201–12.

Montessori, M. (1967). *The Montessori method.* Cambridge, Mass.: Robert Bentley.

Paul, Rhea. (1976). Invented spelling in kindergarten. *Young Children, 31:* 195–200.

Read, C. (1970). *Children's perceptions of the sounds of English: Phonology from three to six.* Unpublished doctoral dissertation, Harvard Graduate School of Education.

———. (1971). Preschool children's knowledge of English phonology. *Harvard Educational Review, 41:* 1–34.

———. (1975). *Children's categorization of speech sounds in English* (Research Report No. 17). Urbana, Ill.: National Council of Teachers of English.

———. (1975). Lessons to be learned from the preschool orthographer. In E. H. Lenneberg & E. Lenneberg (Eds.), *Foundations of language development.* New York: Academic Press.

Rozin, P., and Gleitman, L. R. (1977). The Structure and Acquisition of Reading. Part II. The reading process and the acquisition of the alphabetic principle. In A. S. Reber and D. Scarborough (Eds.), *Toward a psychology of reading.* Hillsdale, N.J.: Lawrence Erlbaum.

8

MONTESSORI AND LEARNING DISABILITIES

American education is currently under attack from many quarters. The nation now recognizes the need for a more literate society, which will require modifications in the educational system. Almost one-third of our children will join the ranks of the illiterate unless they are provided with instruction that meets their needs. Many of these youngsters will be dyslexic or have learning disabilities. Others will not—but they will need appropriate instruction.

This paper will first discuss the major characteristics of learning disabilities and then describe Dr. Montessori's approach to education. Hopefully, the reader will grasp the significance of the Montessori principles and practices as they may be applied in the education of children with language-learning disabilities.

LEARNING DISABILITIES

All children with learning problems do not necessarily have specific learning disabilities. Diagnostic terminology in this field can be extremely confusing. A number of terms are used freely by educators, the lay public, as well as the medical profession.

In 1988, the National Joint Committee on Learning Disabilities (NJCLD), a national committee representing nine organizations concerned with individuals with learning disabilities, provided what may be the best definition, which has also had wide acceptance among professionals:

Learning disabilities is a general term that refers to a heterogeneous group of disorders manifested by significant difficulties in the acquisition and use of listening, speaking, reading, writing, reasoning, or mathematical abilities. These disorders are intrinsic to the individual, presumed to be due to central nervous system dysfunction, and may occur across the lifespan.

Problems in self-regulatory behaviors, social perception, and social interaction may exist with learning disabilities but do not by themselves constitute a learning disability.

Although learning disabilities may occur concomitantly with other handicapping conditions (for example, sensory impairment, mental retardation, serious emotional disturbance) or with extrinsic influences, (such as cultural differences, insufficient or inappropriate instruction), they are not the result of those conditions or influences. (NJCLD, 1988).

Children with specific learning disabilities are of at least average intelligence. Boys outnumber girls by approximately four to one, which happens to be the approximate ratio of boys to girls in relation to language disorders and stuttering. There is usually a family history of learning disabilities, especially among the dyslexic population. These children demonstrate disorders of varying degree in one or more of four areas: coordination, language, attention, and perception.

DISORDERS OF GROWTH AND/OR FINE-MOTOR COORDINATION

The child with learning disabilities may be quite clumsy. Although not a cause of learning disabilities, clumsiness is frequently an associated symptom that can be devastating for a child. This is the youngster who bumps into everything, spills the milk, trips over a thread in the carpet. Of course, there are many clumsy adults who have never had any learning problems, and clumsiness may not be a major concern from the adult point of view. Clumsy children who have difficulty hopping, skipping, running, riding a bike, or playing ball, however, probably don't feel very good about themselves. They are rarely chosen to be on anyone's team and they get in trouble at home because they break things. They easily develop a low self-image—in itself an impediment to learning.

Children with poor fine-motor coordination are unable to coordinate the small muscle groups, particularly in their hands. They may have difficulty dressing and undressing, learning to button, tie, and zip. In school, they will have difficulty using a crayon, scissors, and a pencil. Children with fine-motor incoordination become dependent on others to cut up their food, to help them dress, and so on. This poor coordination is indeed a handicap, since one of the major requisites for school success is independence so that children may assume the responsibility for their own learning.

Gross- or fine-motor incoordination is not the crux or the cause of any specific learning disability, but may nonetheless prevent children from meeting the normal demands of school in all aspects—academic, social, and emotional.

DISORDERS OF LANGUAGE

The language problems of children with specific learning disabilities may be extremely complex. Because they are not visible, unlike problems in coordination or behavior, they are less likely to be discovered or diagnosed. We are not discussing speech problems alone. Speech, like writing, is the motor act of self-expression. Language and thought are related processes, and the term *language* includes both spoken and written language. In order to acquire competence in reading we must build on proficiencies made available in the primary (spoken) language system.

Children with learning disabilities may have problems with any of the several components of language, especially those that affect reading: *phonology,* the sound structure of our language, which includes syllables as well as phonemes; *syntax,* the rules that govern the sequential ordering of words, phrases, and sentences; *semantics,* the meaning system that is attached to words and phrases as a result of experience in many contexts; and adequate *short- and long-term memory capacities.* Many youngsters with learning disabilities have considerable difficulty bridging from speech to print, establishing sound/symbol correspondence in beginning reading—a task that draws on their phonological awareness and memory and also is dependent on the discovery that words are made up of smaller units.

Delay in the acquisition and use of spoken language may be the sole forerunner of a learning disability. Most children with reading and writing problems will have had a history of late or impaired speech and/or language development. These limitations make it difficult for them to learn, in or out of school.

Children with learning disabilities may not have much trouble with articulation, although they may have "cluttered" speech, speech that sort of falls on top of itself. Speech therapy is helpful for such youngsters but other language problems are usually involved as well.

It is important to note that children, upon school entrance, do not possess equal levels of competencies in the critical language areas. Since success in beginning reading, and consequently in beginning school, depends upon the adequate development of the functions of spoken language, early school experiences should be directed toward oral language development as well as reading instruction.

DISORDERS OF ATTENTION

Disorders of the functions of attention include short attention span, distractibility, impulsivity, hyperkinetic behavior or activity decontrol, and disinhibition. The label often given to such behaviors is Attention Deficit with Hyperactivity Disorder (ADHD). Many children called hyperactive are attentive when their activities are of interest to them or when they are doing things that they *can* do. We must distinguish between the child whose hyperactivity is neurologically based and the child who is hyperreacting to stress.

Some children have attentional problems that are secondary to receptive language disorder or to a memory deficit. Some "hyperactive" youngsters simply have very high intensity temperamental attributes (Thomas & Chess, 1977). The importance of attention in learning cannot be overestimated. Attention means close or careful observing or listening. The child with a disorder of attention has difficulty in attending *selectively* to pertinent stimuli. Later in this chapter I will address the ways in which attention can be trained.

DISORDERS IN THE FUNCTIONS OF PERCEPTION

A perceptual disorder is a defect in the way our mind interprets what we see or hear or take in through our other senses. Children with normal vision and hearing acuity may misinterpret or misperceive what they see or hear. The functions of perception can be related to the visual, auditory, tactile, kinesthetic, or other senses. Visual perception is often tied to movement and space while auditory perception refers to that which is temporal and sequential.

Some children may have a visual-motor mismatch. In trying to copy letters or shapes, they are unable to guide finger movements accurately according to what they see, and so drawing and writing are impaired.

Visuospatial perception is closely tied to children's growing organization of their physical environments, which is based on the vantage point of their own beings, whether objects are far from them or near, larger than they are or smaller. There may be confusion about direction—up and down, right and left, front and back. Children with learning disabilities may have difficulty tying objects into a unified whole; their possessions may be scattered in complete disarray. Lack of organization is a major problem. They may demonstrate persistent reversals or erroneous sequencing of letters and words when reading, spelling, or writing. They may also mix up their words, like Sheridan's Mrs. Malaprop.

A great deal of learning is dependent upon early sensorimotor integration and perceptual maturation. Children learn first through their own movements and manipulations, which then become associated with the sensory information that they receive and perceive. Sensorimotor development occurs primarily in the first two to four years of life, but later academic learning is dependent upon the development and integration of these skills. Piaget (1952) wrote: "Sensori-motor intelligence lies at the source of thought, and continues to affect it throughout life through perceptions and practical sets. . . . The role of perception in the most highly developed thought cannot be neglected" (p. 326).

The child's coordination, language, attention, and perception are all interrelated. No learning disabled child is exactly like another. There is no single symptom; the symptoms occur in clusters and vary from child to child. The importance of any particular problem within the symptom complex can change as the child proceeds through school. Learning disabilities change over time and have lifelong effects.

To summarize briefly, the four major disorders demonstrated by children with learning disability are disorders of fine and gross motor coordination, language, attention, and perception. These are not isolated but interdependent functions. They are present from birth through the lifespan of the individual in changing order of importance and in varying degree.

Special education principles and practices address these problems after a child has been identified in school, but I believe that intervention in the school-age years is too little and too late. Much can be done in early childhood education programs to prevent or ameliorate the anguish suffered by the children before assistance is provided in school. I believe that Montessori offers one answer for these children.

MONTESSORI METHOD

Maria Montessori (1870–1952), the first woman to receive a degree in medicine from the University of Rome, has had a tremendous influence on the education of young children, yet she is rarely cited as the author or advocate of the large number of ideas and practices characteristic of her teaching, which are now standard fixtures in the early education scene in America. Dr. Montessori was strongly influenced by Rousseau and Pestalozzi; by Itard, a doctor at the time of the French Revolution who became the "father of otolaryngology"; and by the teacher and physician Edward Sequin, who was the first person to provide a thorough educational system for mentally defective children. Sequin's book, *Idiocy and Its Treatment by the Physiological Method*, was published in New York in 1866. Montessori first applied Sequin's principles of education to mentally defective children in Rome, during which time she also made her own modifications and amplified his theories until they were extended to the education of normal children.

Montessori became known for her lifetime endeavors on behalf of the child, developing a system of education that included programmed preparation for learning, unique methods, and the only systematic collection of educational devices, many of which are auto-educational. In an era when education was stereotyped and discipline in the schools was almost brutal, an era that exploited child labor and placed retarded children in insane asylums, she fought for early childhood education as well as for education of the retarded; she proposed revolutionary changes in curriculum and methods for teaching both retarded and normal children.

In her classic work, *The Montessori Method* (1912), she stated: "The method used by me is that of making a pedagogical experiment with a didactic object and awaiting the spontaneous reaction of the child" (p. 167). She thus went through a set of inductive operations and derived certain conclusions from her observations. She did not try to make the child fit any preconceived notions. Guided by the works of the pioneers, Itard and Sequin, Montessori designed and had manufactured a large variety of didactic materials. She states, however, that "unless these materials were rightly presented they failed to attract the attention of the deficients" (p. 170).

Both Sequin and Montessori believed that the basis of all work with children was primarily spiritual—that is, the love, respect, understanding, and patience of the teacher must awaken the spirit of the child. They considered the moral preparation of the teacher to be the key to successful teaching. Both stressed that mechanical teaching, whereby the teacher follows the rules to the letter in using a particular apparatus, is rarely successful. It is still true today that materials and techniques are ineffective unless the teacher understands the reasons for their use and can also awaken the child's interest in working with them.

There have been many modifications and adaptations of Montessori in America to accommodate cultural differences and change. The basic philosophy and principles of instruction, however, generally remain constant. It is not the purpose of this presentation to discuss the variations on the theme to accommodate the differing needs of children, but rather to point out how Montessori principles and practices pertain to the education of the high-risk child.

Montessori's method is largely based on a concept described by Sequin (1907): "To lead the child, as it were, by the hand, from the education of the muscular system, to that of the nervous system, and of the senses . . . and then from the education of the senses to general notions, from general notions to abstract thought, from abstract thought to morality" (p. 144). In *Dr. Montessori's Own Handbook* (1965), she states: "The technique of my method, as it follows the natural physiological and psychological development of the child, may be divided into three parts: (1) Motor education; (2) Sensory education; and (3) Language or intellectual education. The care and management of the environment itself afford the principle means of motor education, while sensory education and education of language are provided for by my didactic material" (pp. 49–50).

PREPARED ENVIRONMENT AND EXERCISES IN PRACTICAL LIFE

Montessori believed that the child's environment should be "prepared" and maintained by the teacher. She saw the teacher as the caretaker of the environment and as the child's guide.

Montessori designed the furniture in the first Casa dei Bambini (Children's House) to be light, child-sized, and easy for the children to move, arrange, or wash with soap and water. She believed that education should have as its object the development of independence in the child, and she stressed that every unnecessary aid to a child is an impediment. Thus, the "prepared environment" includes the opportunity for movement and motor training, and, of major importance, the provision for order. Children are to be guided from the start by presenting them with activities that they are prepared to do, at which they can be successful, and that thereby capture their attention. The concept of order is particularly applicable to the education of children with learning disabilities.

The "prepared environment" contains objects designed through their use to achieve a definite purpose, to allow the child to carry out a real piece of work having a practical objective. These activities are called "exercises in practical life." Each activity is made up of a graded series of movements to be performed in logical sequence. Montessori broke down each exercise of practical life into "points of interest," specific points within each exercise to which the children's attention is drawn. As the children are taught each "exercise," such as washing hands, polishing shoes, or cutting vegetables, each step of the operation is presented by the teacher verbally and by demonstration in logical, orderly sequence. The children learn to focus their attention and to analyze their body movements as they repeat the sequence each time. As the children's attention is directed to proprioceptive and external cues, they are learning to recognize and to use feedback. All of this helps the children to develop efficient motor patterns as well as selective attention.

The Soviet research psychologists Zaporozhets and Elkonin (1971) found that to teach children how to carry out a complex task, one must make sure that they are also taught how to organize their orienting responses (attention). They must learn what to look at; their action must be directed to the right cues, both external and proprioceptive. Thus, they must learn to make use of feedback from the external situation and from their own actions; the teacher must help them to do this. Several experiments have shown that a task can be learned more rapidly if orienting behavior (attention) is specifically trained through motor mediation. The Montessori exercises in practical life involve both verbal and motor mediation and are invaluable aids in helping the child to attend and to coordinate movements.

The exercises in practical life, including exercises in social behavior, are described as follows: "the primary movements of everyday life such as walking, rising, sitting, handling objects; care of the person; management of the household; gardening; manual work; gymnastic exercises; and rhythmic movements" (p. 53). Montessori designed materials for learning to dress and undress such as buttoning, tying, hooking, and lacing. These materials, now found in most preschools, assist the child who has difficulty with fine-motor coordination as described earlier in this paper; they serve also as indirect preparation of the hand for writing.

The importance of the exercises in practical life cannot be overemphasized in working with learning disabled children. Through these exercises they can develop self-respect and some independence. The self-assurance that comes with the knowledge that they can care for themselves and their environment will help them to withstand the many difficulties they will encounter later in their academic struggles.

SENSORY EDUCATION

Montessori provided much material for sensorimotor training. The sensorial materials are designed to attract children's attention, to "educate the senses," and to allow manipulation by children. The goal is to assist the children in creating order and sequence in sensory input by presenting a carefully constructed sequence of experiences that proceeds very slowly from the concrete to the abstract. These materials are grouped according to sense: auditory, visual, tactile, baric (weight), gustatory, olfactory, and stereognostic. They are subgrouped according to specific qualities such as sound intensity, pitch, form, dimension, color, texture, weight, taste, and odor. Contrasts are presented to the children first, then identities are established through matching and finally, gradations of quality are presented for further discrimination.

When one "educates" the senses, one is not trying to make the children see or hear or touch better, but is helping them to know what it is that they see, hear, or touch. By providing strongly contrasted sensations, followed later by various graded series of sensation, one teaches the child to discriminate. For example, if we teach them first red and then blue, then several shades of blue or several shades of red, we are teaching what is red and what is blue. At the same time they are learning to contrast, to compare and match, to discriminate, to distinguish different sense impressions, and to put them in some sort of order. This is the beginning of a conscious awareness of the environment as opposed to the unconscious knowledge they already have. As they isolate the sense impressions and the qualities perceived, the children gradually build up abstract concepts—first the general category of color, then redness and blueness, darkness and lightness, and so on.

The idea of always presenting two contrasting stimuli rather than a single one was derived, as were so many of Montessori's activities, from Sequin: "We must never confine to automatic memory what can be learned by comparison, nor teach a thing without its natural correlations and generalizations; otherwise we give a false or incomplete idea, or none, but a dry notion with a name" (1907, 66). Sequin also developed the "Three Period Lesson" to associate an object or a quality with its name. The first period consists of establishing identity, associating the sense perception or the object with its name. The second period tests the child's recognition of the object corresponding to the name. The third period establishes that the child can recall the name corresponding to the object. During these lessons the teacher may work on correct articulation, and a good bit of repetition of the first two periods may be necessary before recall is accomplished. The interval between success in the second and in the third period (i.e., between recognition and recall) may be quite lengthy and provides a striking illustration of the amount of time and repetition required for a child to establish the associations so necessary in language development and learning (Richardson, 1969). Current educational practice of telling and testing is absurd, even for children without learning disabilities.

LANGUAGE

Montessori effectively links language development with sensorimotor education, one facilitating the other. She did not devise a method for teaching reading. In fact, in her handbook, the table of contents does not mention reading; there is one section on the material for the preparation for writing and another on exercises for writing "alphabetical signs."

Written language is viewed as an extension of oral language: "To train the child's attention to follow sounds and noises which are produced in the environment, to recognize them and to discriminate between them, is to prepare his attention to follow more accurately the sounds of articulate language" (1965, p. 123). Such attention (listening) aids the child in the development of phonological awareness.

Children are taught the precise nomenclature for the sensorial materials, the names of the objects and words describing the specific attributes. For children with language learning disabilities this is imperative, because we know that one of the factors most characteristic is a deficit in naming. Sequin's Three Period Lesson is used for nomenclature. The children learn the language of forms and dimensions. They learn gradations of quality. For example, colors are graded according to tint and to richness of tone, silence is distinct from nonsilence, noises from sounds, and everything has its own exact and appropriate name.

Montessori stated: "The didactic material, in fact, does not offer to the child the 'content' of the mind, but the *order* for that content. It causes him to distinguish identities from differences, extreme differences from fine gradations, and to classify, under conceptions of quality and of quantity, the most varying sensations appertaining to surfaces, colors, dimensions, forms and sounds. The mind has formed itself by a special exercise of attention, observing, comparing, and classifying" (1965, p. 136). Such vocabulary building, with precision, is part of the preparation for reading and writing: "Language comes to fix by means of exact words the ideas which the mind has acquired. These words are few in number and have reference, not to separate objects, but rather to the order of the ideas which have been formed in the mind" (p. 137).

In current studies there is evidence that the underlying neuropsychological deficit in dyslexia appears to be a problem in phonemic segmentation or phonemic awareness skills. Thus, one can appreciate the significance of Montessori's early language exercises. The analysis of sounds relative to speech are essentially auditory-visual-tactile-kinesthetic exercises connected with the learning of the alphabet. Sandpaper letters are provided for the children to look at and trace with their fingers as they voice the sound of the letter, thus utilizing a multisensory approach. Later they will use a movable alphabet to build words; these are letters which the children can hold in their hands and manipulate themselves.

The multisensory approach to writing and reading was not new. Various forms of this date back to Plato (427–347 B.C.), who taught boys to write by tracing; Horace (65 B.C.), who taught children by means of pieces of pastry made in the shape of letters; and Quintillian (A.D. 35–100), who suggested learning the form and the sound of letters simultaneously (Richardson, 1989).

Montessori viewed graphic, or written, language as offering to the child an essential tool for communication with others as well as a means of perfecting spoken language. This reciprocal function of speaking and writing is an essential point that is overlooked in education and has surfaced only recently in language research.

Montessori saw that the indirect preparation for written language would include all of the child's previous experience: the exercises in practical life, which begin to prepare the hand for writing and which help to establish control of movement and eye-hand coordination; and the sensorial materials, which develop the child's perceptual abilities, visual and auditory discrimination, ability to compare and classify, all of which are necessary for written language. Through practice, with the metal insets, the hand learns to control the pencil, and the sandpaper letters provide the kinesthetic sense with the memory for forms pertinent to written language. At the same time, sounding out the letters reinforces oral kinesthetic memory, increases auditory discrimination and auditory memory, and assists the child in the final perfection of speech itself.

Liberman has pointed out quite clearly that if readers and writers are to use the alphabetic principle productively they must be aware of the phonological structure the letters represent. Liberman also hypothesizes that the weakness in phonological awareness displayed by children who have difficulty learning to read may reflect a more general deficiency in the biological specialization that may process phonological structure in speech (1989). Difficulty in, or a lack of, phonological awareness is a cardinal sign of dyslexia or specific language disability. Liberman (1989) also points out that phonological awareness can be taught. This can be seen in Montessori preschools where children are aided by the sensorial and language materials in their development of attention, phonological awareness, and subsequent reading achievement (Lillard, 1973).

Bradley and Bryant (1983) found high correlations between preschoolers' phonological awareness in response to writing tasks and their later reading and spelling achievement. Those children who were trained in the phonological classification of words and in phoneme-grapheme correspondence were superior later in reading and spelling to children who did not have this training.

When children work with the sandpaper letters, they are exploring the sounds of language and the shapes of the symbols for these sounds; this is neither an exercise in writing nor an exercise in reading.

Through their increasing ability to analyze spoken words into component sounds, and through their mastery of the association between sound and written symbol, the children are led into the process of building words with the moveable alphabet. This is a box divided into compartments that contain cardboard letters of the alphabet—the consonants in red and the vowels in blue. The moveable alphabet enables children to build words but, again, this material is not used to encourage reading or writing but simply the mechanical production of the children's words and later their phrases and sentences as well. Montessori says, "Touching the letters and looking at them at the same time, fixes the image more quickly through the cooperation of the senses. Later, the two facts separate: looking becomes reading, touching becomes writing. According to the type of individual, some learn to read first, others to write" (1912, p. 325). Thus, when children place the cardboard letters in the sequential order in which they hear them in the spoken word, they can build a visual image of the written word for themselves. Then children are led to analyze the written word into its component parts, to articulate them, and to blend them together to form the spoken word—the process of mechanical reading.

Children who can compose a word with the letters of the moveable alphabet are not writing, but they are ready to write—they are prepared. To summarize, the basic steps in teaching the child to write are (1) indirect preparation of the muscular mechanism for holding and using the pencil; (2) use of the sandpaper letters to establish the visual-motor image of the graphic symbols and to establish the kinesthetic memory of the movements necessary to writing, associating these with the sounds of the letters; and (3) use of the moveable alphabet to compose words that are first "sounded out" by the child.

Montessori found that "in general, all children of four are intensely interested in writing" and that "writing is one of the easiest and most delightful conquests made by the child" (1912, pp. 293–94).

We have discussed briefly the development of writing and mechanical reading, or decoding. In order for the child to read with comprehension, however, further work of a different nature is required: "I do not consider as reading the test which the child makes when he verifies the word he has written. He is translating signs into sounds, as he first translated sounds into signs. . . . What I understand by reading is the *interpretation* of an idea from the written signs. . . . So, until the child reads a transmission of ideas from the written word, he does not read" (Montessori, 1912, p. 296).

When the child can read back the words he has made with the moveable alphabet, the teacher introduces the phonetics object game. A box is presented that contains small objects, each with a consonant-vowel-consonant combination, such as pin, cup, cat. The teacher writes one of the words on a slip of paper and asks, "Can you give me the one I want?" If so, the child can then take off, matching objects and labels. Most Montessori classrooms have an enormous number of these object games available, and the children love decoding the labels and placing them with the correct objects.

Next, phonogram cards and "puzzle words" (nonphonetic) are introduced and, later, the roots of words are explored. Usually the children are between six and nine years of age when they become interested in the source of words, although this isn't true of those with learning disabilities.

Gradually, the children begin to explore the functions of words. This is the first time that Montessori uses the term "introduction to reading." She states: "Before the child can understand and enjoy a book, the *logical language* must be established in him. Between knowing how to read the *words,* and how to read the *sense,* of a book there lies the same distance that exists between knowing how to pronounce a word and how to make a speech" (1912, p. 304).

The many grammar games first introduce "naming" words—nouns and their modifiers (articles, adjectives, and prepositions) and then the dynamic "doing" words—verbs with their modifiers (adverbs and prepositions). Finally, the children explore sentence analysis and composition. They learn the names of parts of speech, their functions, and place in the sentence.

Dr. Montessori believed that elementary school should begin with "children who possess, besides a perfect mastery of articulate language, the ability to read written language in an elementary way, and who begin to enter upon the conquest of logical language" (1912, p. 308). She was too wise to specify an age. However, our children with learning disabilities will move very slowly through the language exercises. In fact, it may be necessary for the teacher to lead such children by the hand into these areas when they are reluctant or resistant. The Montessori teacher should know the developmental stages of reading and how to extend or modify them as needed.

Montessori's method may have undergone modification and the schools may be quite diverse. The points I have raised should not be forgotten, however, because they pertain to the education of children who are at risk academically for any reason.

Children with specific language learning disability can profit from this carefully programmed sequence of learning experiences, from the concrete exercises in practical life to the final abstract acts of interpretive reading and writing. A multisensory approach is a requisite in the instructional approaches for children with language learning disabilities or differences.

There are many excellent multisensory remedial programs for children with dyslexia, most of which are offshoots of the Orton-Gillingham approach (Richardson, 1989). June L. Orton (1957) has summarized these approaches in two basic principles: (1) Start the language training with small units that the pupils can handle easily and then proceed by orderly steps from the simple to the more complex. Be sure to teach the blending of the separate units into syllables and words for recognition in reading and recall in writing, (2) Use an "integrated, total language approach. Each unit and sequence is established through hearing, seeing and writing it" (p. 6). These various patterns provide for the individual differences among the students.

The similarity between these remedial approaches and that of Montessori are clear. Why then have we not initiated such preschool programs for children at risk academically, programs that can continue through the primary grades, or longer if necessary?

Not all children who have difficulty learning in the primary grades actually have learning disabilities. Many are overplaced, "unripe" youngsters who need more time for sensorimotor development. When the system insists on force-feeding them, they will soon look and act as if they have learning disabilities. It is, I think, a form of child abuse to allow children to fail the first grades of school before we find a label that will allow them to receive "special" education. We must not continue to punish children who can't learn what we want them to learn, in the way we teach them, and in the time we give them.

To recapitulate: Montessori's approach to early childhood education is developmental—it utilizes techniques and materials that would assist the intelligent child who demonstrates deviant development of coordination, language, attention, and perception—the child who is at risk academically. The sensorimotor foundations of language development are built in an orderly, logical fashion. Training is provided in the motor bases of behavior and learning such as posture and coordination, the development of directionality and laterality, and the development of body image. There is training in perceptual skills such as form perception, space discrimination, stereognosis (the ability to identify objects by touch or feel), and recognition of texture, size, and structure. The child receives training in auditory (listening), visual (looking), and kinesthetic perception (muscular memory of movement, positions, and postures). These provisions assist the child to develop the prelinguistic and preliteracy skills that are among the requisites for the development of symbolic language, spoken and written.

Montessori provided an environment prepared, physically and psychologically, for the child. We must insist that this be done for the child with a learning disability, whether in preschool, elementary school, or in the home; these youngsters require order and structure.

Montessori demanded humility and careful clinical observation on the part of the teacher. She had deep respect, a reverence, for children and their work. So must we all. Children with dyslexia and other learning differences are only handicapped by us—by a system that fails to provide them with access to an appropriate education that meets their learning needs.

REFERENCES

Bradley, L., & Bryant, P. E. (1983).Categorizing sounds and learning to read—A causal connection. *Nature, 30,* 219–241.

Liberman, I. Y. (1989). Phonology and beginning reading revisited. In C. Von Euler (Ed.), *Wenner-Gren International Symposium Series: Brain and Reading* (pp. 135–145). Hampshire, England: Macmillan.

Lillard, P. P. (1972). *Montessori: A modern approach.* New York: Schocken.

Montessori, M. (1912). *The Montessori method.* New York: F. A. Stokes.

———. (1965). *Dr. Montessori's own handbook.* New York: Schocken.

NJCLD (1988). Position paper on Definition of Learning Disabilities. Baltimore: The Orton Dyslexia Society.

Orton, J. L. (1957). The Orton story. *Bulletin of the Orton Society, 7,* 5–8.

Piaget, J. (1952). *The origins of intelligence in children.* (Margaret Cook, Trans.). New York: International Universities Press. (Original work published in 1936)

Richardson, S. O. (1969). In R. C. Orem (Ed.), *Montessori and the special child* (pp. 73–81). New York: Capricorn.

———. (1989). Specific developmental dyslexia: Retrospective and prospective views. *Annals of Dyslexia, 39,* 3–23.

Sequin, E. (1907). *Idiocy and its treatment by the physiological method.* New York: Columbia University Press.

Thomas, A., & Chess, S. (1977). *Temperament and development.* New York: Brunner/Maizel.

Zaporozhets, A., & Elkonin, D. (1971). *The psychology of preschool children.* Cambridge, Mass.: MIT Press.

9

UNITY OF THOUGHT AND EMOTION IN MONTESSORI'S THEORY

The child should love everything he learns, for his mental and emotional growth are linked.

—Maria Montessori, *To Educate the Human Potential*

COGNITIVE MODELS IN DEVELOPMENTAL PSYCHOLOGY AND EDUCATION

During the last three decades, developmental psychology has become a decidedly cognitive enterprise. Piaget no longer dominates the field as he did fifteen or twenty years ago, but another cognitive approach—information processing—has taken over. Inspired by the success of computer technology, information-processing psychologists believe that the workings of the mind can best be described in terms of encoding, storage, retrieval, and other computer concepts. Few disagree. Indeed, in a society as committed to computer technology as ours, computer models of thinking are likely to be popular for years to come.

A major consequence of this new cognitive trend has been the separation of thought from emotion. For example, information-processing psychologist Robert Siegler (1983) observes that computer models have difficulty capturing emotions: "People's feelings of love, hate, anger, fear, and joy are perhaps the ways in which they differ most from computers" (p. 201). But Siegler is unfazed. He says it will be quite sufficient for computer models to explain cognitive functioning, and he assumes that computer models do not need to refer to emotions to do so.

Some psychologists, to be sure, believe that computer models can account for emotions—if not now, in the future (Johnson-Laird, 1988, chap. 20). But one wonders how successful they will be. The information-processing picture of humans is fragmented; it typically views people as bundles of fairly independent computational devices. Many information-processing theorists (e.g., D. A. Allport, 1980; Jackendoff, 1987) even doubt that people possess anything like a self, even though people normally sense that they possess some core self or self-identity that is at the center of their emotional lives (G. W. Allport, 1961, p. 127; White and Watt, 1981, pp. 148–52).

In any event, at present the vast majority of information-processing psychologists are content to concentrate on cognitive processes. As Sigel (1986) has noted, one can read important collections of essays and literature reviews in this field (e.g., Sternberg, 1984; Klahr, 1989) without coming across terms such as *emotion* or *affect*.

In education, the latest cognitive trend is the "thinking skills" movement (Costa, 1985). Here again, writers generally assume that they can focus on cognitive processes without much reference to emotions.

Thinking skills programs typically have a clear goal: they want to teach students the rational, analytical thinking tools they will need as adults in our increasingly technological world. Pursuing this goal, the programs divide thinking into numerous specific "skills," such as observing, predicting, sequencing, and hypothesizing. Some programs list more than one hundred skills. The programs then attempt to teach the skills one at a time.

As a rule, thinking skills specialists do not devote much attention to the theoretical assumptions underlying their programs, but they almost invariably see themselves as part of the new, computer-inspired cognitive revolution. Whenever possible, they sprinkle their writings with computer terminology (for example, using headings such as "input skills" and "output skills") and they often attempt to teach overarching cognitive strategies, such as goal-setting and self-monitoring, derived from computer technology (see, for example, Costa, 1985, chap. 12 and 13).

Some thinking skills specialists refer to the emotional aspects of thinking, but they generally assign feelings and attitudes a peripheral role (see Nickerson et al., 1985, pp. 337–40). For example, Arthur Costa is a thinking skills authority who is unusually sensitive to the importance of emotion, but he does not really integrate it into his model. In one essay (1985, chap. 20), Costa prints a physicist's account of what he did and how he felt when working on a problem in optics, and Costa provides his own running commentary "intended to illuminate the mental processes that are prerequisite and pervasive throughout the scientific process of inquiry" (p. 114). What is striking is the difference between the two accounts. Whereas the scientist's self-report is full of emotional drama,

Costa's comments focus primarily on cerebral processes. The scientist writes that he at various times "hurried to the lab," "struggled with alternatives," "became disgusted with the whole affair," "was struck with another idea," again "hurried to the lab," and was "thrilled" by the outcome. During all this, Costa primarily sees the scientist formulating, rejecting, and accepting hypotheses. For example, when the scientist says, "My theory was no good, and I went to bed disgusted with the whole affair," Costa comments, "He rejects his theory." When the scientist says, "This time it worked!" Costa says, "The data he collected supports his explanation" (1985, pp. 115–17). Costa's analysis notwithstanding, what distinguishes the scientist is not his use of hypothetico-deductive reasoning, but his intense, personal involvement in his work.

Indeed, as numerous creative people have reminded us, it is a passion for one's work, above all else, that is essential. Einstein likened the mind of the creative physicist to that of the "religious worshiper or the lover." The creative scientist, he said, could not possibly put forth the tremendous daily effort that the work requires unless the effort comes "straight from the heart" (Hoffmann, 1972, p. 222). Creative people in other fields have made similar comments (John-Steiner, 1985). Yet emotion is today neglected.

The second-class status of emotion in current educational policy is illustrated by a recent report of the New Jersey School Boards Association (Seiden, 1989). Studying the impact of standardized testing on New Jersey schools, a school board committee expressed concern that "teaching has become mechanical; school has become more boring; love of learning is not encouraged by emphasis on passing tests" (p. 4). Nevertheless, the committee recommended changes that would increase the impact of standardized testing. Testing, the committee decided, had improved basic skills, and basic skills are "the most important thing that students should learn in school since these are the tools necessary for all further learning" (p. 5). Apparently the committee overlooked the possibility that by the time students have mastered a sizeable number of basic skills they will have lost all interest in further learning.

THE ROLE OF EMOTION IN PIAGETIAN THEORY

From the perspective of traditional developmental theory, from Rousseau to Dewey and Piaget, the current neglect of emotion is unfortunate. In Piagetian theory, for example, emotions—especially interest and curiosity—are the driving forces behind developmental change. Children become interested in things and ideas that they cannot quite fit into their cognitive structures and are therefore motivated to change their structures to incorporate them. For example, a baby girl who tries to grab a piece of chalk might find that it keeps slipping from her palmar grasp. The baby's difficulty challenges her to try new ways of grasping, and in the process she constructs new structures for dealing with the world.

In a sense, the centrality of emotion in Piaget's theory is easy to over-look. Piaget devoted a great deal of attention to the logical and mathematical features of his stage structures, and these descriptions are theoretical and dry. He spent far less time on the process of cognitive change, which is where emotions such as interest and curiosity come into play.

Piaget's writings on education (1971, 1973) were relatively sparse, but his concern for emotions, attitudes, and personal characteristics was clear. In these writings, Piaget hardly mentioned cognitive structures. He emphasized, instead, children's need to think for themselves. Children cannot develop mentally, he said, if they are dominated by adults—if, as Kamii (1973) puts it, they must believe that the answers must "always come from the teacher's head" (p. 234). Children must figure out problems for themselves, and they will do so only if the problems are sufficiently interesting to set their minds in motion. Thus, the goal of education becomes that of fostering interest and independence—of producing people who do not merely accept what others tell them, but who are "creative, inventive, and discoverers" (Piaget, 1964, p. 5).

Constance Kamii, a Piagetian early childhood specialist, says that with respect to learning,

> we would like children to be alert, curious, critical and confident in their ability to figure things out and say what they honestly think. We would also like them to have initiative; come up with interesting ideas, problems, and questions; and put things into relationships (1980, p. 12).

Here again, the emphasis is on children's feelings and attitudes toward learning, not on school subjects such as math or reading, or even on Piagetian capacities such as classification or seriation.

EMOTION IN MONTESSORI'S THEORY

Montessori would not have disagreed with the Piagetians. From her perspective, however, the Piagetian view of the emotions involved in learning is still a bit cerebral. For Montessori, the child's emotional involvement in real learning goes to the very core of the personality, to the child's "innermost self" (1967, pp. 102, 218), or, as she sometimes said, to the child's very "soul" (e.g., 1967, pp. 9, 62, 272). To demonstrate her point, she often called attention to the child's early language learning.

LANGUAGE ACQUISITION

Montessori, anticipating Chomsky (1965), observed that the child's ability to master a human language is an amazing fact. What is most incredible is not just the development of an enormous vocabulary, but the mastery of a grammar—a set of rules for putting words into their proper order. These rules are in all languages so complex and abstract that linguists are still trying to figure them out. Nevertheless, children spontaneously acquire a working knowledge of most of them by the age of five or six years.

To explain language acquisition and other learning in the first six years, Montessori proposed the concept of the absorbent mind—a special power that enables children to tirelessly incorporate aspects of their surroundings.

In the first three years, Montessori said (1967, pp. 6–7, 167–68), children absorb the environment in a largely unconscious and profound manner. They become so moved by certain impressions that they take them into themselves and in this way build core elements of their personalities. This process, Montessori emphasized, is not just mental. Certain impressions "awaken so much interest and so much enthusiasm that they become incorporated into [the child's] very existence. The child *absorbs* these impressions not with his mind but with his life itself" (1967, p. 24). Montessori proposed that a "biological or psychochemical change" (p. 101) takes place as these impressions "incarnate" themselves into the child's innermost self (pp. 62, 102).

Through the absorbent mind, then, infants and young children begin acquiring basic aspects of their language. The sounds of speech, Montessori hypothesized, make far deeper impressions on infants than other sounds. "These impressions must be so strong, and cause such an intensity of emotion—so deep an enthusiasm as to set in motion invisible fibers of his body, fibers which start vibrating in the effort to reproduce those sounds" (1967, p. 24). Montessori would have been gratified by the research of Condon and Sander (1974), whose careful film analyses showed that newborns almost imperceptibly "dance" to the sounds of human speech, but not to other sounds.

In any case, we see that early language acquisition, in Montessori's view, is hardly just an intellectual process, which is what learning so frequently is for adults. Children need language—and positively yearn for it—to build their psychic structures. The impressions the child receives, Montessori said, "are not just remembered; they form part of his soul" (1967, p. 62).

At the age of about three years, the first period for the absorption of language ends. Between three and six years, children still have a special ability to absorb language—they are still in the sensitive period for language acquisition—but their efforts are now more conscious and deliberate, and they no longer absorb the fundamental structures of language so deeply into their psyches.

Because Montessori believed the first period is the more powerful and mysterious, she searched for analogies to describe it. In one passage (1967, p. 112) she likened the early absorbent mind to the process by which photographic images are permanently imprinted on a plate. She was not entirely satisfied with this metaphor, but the related concept of imprinting, as used by ethologists, seems apt. Imprinting is the process by which the young in many species fill in irreversible images during an early critical period. For example, mallard ducklings, during an early period of intense searching and following, form a permanent image of their mother-figure, whom they will follow for months thereafter. In a like manner, human infants, during an initial period of intense concentration, form a deep and lasting imprint of the basic patterns of their mother tongue (see Leyhausen, 1973, and Crain, 1992, pp. 34–37 for discussions of imprinting and imprintinglike phenomena).

Although early language learning is the most impressive example of the absorbent mind, the concept also applies to other learning in the first three years. Through the power of the absorbent mind, Montessori (1967, pp. 63, 102) said, children acquire the musical patterns and the distinctive physical gestures and expressions that form part of their cultural identities. Children also develop a deep identification with their native geographical surroundings. For example, adults who grew up by the sea frequently feel most relaxed and at home when they return to the seashore. They feel that the sea is somehow a part of them, that it is "in their blood." It is as if they have imprinted upon it. It has become a basic part of their personal identity.

INTEGRATING THE PERSONALITY

During the first three years of life, when children are absorbing impressions unconsciously, their various capacities develop separately. For example, language develops separately from control over the limbs (Montessori, 1967, p. 165). During the next three years, children organize their capacities, and they work with great intensity on tasks that enable them to do so. For example, by cutting vegetables with precision, they coordinate hand, eye, and mind. Through writing and drawing, they organize language with hand and eye (p. 203).

During this period, the child's activities become more conscious and deliberate. Whereas younger children frequently act as if they are governed by an impersonal force as they take in the world about them, three- to six-year-olds seem to be exercising their wills. The child in this age range, Montessori said, "is now guided by his conscious 'I,' his personal self, and we see that his hands are busy" (p. 167).

Vygotsky (1934), whose work has recently generated wide interest, described how children of this age use speech to consciously regulate their actions. While working or playing, they frequently talk aloud and give themselves directions. For example, a boy says, "Where's the pencil? I need the blue pencil. Never mind, I'll draw with the red one and wet it with water. It will become dark and look like blue" (p. 30). The child talks aloud to solve the problem and guide his actions.

Paradoxically, at the very time when children are gaining conscious control over their actions, their work is most profoundly characterized by a capacity for deep concentration in which they seem to lose self-consciousness. When children find tasks that enable them to integrate their separate capacities, they often become completely engrossed in them, entering into a kind of meditation (Montessori, 1965, p. 220). Montessori frequently told, for example, about the little girl whom she first saw become totally absorbed in work with cylinders. The girl couldn't be distracted as she repeated the exercise over and over, and when she finally finished the exercise, she appeared fresh and rested, as if awakening from a pleasant dream (1970, pp. 53–55; 1972b, p. 119).

The child who concentrates deeply, Montessori argued, is not merely satisfying her curiosity or learning in any narrowly cognitive sense. The child is achieving a new psychic integration; she is unifying her personality as a whole. The depth of the personality transformation is evident in the child's emotional behavior. Before children learn to concentrate, they are restless and distractible. "The hand moves aimlessly; the mind wanders about far from reality; language takes pleasure in itself; the body moves clumsily" (1967, p. 203). Energies go off in separate directions. The child behaves as if she lacks a personal center of gravity.

Children who have learned to concentrate, in contrast, act as if they have found themselves. They are happy and possess a new serenity, an inner assurance that comes from their knowledge that they can now bring all their energies to bear on focused work (1967, p. 75).

The inner fulfillment achieved through concentration also seems to release affectionate feelings outward to others. When children enter into states of deep concentration, they are oblivious to their surroundings. For the time being, Montessori said, the child's "spirit is like that of a hermit in the desert" (1967, p. 272). But when the child

> . . . comes out of his concentration, he seems to perceive the world anew as a boundless field for fresh discoveries. He becomes aware of his classmates in whom he takes an affectionate interest. Love awakens in him for people and for things. He becomes friendly to everyone. (1967, pp. 272–73)

It is apparent, then, that concentration produces a major personality transformation. Montessori said that concentration "normalizes" the child; it enables children to integrate their capacities and their personalities and to become more truly themselves (1967, pp. 204–7).

In some ways, the concentration of early childhood is unique to this period. In contrast to adults, young children put as much effort as possible into their work, probably because the effort solidifies and unifies their powers. Nevertheless, the power of concentration is retained in highly creative individuals, and Montessori said that we all need creative work, into which we can pour all our energies, to actualize our potentials and express our individuality (1972b, p. 186).

EMOTIONAL DISTURBANCES

I have highlighted ways in which cognitive development is, in Montessori's view, a very emotional process. When children learn language, they are profoundly moved by the impressions they receive, and when they find tasks that enable them to coordinate their separate capacities, they enter into states of deep concentration, from which they emerge refreshed, tranquil, and friendly. Children display such a range of emotions because they are developing not just their minds, but their whole personalities.

In fact, Montessori believed that cognitive development is so directly related to the growth of the whole personality that when cognitive work is impeded, emotional disturbances result. In this section, I will outline Montessori's view on how healthy development goes awry and emotional disturbances arise.

Healthy development, Montessori said, comes from within. It is not adults who mold and form children; children construct their own minds and selves through their own efforts. In this process, an inner biological guide prompts them to select from the environment the activities they need and to work tirelessly on them. Adults provide an environment that gives children opportunities for self-development, but the work must be done by the children themselves (1970; 1967, chap. 22–26).

Unfortunately, this is not the way things usually happen. Adults are frequently insensitive to the objects and activities that children need, even though children's spontaneous interests usually make these readily apparent. Moreover, adults constantly interfere with the work the child finds meaningful. If a child is exploring an object with her hand, she is told, "Don't touch." If she is trying to feed herself, an adult comes along and feeds her (Montessori, 1965, p. 20). If she is trying to walk at her own pace, taking pleasure in her growing power, an adult swoops her up, puts her in a stroller, and moves her along (1972b, p. 77).

In Montessori's view, children are small, delicate people surrounded by giants who dominate and control them. Because children's activities are prompted by an inner, vital need to develop themselves, they experience the adult's domination and intrusiveness as severe violence. The child, Montessori said, might well think: "Why does she, whom I love so dearly, want to annihilate me?" (1965, p. 193).

Adults also undermine the child's independence through the use of rewards and punishments. Teachers, for example, try to motivate children through praise, good grades, criticism, threats, and so on. These external inducements usually make learning a miserable experience. Children become so worried about external evaluations—so afraid of getting wrong answers or looking stupid—that they cannot concentrate deeply on their work. Moreover, external evaluations take children away from themselves. Children begin looking to grownups to determine if they are giving the right answers. Soon they turn to others to know what they are supposed to do and say. Rewards and punishments socialize children into the conventional social order, but they drown out the inner voice that guides them toward the full development of their potential (Montessori, 1972a, pp. 14–18).

When children are deprived of the activities they need to develop themselves, Montessori said, they display various "deviations" or emotional problems. Montessori's descriptions of these problems was extremely impressive. Without missing a beat, her writing moved into psychoanalytic theory, as if it were second nature to her. Some of Montessori's thoughts on emotional problems were in an Adlerian vein. For example, she pointed out how children sometimes respond to adult domination by using their own weakness to exploit the adult. Children use their tears, entreaties, melancholy looks, and childhood charm to get adults to do their bidding (1972b, p. 165). More fundamentally, though, Montessori's discussions frequently anticipated the imagery and spirit of contemporary self-psychology, especially that of D. W. Winnicott.

Montessori and Winnicott.

Before outlining their shared views on pathology, it would be useful to give a brief introduction to Winnicott's theory of normal development. Unfortunately, Winnicott's writing, while poetic, was so unsystematic that it would be impossible to do so in any short space. But I would like to make a couple of general points.

Winnicott is currently popular among psychoanalysts for his insights into the development of the healthy self, which he thought of as the sense we get when we are not complying with others' expectations, but are acting spontaneously and creatively. At such times, we feel that we are most real and are expressing our true nature (Winnicott, 1971, pp. 54, 68–69; 1965, pp. 145–48). This view resonates well with that of Montessori, who also emphasized our need for creative work to draw upon our full powers and express our individuality (1972b, p. 186).

This is not to say that the views of Winnicott and Montessori on creativity and development were identical. Whereas Montessori saw healthy development occurring primarily through work with physical objects, Winnicott focused on the mother/infant relationship. Winnicott also had a much higher regard for the benefits of imaginative play.

Nevertheless, their overall orientations to normal development were strikingly similar. Both believed that the impetus for healthy development comes from within; children are biologically motivated to organize their capacities and develop a coherent sense of themselves as creative beings. Both hoped the environment would facilitate this process, but both worried about the ways in which adult neglect and interference impedes healthy development. The following are some of their shared impressions of what can happen when things go wrong.

1   Winnicott said that when adult interference is severe, depriving children of the spontaneous experiences they need to develop themselves, children often feel threatened with "annihilation" (1975, p. 303). Montessori, as we have seen, suggested the same thing (1965, p. 193).

2   Winnicott (1965, p. 150) observed that when children have been unable to integrate their personalities, they often manifest outward symptoms of restlessness, distractibility, and a lack of concentration. Montessori pointed to the same symptoms, arguing that what children need are opportunities to concentrate deeply on work that will enable them to bring their capacities together (1967, pp. 203, 265–67).

3   Both Winnicott and Montessori saw many childhood behavior problems as the children's effort to protect their growing selves from adult intrusions. For example, both questioned the common assumption that childhood disobedience indicates some problem in children. Instead, rebelliousness may represent a positive effort by children to protect their right to self-construction. Rebellious children may be fighting against domineering adults who prevent them from developing their will and their character (Winnicott, 1986, pp. 65–70; Montessori, 1965, p. 29).

4   Winnicott observed that many of his patients (both child and adult) had reacted to adult intrusiveness by creating an "inner hiding place" to keep their true selves and feelings concealed from others. He believed that we all do this to some extent: "At the center of each person is an incommunicado element, and this is sacred and most worthy of preservation" (1965, p. 187). Some patients, however, need to wall themselves off from others to a strong degree.

Similarly, Montessori saw many children building "psychic barriers" against the world. Externally, these children seem dull, listless, and unresponsive. But they are really barricading themselves against adult intrusions. They refuse to listen to those who would prevent them from following their inner urges, and they build an inner wall "which closes the spirit and conceals it as a defense against the world" (1972b, p. 160).

5   Perhaps the most characteristic disorder of our time does not always appear to be a disorder at all. This is an excessive conformity to social expectations. Winnicott observed that even healthy individuals conform to social pressures to some extent; they frequently compromise between behavior that reflects their true feelings and behavior that others expect.

In Winnicott's terms, people compromise between the "true self" and the "false self" (1965, ch. 12). The problem is that in recent decades mental health professionals have increasingly found themselves treating clients whose false or socially compliant selves are far too dominant. These clients, suffering from "narcissistic personality disorders," report feelings of inner emptiness, fragile self-esteem, and a preoccupation with how they appear in the eyes of others (American Psychiatric Association, 1987, pp. 349–51; Lasch, 1979, p. 81).

Montessori, you will recall, pointed to the development of the same general problem in her discussion of rewards and punishments (1972a, pp. 14–18). When we try to motivate children through external inducements, we make them dependent on the approval of others. Children begin looking outside themselves for the sources of truth and stop relying on their own judgment. Through rewards and punishments, we enslave children to the conventional social order, teaching them to think and behave as they are supposed to, regardless of their true feelings (Montessori, 1972b, pp. 175–76).

Montessori was particularly concerned about this last problem—an excessive dependence on the approval of others—and she believed her schools were counteracting it. In her schools, children were finding deep gratification in intrinsically meaningful work, and they were making their own discoveries. Thus, they had no reason to look to adults for rewards or for right answers. They were becoming self-assured and independent. In fact, Montessori noted that children who graduated from her schools frequently got into trouble because they spoke their minds instead of saying what others wanted to hear (1972b, pp. 170, 175).

Why, though, is the need for social approval apparently on the rise today? An answer would require sociological analyses, and neither Winnicott nor Montessori went into such analyses in any detail. But Montessori did point to the lack of intrinsic satisfaction in modern work. Most employees, she noted, are motivated solely by external inducements, such as promotions and social status (1972a, p. 14; 1972b, p. 186). In addition, the recent increase in service professions may be a factor. In today's people-oriented occupations, what one produces counts for less than the impression one makes on others (Lasch, 1979, p. 96). Thus, the occupational world increases people's feeling that only external approval really matters.

Sociological speculations aside, what I want to emphasize here is how much Montessori had to say about the central disorders of our time—disorders in which people fail to develop a solid sense of themselves as independent, creative individuals. The fact that Montessori anticipated several of Winnicott's key insights into the disorders of the self shows that her theory went far beyond the realm of the intellect alone and spoke to the development of the whole personality.

THE COSMIC PLAN

So far, my discussion of Montessori's developmental theory has been confined to the behavior and experiences of children from birth to six years of age. At the age of six, Montessori said, children undergo a change. They are no longer so energetically engaged in work that primarily develops and integrates their own capacities. Instead, their focus turns outward. They become interested in exploring nature and the social environment. Most fundamentally, there is a kind of philosophical awakening, a sensitivity to what is good and noble (Montessori, 1948).

To meet this sensitivity, Montessori proposed a curriculum centered around the cosmic plan, a history of the earth and its life forms in which everything the children study fits into an interrelated whole. The cosmic plan tells a majestic story of progress designed to inspire children as they learn. "Our aim," Montessori said, "is not merely to make the child understand, and still less to force him to memorise, but so to touch his imagination as to enthuse him to his inmost core" (1948, p. 15).

This kind of inspiration seems terribly important. The most creative people possess, in addition to the young child's powers of concentration, an enthusiasm for their work that has a kind of spiritual element. Creative people work with such intensity because they are reaching for something more noble or beautiful than has yet been expressed or produced (John-Steiner, 1985, pp. 60–68).

The specific content of the cosmic plan, however, is no longer persuasive. The plan combines an appreciation of ecology with an enthusiasm for technological progress. Today, the contradiction between these two themes is very clear: technological progress has occurred at the expense of the natural environment. As humans have created their industrial and technological wonders, they have poisoned the air, polluted the waters, destroyed large forests, and brought numerous species to the point of extinction. Ecologists wonder whether the planet will remain habitable for future generations.

Today, those embracing environmentalism tend to be romantics who sometimes speak in the same poetic terms that Montessori did. Like her, they would say there is something that "emanates from trees which speaks to the soul" (Montessori, 1976, p. 35). The proponents of technology, in contrast, would never use such words. Indeed, as noted in the beginning of this paper, many computer-oriented psychologists do not even believe that humans have anything like an inner self or a unified personality—a view that seems to be spreading to college-age computer enthusiasts (Turkle, 1984). The proponents of computer technology also would bring computers into the schools in an extensive way, even though computers lock children into a closed, mechanical world, isolating them from nature and full interactions with others.

I believe that today Montessori would reformulate the cosmic plan. Nevertheless, such a plan is needed. Students need the feeling that their studies will put them into contact with ideas that are meaningful, beautiful, and ennobling. Thus inspired, they will become deeply involved in their work.

SUMMARY

In recent years, developmental psychology and education have been strongly influenced by computer models, which generally neglect the emotional aspects of thinking. Piagetian theory recognizes the role of emotion in cognitive development, but an especially rich account of the emotional nature of cognitive development is found in the work of Montessori.

Montessori suggested, for example, that the child's acquisition of language, a highly symbolic activity, begins as an intensely emotional, physical process. Patterns of sound make profound impressions on young children, and they absorb these impressions into their "innermost selves."

The emotional intensity underlying cognitive development is also seen in the way three- to six-year-old children concentrate so deeply on tasks that enable them to integrate their cognitive capacities. This concentrated effort produces a new serenity and self-assurance in the child and releases affectionate feelings toward others.

Montessori believed that the child's spontaneous cognitive work so directly affects the development of the whole personality that adult interference with this work creates emotional problems. Her descriptions of these problems, moreover, anticipated central themes in the psychoanalytic self-psychology of D. W. Winnicott. Like Winnicott, for example, Montessori called attention to the ways in which children barricade themselves against adult intrusions, hiding their spontaneous feelings within.

Both theorists also were concerned with the ways in which people lose faith in themselves and their powers and become slaves to social approval.

Developing a curriculum for children after the age of six years, Montessori tried to inspire students with a majestic story of nature and human progress. Today we can question Montessori's unbridled admiration for technological progress, but we cannot question the need for a curriculum that inspires love and enthusiasm for its subject matter.

REFERENCES

Allport, D. A. (1980). Patterns and actions: Cognitive mechanisms are content specific. In G. Claxton (Ed.), *Cognitive psychology: New directions*. London: Routledge & Kegan Paul, pp. 26–64.

Allport, G. W. (1961). *Pattern and growth in personality*. New York: Holt, Rinehart and Winston.

American Psychiatric Association (1987). *Diagnostic and statistical manual of mental disorders* (3rd ed., rev.). Washington, D. C.: American Psychiatric Association.

Chomsky, N. (1965). *Aspects of the theory of syntax*. Cambridge, Mass.: MIT Press.

Condon, W. S., and Sander, L. W. (1974). Neonate movement is synchronized with adult speech: Interaction participation and language acquisition. *Science, 183*, 99–101.

Costa, A. L. (1985). *Developing minds*. Alexandria, Va.: Association for Supervision and Curriculum Development.

Crain, W. C. (1992). *Theories of development: Concepts and applications* (3rd ed.). Englewood Cliffs, N.J.: Prentice-Hall.

Hoffmann, B. (1972). *Albert Einstein: Creator and rebel*. New York: New American Library.

Jackendoff, R. S. (1987). *Consciousness and the computational mind*. Cambridge, Mass.: MIT Press.

John-Steiner, V. (1985). *Notebooks of the mind*. New York: Harper & Row.

Johnson-Laird, P.N. (1988). *The computer and the mind*. Cambridge, Mass.: Harvard University Press.

Kamii, C. (1973). Piaget's interactionism and the process of teaching young children. In M. Schwebel and J. Raph (Eds.), *Piaget in the classroom*. New York: Basic Books, pp. 216–30.

———. (1980). Why use group games? In C. Kamii and R. DeVries (Eds.), *Group games in early education*. Washington, D.C.: National Association for the Education of Young Children, pp. 11–33.

Klahr, D. (1989). Information-processing approaches. *Annals of Child Development, 6*, 133–85.

Lasch, C. (1979). *The culture of narcissism*. New York: Warner Books.

Leyhausen, P. (1973). The relationship between drive and will in its significance to educational theory. In K. Lorenz and P. Leyhausen (Eds.), *Motivation of human and animal behavior* (B. A. Tonkin, Trans.). New York: Van Nostrand Reinhold, pp. 37–58. (Original work published in 1951)

Montessori, M. (1948). *To educate the human potential.* Adyar Madras 20, India: Kalakshetra Publications.

———. (1965). *The advanced Montessori method, Vol. I, Spontaneous activity in education* (F. Simmonds, Trans.). New York: Shocken. (Original work published in 1917)

———. (1967). *The absorbent mind* (C. A. Claremont, Trans.). New York: Holt, Rinehart and Winston. (Original work published in 1949)

———. (1970). *The child in the family* (N. R. Cirillo, Trans.). Chicago: Henry Regnery Co. (Original work published in 1936)

———. (1972a). *The discovery of the child* (M. J. Costelloe, Trans.). New York: Ballantine Books. (Original work published in 1948)

———. (1972b). *The secret of childhood* (M. J. Costelloe, Trans.). New York: Schocken Books. (Original work published in 1936)

———. (1976). *From childhood to adolescence* (A. M. Joosten, Trans.). New York: Schocken Books. (Original work published in 1948)

Nickerson, R. S., Perkins, D. N., and Smith, E. E. (1985). *The teaching of thinking.* Hillsdale, N.J.: Lawrence Erlbaum.

Piaget, J. (1964). Development and learning. In R. Ripple and V. Rockcastle (Eds.), *Piaget rediscovered.* Ithaca, N.Y.: Cornell University Press, pp. 7–20.

———. (1971). *Science of education and the psychology of the child* (D. Coltman, Trans.). New York: Viking. (Original work published in 1969)

———. (1973). *To understand is to invent.* (G. A. Roberts, Trans.). New York: Grossman (Original work published in 1948)

Seiden, D. (1989). *Final report: Ad hoc committee to study HSPT/differentiated diplomas.* New Jersey School Boards Association. 413 State St., Trenton, N.J. 08605.

Siegler, R. S. (1983). Information processing approaches to development. In W. Kessen (Ed.), *Handbook of Child Psychology*, Vol. I. New York: John Wiley & Sons, pp. 129–211.

Sigel, I. E. (1986). Mechanism: A metaphor for cognitive development? A review of Sternberg's *Mechanisms of cognitive development. Merrill-Palmer Quarterly, 32,* 93–101.

Sternberg, R. J. (1984). *Mechanisms of cognitive development.* San Francisco: Freeman.

Turkle, S. (1984). *The second self: Computers and the human spirit.* New York: Simon and Schuster.

Vygotsky, L. S. (1934). *Thought and language* (A. Kozulin, Trans.). Cambridge, Mass.: MIT Press.

White, R. W., and Watt, N. F. (1981). *The abnormal personality* (5/ê). New York: Wiley.

Winnicott, D. W. (1965). *The maturational process and the facilitating environment.* New York: International Universities Press.

———. (1971). *Playing and reality.* New York: Basic Books.

————. (1975). *Through pediatrics to psycho-analysis*. New York: Basic Books. (Original work published in 1958)

————. (1986). *Home is where we start from* (essays compiled and edited by C. Winnicott, M. Shepard, and M. Davis). New York: W. W. Norton.

10

QUESTIONS ABOUT MONTESSORI EDUCATION TODAY

Although I am not a Montessori educator, I come to the topic of this symposium with a very soft spot for Maria Montessori and for the American Montessori Society with its commitment to providing a sound education for our young children. Indeed, how could anyone in early childhood education not have a soft spot for Maria Montessori? The entire early childhood profession owes so much to her. But of course, there is no need for me to tell this audience about the importance and significance of Montessori's ideas and practices. My role and my goal in this presentation is to pose questions that will provoke you into explicating what you are about, and what you really mean when you use your "inside" language among yourselves so that the rest of us in early childhood education can gain a fuller understanding of Montessori education today.

KINDS OF QUESTIONS

Because my assignment is to pose questions, I want to say a bit about three kinds of questions and their functions. The first kind, commonly used by teachers at every level of education, is *interrogation,* in which the questioner looks for a predetermined, right answer (e.g., What was the date of the Louisiana Purchase? What did I just say? What color is your shirt?). These are questions that have correct answers; guessing or approximating would not be acceptable responses. Such interrogations can be quite intimidating; they often make respondents feel somewhat powerless. Furthermore, because the questioner already knows the answer, such questions also seem phony. I once observed a teacher of four-year-olds leading a debriefing discussion following a field trip to an aquarium. When she asked the group, "How did the fish get in the tank?" one of them responded, "Have you forgotten already?" This youngster had not yet learned to play the question-answer games typical of the school culture. Perhaps there is a place for such questions in teaching, as for example when a teacher wants to check whether children know their address or phone number. In such cases phoniness can be avoided by the teacher saying straightforwardly, "I want to know if you know your address and phone number. Please say it to me."

The second kind of question, mostly used in conversations, discussions, and interviews, *solicits* ideas, views, or opinions that the questioner does not know in advance (Is the blue shirt one you like?).

A third kind of question—sometimes called *illuminating* questions—requires respondents to flesh out the ellipses in their written and spoken expressions—the ends of sentences left unsaid that are understood by insiders and not by outsiders. For example, I recently met a school superintendent who proudly declared that his district is committed to the goal that "Every child will have success." When I asked him, "Success at what?" I was provoking him to complete the sentence and thereby to help me understand what the children were to be successful at. The superintendent was quite puzzled by my question; most of the people he interacts with apparently fill in the ellipses of the sentence without difficulty. But to an outsider like myself the end of the sentence was missing and I did not know what meaning to give it.

I propose to use all three kinds of questions, but I shall try to employ illuminating questions as much as possible because I believe they aid the process of self-scrutiny, which I take to be one of the main purposes of this symposium. My presentation is divided into three general sections. The first offers some introductory comments about Montessori education, especially as perceived by outsiders. The second part is a list of my questions about Montessori education, and the third part is a discussion about contemporary Montessori methods education.

GENERAL OBSERVATIONS ABOUT MONTESSORI EDUCATION TODAY

As part of my preparation, I did some catching up on the recent Montessori literature and revisited some of Maria Montessori's own writing as well. In addition, I interviewed as many students, colleagues, and teachers as I could about their opinions, perceptions, and especially their own direct experiences of Montessori education. Two of my respondents were qualified Montessori teachers, but had left the fold for a variety of reasons. I interviewed about thirty people in this process, but unfortunately my sampling was *not* systematic.

On the whole my findings were somewhat puzzling. Many people whose own children had been in Montessori preschools were pleased with their experience. Of about a dozen parents interviewed, only two of them were unsure that Montessori was "right" for their particular children.

Even more interesting to me were the comments made by graduate students, colleagues, and teachers in the wider early childhood education community. Their responses to my probing gave me the impression that there is a fairly strong stereotype of Montessori practices, teachers, and advocates in the general community of early childhood educators; there is even a trace of hostility attached to it. You may have some guesses about why this is so. I am not sure how to account for it. But it is useful to keep in mind that any method of teaching can be done well or poorly; no doubt you know of embarrassing cases of Montessori education! It could be that my informal sample included a few who were exposed to poorly implemented Montessori education. I doubt whether you will be surprised by any of the general views expressed by my interviewees. The main comments were as follows:

- Montessori methods place too little emphasis on children's social development.

- Montessori educators underestimate the value of pretend play.

- In Montessori classrooms children are not sufficiently spontaneous; they seem restrained and restricted.

- Montessori philosophy talks a lot about liberty, but Montessori teachers seem to be very controlling.

- Teachers in Montessori classrooms often seem unnatural; teachers' talk is stylized, pre-scripted, and proscribed.

- Montessori teachers seem rather distant and cold in their relations with children; they are not supposed to touch the children, for example.

- In a Montessori classroom the children have to use the same self-correcting materials all year; the range of available materials is too narrow.

In the course of my informal investigation and discussions I often pointed out to my respondents that even though the available relevant research has many problems, it generally gives Montessori methods good marks; I know of little in the way of negative findings about the effects of Montessori education. But my respondents remained unimpressed by the evidence!

Perhaps some of the distance between Montessori and other early childhood educators is due to insufficient contact between Montessori and the wider early childhood education community. Perhaps some people acquired their stereotypes of Montessori and her disciples from history of education courses or from frustrating attempts to read Maria Montessori's own words without benefit of knowledgeable modern interpreters.

My hunch is that the central issues that divide the general early childhood community from Montessorians are ideological rather than scientific, theoretical, or even philosophical. Ideologies are sets of beliefs concerning the things about which we are the most passionate and of which we are least certain (Katz, 1977). We know that we have touched a person or group's ideological nerve when they take what we say about their views or positions personally rather than conceptually or philosophically. Furthermore, people who share an ideological commitment tend to use a special language—esoteric "in" words or dialects not used or understood in the same way by outsiders. In addition, the insiders tend to remain separate, exclusive; they keep to themselves.

In principle, any field with a weak or unreliable data base suffers from a vacuum that is filled by ideologies that are typically promoted by attractive or charismatic leaders. Competing schools of thought tend to emerge about the most basic but elusive concerns of the field; sometimes factions, camps, or cabals develop to preserve and advocate various versions of the truth. Ideologies tend to be related to an ideal conception of humanity and the good life. Although the term *ideology* usually carries with it derogatory connotations, ideologies serve important functions and are probably indispensable (Katz, 1977).

Early childhood education inevitably suffers from a weak data base for two reasons. First, the object of our concern—the young child—is by definition immature. This means that the object of our inquiries and investigations is unstable and changing at such a rapid rate that generating valid and reliable longitudinal empirical data is problematic. The younger the subject, the more true it is that empirical studies must be reported with qualifiers about their validity and reliability. Second, the definitive experiments needed to settle the most troubling theoretical and pedagogical disputes would be unethical to conduct. As long as we have any sound reason to believe that something is "good" for children, it would be unethical to withhold it from them just for the sake of the advancement of science. In the same way, as long as we have any sound reason to believe that something might be harmful to children, it would be unethical to subject them to it as well. Thus we are always at the mercy of slippery data that are open to dispute and disagreement.

In any ideology-bound discipline there is a strong tendency to resist and deny evidence (however slippery) that runs counter to our deep beliefs. Ideologies also generate strong temptations to become doctrinaire, to adhere slavishly to the words and pronouncements of the founding fathers and mothers, and to interpret the sacred texts more rigidly than the founders themselves did.

One way of coping with the inherent temptations and difficulties of being in a field characterized by several competing ideologies and doctrines is to take advantage of all possible opportunities to put our ideas out into the public arena to be analyzed, criticized, examined, cross-examined. One way of keeping ourselves "clean" is to expose our beliefs and allow them to be pulled apart, challenged, and evaluated in the light of other colleagues' experiences as well as our own. I propose to challenge your devoutly held beliefs by presenting a set of questions. I hope that you will share your answers with each other and with other early childhood educators.

QUESTIONS ABOUT MONTESSORI EDUCATION

The questions that follow are based on a limited experience and knowledge of the range of practices within Montessori schools. They also reflect my role as "devil's advocate."

THE ESSENTIALS

- What is the essence in classroom practice without which a program cannot be identified or characterized as a genuine Montessori class? Are some elements of the method optional and some obligatory? Can all of you agree on what these are?

- What is excluded or prohibited in a Montessori class that might be allowed or even encouraged in another early childhood program? What might we see in a High/Scope, traditional, or constructivist classroom that would not be consistent with Montessori principles?

- How eclectic can a teacher be and still be accredited and accepted as a Montessori practitioner?

- How much diversity can the Montessori approach tolerate and still honor the essential principles of the method?

- Is it still a Montessori classroom without multi-age grouping? Why so, or why not? How would single-age grouping be rationalized?

- Is it still a Montessori classroom without a garden? Without animals? How so? What principles are applied to make such decisions?

- If a classroom has the furniture, equipment, and play materials designed and promoted by the Montessori movement, but no other elements of Montessori practice, can it still be called a Montessori class?

Your answers to the questions can illuminate for the rest of us the essence of sound Montessori practices and help us understand their underlying principles.

THE POSITION STATEMENT

- Some of you say that the Montessori approach is not a curriculum model, but a mind-set, a frame of reference, a set of values and attitudes. Are these reflected in the position statement? For example, the position paper (AMS, 1990) states: "The aim of Montessori education is to foster autonomous, competent, responsible, adaptive citizens who are life-long learners and problem solvers." Does an educator have to be a "Montessori person" to subscribe to these aims? Are there early childhood educators who would deny them? If others share these aims, are they thereby Montessori persons? How so, or why not?

- The position paper states that "respect for oneself, others, the environment, and life is necessary to develop a caring attitude towards all people and the planet." Are there early childhood educators who would disavow these aims? Is it a matter of values or distinctive methods of achieving them? Does an educator have to be a Montessori person to subscribe to this view? Does this statement characterize the relationships Montessori people have with each other and with outsiders?

- The position paper states that the Montessori teacher is educated to use "teaching strategies that support and facilitate the unique and total growth of each individual." What specific or uniquely Montessori strategies, for example, promote these aims? Does a teacher have to be Montessori educated to acquire these strategies and value these goals?

- What does the term "cosmic values" mentioned in the position statement mean? Does the position statement use the term *cosmic* in a special way? Does this refer to the traditional Montessori concern for education for peace, brotherhood, and geographic literacy? Does one have to a Montessori educator to adopt these goals? I am not entirely convinced that these goals are developmentally appropriate at the preschool and kindergarten level. It seems to me developmentally appropriate for preschoolers to be ethnocentric, and the correct developmental sequence may be to grow from seeing one's own home or culture as superior to transcending these to accept those of others. Thus, as they develop, children should become adults who have outgrown their ethnocentrism and become allocentric. Why assume that young children are better at peace and brotherhood than mature well-educated, widely traveled adults?

■ The position statement also emphasizes autonomy and self-sufficiency. This seems consistent with Montessori's concern with inner or self-discipline. Why is that so important? It is understandable that Maria Montessori would work toward helping the children in Rome, for whom she originally developed her methods, to become more self-reliant. But I am not sure it is so important for modern American children who tend to become not so much prematurely independent as nondependent. It seems to me that one of the big issues for contemporary child rearing and education is to learn how to achieve *inter dependence*. What is the hurry to be autonomous? Parents of adolescents are not usually so thrilled to see their young become independent of them before they have acquired the wisdom and maturity that constructive use of freedom and independence requires.

GENERAL QUESTIONS

■ Montessori educators have traditionally emphasized learning through the senses. What does that mean? In contrast to what other ways of learning? When a teacher uses a direct instructional method to teach phonics (e.g., Distar), are children not learning through their senses? Are such practices acceptable to Montessori educators? If not, why not? If so, what is unique about the Montessori method?

Children may take in information through their senses, as do adults. But learning may involve making connections between internalized schemas, analyzing the meanings of stories, making sense of observations, and so forth. Let us take the example of a child absorbing information through his senses as he watches other children at play; he may very well be learning what he could and could not get away with in interactions with particular other children, or in the presence of the teacher. Would you call this "learning through the senses"? When a four-year-old experiments with ways to negotiate with peers, is that "learning through the senses?" In what other ways might these social skills be learned?

One of the characteristic materials of Montessori education is the map puzzle. I am not sure of the rationale for including it. But it is clear to me that the true nature of the earth is not directly apprehensible to the senses of young children. To accept the fact that the world consists of continents, islands, and oceans, and so on, and is round is not at all *sensible* (at age four or five or even six)! It must be taken on faith! To speak of this kind of learning as learning through the senses seems to me to oversimplify it seriously, and to underestimate the kind of intellectual work young children constantly engage in.

Furthermore, if children learn through their senses, all children do. But they do not all learn the same things. What are the things Montessori educators especially want all of them to learn? Answers to these questions could help explicate the basic assumptions you make about how children process information in their environment. I think it is useful to keep in mind that the term *learning* is morally neutral: one can learn to trust and/or mistrust, to cooperate and/or to compete, and to help and/or hurt—all of these things are learned! Are some learnings more important to Montessori educators than some others?

- Montessori literature frequently alludes to the "universals" of development. What are they? Do they include for example, the Oedipal conflict? The anal stage? How do these kinds of universals fit into Montessori conceptions of development?

- Montessori literature puts great emphasis on the "prepared environment." As long as an environment is prepared, is it acceptable? Many teachers prepare their classrooms carefully with learning centers, tables piled high with workbooks or worksheets, flash cards, and dittoed materials. Some are very carefully prepared indeed. Do such classes meet Montessori criteria? If not, why not? What principles are applied by which a "prepared environment" is classified as acceptable Montessori education?

- What does "constructivist" really mean? What principles of practice can be derived from asserting that children construct their understandings of the world? Presumably all children construct their understandings, regardless of whether adults get involved in the constructions or not. Is there any other way for children to make sense of their experience other than to construct the best sense they can out of it? Are some constructions of children better than some others? Presumably the environment is specially prepared for the children so as to increase the likelihood that some constructions will be developed or at least be facilitated more than others. Which ones are most highly desired by Montessori educators, and why so? Does one have to be a Montessori educator to promote those constructions? By way of example, Piagetians have been discussing children's acquisition of one-to-one correspondence for decades; presumably all children eventually, sooner or later, acquire the relevant schema. So why should an educator bother to prepare the environment to ensure that children learn it? Why not get on with other more useful and interesting investigations, explorations, and learnings?

- What does it feel like to be a child in a Montessori class? When adult observers describe a class they provide a view "from above" of what transpired within it, what it contains, and so forth. However, to make reliable predictions of the impact of early experiences, we need to make good inferences about the view "from below," that is, what it feels like to each individual child to be in a given physical and social environment. In other words, we need to make good estimates of the *quality of life experienced* by the children to evaluate a teaching/curriculum method properly. We want to know whether the view from below is that the environment is interesting or boring, engaging or frivolous, challenging or amusing, satisfying or entertaining, and so forth.

  Early childhood educators frequently justify their practices on the grounds that "the children love it"—whatever "it" is. Or they declare that the children are fascinated or excited by a particular activity. But feelings of amusement, fascination, or excitement are not criteria of appropriateness for activities, materials, or experiences offered in classes for young children. Children love many things that are not good for them (TV shows, toy weapons, and so on). Enjoyment is not an appropriate goal for education; it is the goal of entertainment. The goal of education is to engage the mind so as to help the learner make deeper, and more accurate sense of his or her experiences and environment and to strengthen the disposition to go on learning worthwhile things.

MADAME MONTESSORI TODAY

- What would Montessori say about today's children? How might she address their exposure to television cartoon violence and high-tech toys? Would Montessori have allowed children to play Batman in the classroom?

  Perhaps she was on the right track with lessons on silence! They may be just as appropriate for modern American big-city children as they were for Montessori's young Romans.

- What would Montessori say about the expanding adoption of the High/Scope curriculum, of the achievement gains reported by the developers of the DISTAR approach to teaching reading?

- I have learned during this symposium that a few decades ago the incorporation of pretend play activities into the Montessori classroom was a new phenomenon. What is it today? What are the new features of Montessori practices? What fresh precepts or concepts are being investigated, experimented with, and proposed for the near future?

- What would Montessori be working on if she were among us today? Certainly she would be interested in the constant struggle to intervene in the early years of the children of poor families. But what teaching strategies might she propose in light of all that has been learned about children since she first began?

Would she have something fresh to say about teaching strategies that would facilitate language development in view of all that has been learned about it in the last quarter-century?

- What would Montessori say about including project work as I have described elsewhere (Katz and Chard, 1989) in the daily classroom life of young children? In project work, usually working in small groups, children undertake an extended study of a topic related to their own environments and worth knowing more about. Invariably projects involve children in excursions outside their own classroom, collecting objects to handle and inspect closely. Children are encouraged to follow their emerging interests and to work collaboratively. The full scope of the work undertaken cannot be fully predicted from the outset.

- Why should Montessori education change at all? The results of the available research are generally positive. Montessori education seems to be thriving, expanding into public school systems, and attracting a good deal of attention. I suppose a big question for which we shall have to await the answer is, Can others adopt features of Montessori practices and still get positive results?

- Do Montessori methods fit into the developmentally appropriate practices guidelines developed by the National Association for the Education of Young Children (Bredekamp, 1987)? What are some ways they vary from the guidelines?

Your responses to these questions could strengthen the contribution of Montessori educators to early childhood education in general and could also enhance outsiders' understandings of your position on the complex issues that confront all of us.

THE FUTURE OF MONTESSORI EDUCATION

As I indicated at the outset, I myself am not a Montessori practitioner. But there are many Montessori ideas and practices that to me seem to continue to be highly appropriate in the light of experience and research on how young children grow, learn, and develop. I want to encourage you to hold on to these as steadfastly as you can.

To begin with, I want to urge you to hold on to your insistence on the importance of intrinsic motivation. In general the education of young children in our country is plagued by the excessive use of extrinsic rewards, which I believe has negative consequences in the long term.

I hope also that you will maintain your commitment to unobtrusive, firm but gentle guidance of children. Keep your strong focus on the children as workers as well as players. I am more convinced than ever that Montessori was on the right track when she encouraged us to take children's thinking and work seriously and to treat their efforts with respect. I am not as keen on the autodidactic materials as most of you are, but they surely cannot hurt. I just hope that you will add to the standard Montessori equipment more art work along the lines we have seen in Reggio Emilia in Italy (Katz, 1990) and much more project work as Sylvia Chard and I have described it (Katz & Chard, 1989).

I have a strong hunch that one of the great assets of the Montessori method is that, when properly implemented, the adults give children very clear signals about what is valued, expected, acceptable, and unacceptable. I believe that most young children benefit from having clear signals from the adults around them. Furthermore, when adults are unclear about what really matters, children push against them with all their might in order to find out!

In so many preschools, child-care centers, and kindergartens, children and their efforts are frequently admired as "cute" but are not taken as seriously as they should be. I think Maria Montessori understood intuitively very early the importance of treating children's thoughts and feelings seriously. I hope you safeguard that quality of the approach.

I hope also that you maintain your commitment to eschewing fantasy and fanciful products and decor. I believe the majority of our young children suffer from a surfeit of adult-generated fantasy. It is one thing to encourage children's own rich fantasies and imaginations, but quite another to impose those of adults and various industries (Disneyworld, Barbie Dolls) upon them from above. We have reached a stage that I call the abuses of enchantment; it is another aspect of treating children like silly empty-headed pets that have to be amused and titillated.

I want to encourage you to keep your commitment to being direct and authentic with children. Some colleagues and students I spoke to about Montessori before the symposium complained that Montessori teachers don't speak naturally to children. I have not observed this myself in a Montessori class, though I have in others. I just want to emphasize that it is important to speak to children as people with lively minds, to appeal to their good sense, and to ensure that your interactions with them are authentic rather than phony and stylized.

SUMMARY

I hope that you will be able to take time to address the questions presented and develop a model of teaching that includes some of the aspects of others' contemporary practices that I have just listed. I hope you will incorporate project work into the curriculum and emphasize the *intellectual* rather than the *academic* life of the child. I hope you take into account as you develop your model the rich and recent data base that has been accumulating for the last twenty years about development of children's social competence. Keep in mind that social interaction cannot occur in a vacuum; children must be interacting *about* something—something of interest to them, something rich in meaning for them. And I hope you call your fresh approach "modern American Montessori education."

Finally, remember that Montessori people are just like other people. Some do better than others in all kinds of teaching. We in early childhood education have much more in common than not. I hope we will meet again and share what we are all doing in our work with young children, and that modern Montessorians will join with others in the field to address the basic needs of all of the world's children.

REFERENCES

American Montessori Association. (1990). Position Statement. *Montessori Life.* pp. 10–11.

Bredekamp, S. (1987). *Developmentally appropriate practice in early childhood programs serving children from birth through age 8.* Washington, D. C.: National Association for the Education of Young Children.

Katz, L. G. (1990). Lessons from Reggio Emilia. *Young Children* Vol. 45, no. 6, p. 11–12.

————. (1977). "Early childhood programs and ideological disputes." In L. G. Katz (Ed.), *Talks with teachers*, pp. 69–78. Washington, D. C.: National Association for the Education of Young Children.

Katz, L. G., & Chard, S. C. (1989). *Engaging children's minds: The project approach.* Norwood, N.J.: Ablex.

11

SUMMARY OF REPLIES TO KATZ'S QUESTIONS

A RESPONSE TO LILIAN KATZ'S QUESTIONS FOR MONTESSORIANS
David Kahn

THE MONTESSORI ESSENTIALS

The standards of Montessori practice were originally delineated by the Association Montessori Internationale (AMI) in 1929. They represent an integrated body of materials, methodology, psychology, and philosophy that provides Montessori teachers with a common reference point. Montessori training conveys a specific developmental understanding of the child, specific materials that interact with the psychological characteristics and tendencies for each stage of development, and specific principles that underscore belief in the scope and sequence of the Montessori materials.

For every stage of development there is a corresponding educational environment and a trained teacher who "prepares the environment." The child learns independently using the Montessori materials; the teacher, the link between the child and the environment, coaches and observes the child who chooses activities. The learning environment cultivates individual responsibility, freedom of choice, concentration, independence, problem-solving abilities, social interaction, interdisciplinary breadth, and competency in basic skills.

Ms. Katz's query about whether some materials are "optional and some obligatory" in authenticating a Montessori environment harbors an incorrect assumption about Montessori. Montessori includes a defined set of materials and practices. But the application of Montessori principles and learning differs depending on the classroom, the age group, or the particular needs of the children (for example, children with disabilities). A new classroom beginning with three-year-olds, for example, would only include selective materials, as would a classroom for blind children. The Montessori framework then is a constant; the application of the framework is relative to the observed needs of the children and the decisions of the teachers. The curriculum provides keys that Montessori designed in relation to children all over the world aided by her enlightened observation experience as an anthropologist and physician. These keys stimulate children to initiate activities but do not unduly restrict them or displace their native interests. In that way, through a rigorous economy of presentation, the child is then given room to explore. Eighty years of experience have proved that this "key approach" works, with some modifications introduced by practicing teachers.

If the Montessori pedagogical system works based on the "less is more" premise, why introduce a mixed bag of enterprises that may clutter the concepts and undermine their balance? Therefore, Ms. Katz's concern about whether a Montessori teacher can ever be eclectic brings up a complex issue—the skill of being a Montessorian. There are many aspects to the classroom in addition to Montessori's specific pedagogical materials—parent education, nature activities, musical instruments, effective communication with children, and so on. These make the Montessori teacher eclectic. At the same time, the explicit standards and values of Montessori classroom practices suggest that the pedagogical characteristics of Montessori and psychological characteristics of the child are to be emphasized. Yet no two Montessori classrooms are identical, because they reflect the unique personalities of the children and the teachers, who realize the Montessori ideal in their own ways, in keeping with its formula for success.

PREPARED ENVIRONMENT

The "prepared environment" is one of Montessori's great innovations. It implies that there is optimal developmental space for infants, toddlers, elementary, and adolescents, each corresponding to the respective "planes of development."

Children's House

The Montessori preschool classroom is a "living room" for children. Children choose their materials from open shelves with self-correcting materials and work in discrete areas. The prepared environment integrates the psychosocial, physical, and academic functioning of the child. Its curriculum covers practical life, sensorial education, mathematics, language arts, geography, history, science, and other aspects of culture. Adjacent gardens, play, and work areas integrate indoors and outdoors experiences.

Elementary Prepared Environment

The elementary prepared environment builds on the preschool model but reflects a new stage of development. The Montessori classroom offers diversified time lines, picture charts, other visual aids, and practical activities providing a linguistic and visual overview of the first principles of each discipline.

Integrating the arts, sciences, geography, history, and languages inspires the imagination of the children. Live specimens heighten the strong orientation toward zoology, botany, anthropology, geology, and the like, exposing children to scientific laws and new vocabulary. Mathematics is presented through concrete materials that simultaneously reveal arithmetic, geometric, and algebraic correlations. The presence of reference books instead of textbooks reflects the emphasis on open-ended research. Finally, learning ventures outside the school are basic to the organization of the classroom. The students themselves organize these outings as a natural extension of their in-school interests.

In both the preschool and elementary environments the trained educators have in-depth knowledge of the materials and of child development.

Ms. Katz asks what is different about the Montessori prepared environment. "Many teachers prepare their classrooms carefully with learning centers, tables piled high with workbooks, or worksheets, flash cards, and dittoed materials. . . . Do such classes meet Montessori criteria?" The answer is no.

Montessori materials are three-dimensional, aesthetically pleasing, and durable. They permit various layers of exploration and meaning that could not be captured by fill-in-the-blank or multiple-choice materials. Each experience with a Montessori material is reflective and interpretive—there is not one right answer. The emphasis instead is on the relationship between the exercises and extensions of increasing complexity that are implicit in the visual arrangement of the materials. Lastly, the Montessori prepared environment, by virtue of its proportion and balance, by the integral nature of the materials and economy of presentation, creates a deeply felt rapport in the child for the surrounding physical space and activities.

Most important, the Montessori professional receives approximately six hundred hours of preservice training in the integrated use of the prepared environment in relation to the harmonious development of the child. That training is specific to the Montessori materials and their comprehensive, interdisciplinary applications—each subject area incorporates elements from another. Materials can be added or deleted only when they relate to the comprehensive whole.

MULTISENSORY LEARNING

The prepared environment of the Casa dei Bambini offers the world to the explorations of the young child in the first plane of the development (ages three to six) . . . the world is color, size, dimension, shape, form, sound, touch, taste, smell. The child has already come into contact with all these qualities from the moment he is born . . .
—Margaret Stephenson, "The adolescent and the future"

Lilian Katz should glean from the above quote that sensory learning for Montessori has a broad meaning; children live in a world of senses. In order to continue their creative task, children highlight impressions they have already received. Through sight, touch, sound, taste, and smell, the sensorial materials throw a spotlight on reality. For example, the concept of length is derived from the red rods of varying lengths. Language is clarified by discussing long and short. Because the rods are rendered in unit lengths from one to ten, they also provide a basis for mathematical gradation. The use of this one sensorial material demonstrates how a child's experience with materials and their attributes allows for derivation of clearer linguistic expression, abstract operations of comparison and gradation, as well as opportunities for hand-eye coordinated movement. In-depth examination of Montessori's view of the sensorial area indicates that she has considered "the intangible essences" of material objects, along with their ability to capture the essential nature of the outside world and at the same time build abstractions.

Katz's questions regarding sensory learning imply that Montessorians might exclude the sensory intake of social relations at the preschool level or any realities beyond the classification of refined sensorial discrimination exercises. In response, such social realities cannot be removed from the child's perceptions no matter what methodology the teacher might subscribe to.

Most upsetting to Katz is the aspect of presenting the world map to the preschool child: "To accept the fact that the world consists of continents, islands, and oceans, etc. and is round . . . is not at all sensible at age four, or five or even six." If sensory education is linked with exploration of land forms that are in the child's immediate environment (e.g. lakes, islands, gulfs, peninsulas, etc.), if the child sees in the neighborhood or school foreign people who "live far, far away," and if a preschooler has encountered an ocean with a boundless horizon, then, Montessori intuited, a child could "imagine" the earth. Thus a "materialized abstraction" like the globe becomes a synthesis of the child's sensorial experience—a new key that explains the interconnectedness of the human family in relation to land and water. This impression may not be fully understood, but it does impart a universal, multicultural awareness perspective at an age—four, five, and six—when the imagination is beginning to develop. This beginning imaginative power of abstraction has been perceived in children under six for generations, as indicated by the use of fairy tales, folk myths, and religious beliefs in child-rearing practices for children who are preschool age.

DEVELOPMENTALLY APPROPRIATE PRACTICES— DOES MONTESSORI APPLY?

The National Association for the Education of Young Children (NAEYC) has produced several documents defining developmentally appropriate activities, a code of ethics, and a statement on school readiness—all of which are catching up to the precepts of the Montessori method generated at the beginning of our century. Educating the whole child (physical, emotional, social, and intellectual aspects); looking at the variability among children of the same chronological age and the variability within each individual child; organizing instruction around each child's developmental needs, interests, and learning style; emphasizing the processes of learning rather than the product; recognizing that each child follows a unique pattern of development; and affirming the importance of play to the children's total development—these are all aspects of Montessori philosophy for school and home as well as the basis for NAEYC developmentally appropriate practice. Montessori invented developmentally appropriate practice.

Some might say that Montessori had some negative views on play. Montessorians on an odd day might describe the work of the classroom as goal-oriented play, although Montessori was always careful to distinguish work from play. Lili Peller, a Montessori writer, defined work as "any activity of the young child in which he engages with his deepest interests." Surely certain forms of play fall into this category. The Montessori criterion for work is that it must be freely chosen, which is far from the typical understanding of work as product oriented and usually assigned.

MONTESSORI TODAY

Katz asks, "Why should Montessori change at all?" The question is vital to Montessorians who assert that the Montessori formula remains the same because fundamentally human nature is unchanging. This does not, by any stretch of the imagination, eliminate dialogue or changing views and applications of Montessori in changing times.

Today the influence of Montessori can be found at the developmental extremes of the practice. Montessori is working down to prenatal care and upward through secondary education. In both cases the emphasis is on engaging the whole personality of the child and creating educational environments that elicit the child's maximum potential.

Montessori is also expanding in terms of its applications. The ideas and principles of Montessori are affecting urban renewal, magnet public school education, day-care design, catechesis, intergenerational living, bilingual education, special education, parent education, teacher education, educational reform, global education, self-initiated learning, ethnographic research, teacher-managed research and observation, curriculum design, interdisciplinary thinking, humanities and education, and so on. Montessori is a set of keys that opens the human mind to logic and the mystery of the universe in relation to human development. This is a gigantic vision. The Montessori educational ideal is gigantic, because it explores with rigorous consistency the laws of development and laws of life that have application and new meaning in every aspect of human existence and in every age.

REFERENCES

Peller, Lili, E. (1978). *On development and education of young children.* New York: Philosophical Library.

Stephenson, Margaret E. (1989). "The adolescent and the future." *Education for the twenty-first century.* AMI International Study Conference Proceedings. Washington, D.C.: Association Montessori Internationale of the United States Inc.

BASIC CONCERNS ABOUT DR. KATZ'S PAPER
by Marlene Barron

SOURCES OF KATZ'S BACKGROUND INFORMATION

According to Dr. Katz, her paper developed out of her revisiting some of Maria Montessori's own writing, reading recent Montessori literature (it would have been helpful if these references had been listed in her bibliography), and eliciting popular views of Montessori from thirty interviews with students, colleagues, and teachers. No mention is made of her visiting Montessori classrooms. Since it is difficult to know how one can ask meaningful questions or comment on American Montessori education without having seen Montessori in practice, I can only assume that her failure to mention classroom observations was an oversight on her part and not an indication that she missed this firsthand opportunity to answer her own questions.

KATZ'S UNDERLYING PERSPECTIVE

Contrary to her initial statement of purpose, most of her questions are interrogatory rather than illuminating. These interrogatory questions cannot be answered as directly and conventionally as Katz assumes. Real children in real situations in real classrooms do not readily lend themselves to simple responses.

In addition, these questions assume a technical, rational perspective that just does not fit with Montessori's view of education as a social construction process. Katz's questions also suggest that Montessori's approach can be applied mechanically to pedagogical problems. I don't believe that it can.

Montessori, like Katz, frames pedagogical issues in a way that leads to different notions of implementation and of acceptability. I would like to reframe the Montessori educational paradigm into what Vygotsky calls "organized development" (1978, p. 118), rather than viewing the materials and techniques as ways to teach specific skills. Then the Montessori teaching/learning environment (materials, social experiences, and delivery system) can be viewed as composed of instructional scaffolds. These instructional aids provide temporary and adjustable help, well-timed and well-tuned help, which self-destruct gradually as the child's competency grows. In other words, the Montessori approach can best be viewed as providing a host of strategies and experiences that enables each child to learn within his or her own zone of proximal development (Vygotsky, 1978, p. 86).

Vygotsky's zone of proximal development refers to the distance between what learners can do on their own and what they can do with guidance from a more capable person. In Montessori classrooms, intention, initiation, control, and personal meaning become the primary determiners of whether or not a particular experience is effective or useful for a particular child. Thus the framing of Katz's questions and comments about the value of puzzle maps for young children does not fit within this perspective. Katz's a priori sense of significance or importance needs to shift to a holistic perspective that considers how these items (or any items, procedures, or experiences) support each child's development.

OTHER ISSUES

This leads me into the practical issue of teacher education and Katz's question about the education of Montessori teachers. How might teachers be educated to practice from such a transactional perspective in the classroom? A focus on reflective teaching practices and on the notion of instructional scaffolding (teaching within the child's zone of proximal development) provides a solution. Montessori's emphasis on observation as the keystone of her approach underscores the reciprocal relationship between knowing and doing.

As in all complex approaches to real situations, there are certainly some teachers who will be better at educating in this way than others. After all, there are always those who fall back on the security and comfort provided by what they view as preset curriculum and, unfortunately, there are those who manage to do this even within the Montessori framework. My hunch is, however, that the combination of Montessori instructional aids and the emphases in teacher education programs on preparing both the physical and socioemotional environment, on observation, and on reflective teaching lead to more developmentally successful classroom experiences for children than any approach to date.

Katz wonders—if one subscribes to Montessori principles is one, thereby, a Montessorian? The issue is one of set/subset understanding; it is not, as presented, an either/or question. Montessori certainly fits within the larger set of humanistic, constructivist educational paradigms and has much in common with other educational approaches fitting that description. Those who subscribe to these related approaches have much in common with Montessorians.

I dislike Katz's use of the term "correct developmental sequence" (in her reference to cosmic education). Does anyone really know what is correct or true in regard to a child's development? The ability to adopt multiple perspectives is what is needed in today's global environment. Montessori's stress on humility when working with children and her suggestion that development is a mystery together constitute a response to this comment. We, as educators, still have much to learn about human development.

Katz's emphasis on interdependence as one of the "big issues for contemporary child rearing and education" is exactly what Montessori's cosmic education is all about. The notion that we live in one world with all other humans as well as with the natural environment is a basic premise of Montessori's educational philosophy. But autonomy is not the opposite of interdependence; rather it is a prerequisite for interdependence. One first must develop a sense of autonomy to become truly interdependent with others. Otherwise, true cooperation cannot occur.

And it seems to me that her question "What is the *hurry* to be autonomous?" is perhaps her issue—it is *not* Montessori's. Montessori and other theorists—Erikson, Piaget, Vygotsky—are clear that the fullest development of each stage is what is important. Hurry, as a notion, is the antithesis of Montessori principles or practices. We respect and celebrate three-year-oldness and four-year-oldness and five-year-oldness. Autonomy and interdependence take time to construct.

SOME ADDITIONAL RESPONSES

Multisensory education: Multisensory education involves experiential learning that incorporates all the senses. For example, learning about a rain forest might include the unique smells, sounds, temperature, humidity, and visual experiences. These are the kinds of multisensorial experiences that we'd like children to experience throughout the curriculum. It's all part of understanding—from a holistic perspective.

The goal of education: The goal of education, according to Katz, is to engage the mind so as to help the learners make better, deeper, fuller, and *more accurate* sense of their experiences and environment. I would argue with the term *more accurate*—more accurate according to whom or what? I suggest that the goal of education is a collaborative, meaning-making process in a social environment that supports ethnic and cultural diversity.

Building on its keystone of observation, contemporary Montessori practices aim at the development of more classroom-based, teacher-initiated research projects as well as cooperative linkages between university researchers and classroom teachers.

REFERENCES

Erikson, Erik (1977). *Toys and reasons.* New York: Norton.
Piaget, Jean (1973). *To understand is to invent: the future of education.* New York: Grossman.
Vygotsky, L. (1978). *Mind in Society.* Cambridge, Mass.: Harvard University Press.

RESPONSES TO DR. LILIAN KATZ'S QUESTIONS
by Elizabeth L. Bronsil

WHAT ARE THE ESSENTIALS OF A MONTESSORI CLASSROOM?

There are a variety of Montessori programs throughout the country. Some symbols will be common to all physical environments. A quick assessment of the classroom should reveal the following:

1 The room is safe, clean, and the right size for the number of children.

2 There are child-size shelves and furniture.

3 The materials are set up so that children can get them themselves. They do not have to rely on an adult to find what they need.

4 There are developmentally appropriate materials for all areas of the curriculum: practical life, sensorial, art, music, science, math, language, social studies, and movement education.

An aesthetically pleasing environment is just the foundation for the answer to Katz's question of what is essential to Montessori. The essential can be found in the approach of the teacher. What is the teacher's background in philosophy, theory, and child development? Is respect for the child the main principle for action? Does the teacher understand the developmental levels of children? Does the teacher understand Dr. Montessori's writings about the absorbent mind, the sensitive periods, and the four planes of development?

Another essential element of the Montessori environment is the formation of the child's whole personality. In this environment the child uses initiative to make choices. You will see children working independently as well as collaboratively. Children learn from each other and teach each other. Children feel secure in this environment and are free to use the materials to make many new discoveries about the world they live in. They are also free to make discoveries about themselves in relationship to others. The members of this community need to experience independence, interdependence, the essential elements of their culture, integration, the ability to make choices, opportunities for learning, and cooperation. It is essential to prepare children for life instead of just the next grade in school.

WHAT IS THE MONTESSORI PREPARED ENVIRONMENT?

The preparation of the Montessori environment begins with the education of the Montessori teacher. This education begins with self-knowledge and extends to the understanding of human development as defined by Dr. Montessori and other theorists such as Piaget and Erikson. The preparation of the environment is based on the teacher's careful observation of the needs of the children.

Many observers will first notice the obvious structure. The structure frees the child from uncertainty and unpredictability. The prepared environment is a place where the child may live and work in freedom. The teacher sets up this space to meet the child's physical, social, intellectual, and psychological needs.

Children absorb their surroundings. It is the responsibility of the teacher to make the environment safe and beautiful. It must reflect the children's culture, allow them to be independent, give them freedom of movement, and provide many opportunities for social development.

The prepared environment does not remain static. Children grow and change, and the observing teacher will recognize these changes and provide for the children's needs.

There are many teaching strategies unique to the Montessori environment. They provide order for the children and freedom to be comfortable in their own self-construction. Some of these strategies are obvious to Montessori teachers, but without them, there would be chaos for the children and the teacher. I will list some of them:

1   We provide small individual rugs that children use for their work. They define the children's work spaces and help other children respect them.

2   We provide low shelves with organized learning materials. Children find everything they need on the tray or in the basket. Pieces of materials are not scattered throughout the room.

3   We provide materials for taking care of the children's physical needs. These include a place to get snacks, wash hands, and materials for cleaning up.

4   We allow children to choose their own work and to work with it as long as they wish.

5   We ask children to respect other children's rights to work.

6   We allow children to work alone or with others. It is their choice.

7   We encourage children in this multi-age setting to teach each other.

8   We always model grace and courtesy for the child.

The foundation for the prepared environment is that the teachers must trust the child!

IS AUTONOMY AN IMPORTANT GOAL FOR YOUNG CHILDREN?

According to Erikson the first stage of development is trust. The second stage, autonomy, is built on trust. Children must come to believe that faith in themselves and their environment will not be destroyed by adults who are too demanding and refuse to let them make choices for themselves. Children's first lesson in social behavior may come when they say no to something that someone is trying to do for them. "I do it myself" is a toddler's favorite theme song.

Having established strong will power, three-year-olds enter our Montessori environment where their autonomy is respected, and their initiative enriched as they learn to choose their work and their friends. They move about freely; their language is perfected, and they use it to question, to share, to make friends, and to learn new ideas.

Language and motor coordination help the children become independent. They begin to have a sense of themselves. This sense comes from all that they accomplish in an environment where they are allowed to explore, make mistakes, learn new ideas, and be responsible. Erikson characterizes this stage as "I am what I can imagine I will be." Adults must allow autonomy and initiative to be a part of the child's life if we want children to develop healthy personalities.

In her book *Montessori Method,* Dr. Montessori states:

No one can be free unless he is independent; therefore, the first active manifestation of the child's individual liberty must be so guided that through this activity he may arrive at independence. . . . We habitually serve children, and this is not only an act of servility toward them, but it is dangerous since it tends to suffocate their useful spontaneous activity. . . . Our duty toward him is, in every case, that of helping him to make a conquest of such useful acts as nature intended he should perform. (New York: Schocken, 1964, pp. 95–96)

PART THREE

MONTESSORI

AND

CONTEMPORARY

SOCIAL

PROBLEMS

INTRODUCTION

When Maria Montessori introduced her methods in the first Children's Houses in Rome which she had established for that purpose, she was carrying out an experiment to meet a current social problem—the care and education of children of the working poor left to fend for themselves during the day while their parents were away from home.

Because of her enormous success, her ideas and methods soon were adopted by educators and parents around the world; however, instead of being applied to the education of children of poor urban parents, as in Rome, the Montessori schools established following her model usually had as their students children of middle-class or affluent families.

Although many of the first Montessori schools established in this country in the 1960s were also situated in middle-class environments, a number of Headstart programs were set up following the Montessori model. Notably successful programs based on the Montessori model could be found in Chicago, Syracuse, Ithaca, Cincinnati, New York City, and Oklahoma City among other sites; however, the turnover rate of teachers proved to be a problem. Montessori teachers require specialized training and, since funds were limited, teachers often had to be replaced by those without training. Consequently, the model became more diluted with time, and few Montessori Headstart programs remain today.

Nonetheless, there are many Montessori programs currently serving the children of poor and minority families under other public and private auspices, and the number is growing rapidly. The first chapters in this section offer examples of these, representing answers to some contemporary social problems and describing the unique qualities of the Montessori model in meeting these challenges.

In chapter 12, "Beyond Day Care: Full-Day Montessori for Migrant and Other Language Minority Children," Antonia Lopez describes the implementation of a successful Montessori child-care and adult education program in California, under the sponsorship and direction of the Foundation Center for Phenomenological Research, Inc., which serves approximately 1,900 children through funding from the Child Development Division of the California State Department of Education. Ms. Lopez, who grew up in a family of migrant workers herself and who serves as director of education and staff development for the Foundation Center, describes the life of migrant families in the United States and details the history of the evolution of the center's work.

Having started as a group dedicated to providing training and technical assistance to other nonprofit organizations and newly forming groups working with migrant and language minority families, the center now serves children and families directly through a network of eighteen child-care centers and thirty family day-care homes in nine California counties.

As part of its work with families, the center trains adults to work as teachers and in other positions at these centers and offers opportunities for other family members to continue their own education through GED courses and similar means.

Lopez delineates the reasons why the Foundation Center chose Montessori as the curriculum method for its centers, pointing to (1) the possibility of "installing Montessori" over a period of three to five years (thus permitting components to be added to more traditional child development/day-care programs over time while gradually revamping the entire program); (2) the possibility also for teachers to study in meaningful and implementable "blocks" while working full time; (3) the ability of the Foundation Center to budget and plan for the costs and logistics related to the long-term installation of this additive model; and (4) the possibility of relating the philosophy and its implementation (through practical life, sensorial, math, the child's own language, and the cultural subjects of art, music, geography, history and science) to the teachers' and childrens' own families and cultures, as the Montessori methods had so successfully done already in settings around the world.

The second chapter in this part, "Montessori in Public Schools," by Eileen Wilms Buermann, program coordinator of the program at Bennett Park Montessori Center in Buffalo, New York, describes the program in an urban public magnet school serving children and their families from three years of age through grade eight.

The Bennett Park program came into existence in 1976 as part of the Buffalo school system's program of magnet schools. These schools were organized as components of a voluntary desegregation plan developed in response to a federal court order. The Buffalo program grew out of the unique consortium of members of the Buffalo Montessori community, Buffalo public school officials, Buffalo State College professors, and parents.

The Montessori educational approach was chosen because it has a history of success in urban education beginning with the original Children's Houses in Rome and because it has been able to adapt to various cultural settings.

During the fourteen years of its existence, the program has been an unqualified success. In this article, Ms. Buermann, the program coordinator, provides us with a timely glimpse into the life of this school.

These two chapters, one on child care and one describing an urban school setting, have been chosen to represent the many other Montessori-based programs providing service to families and children that were presented at the symposium. These included public school programs in Houston, Texas, Cincinnati, Ohio, and the Chicago area; corporate-sponsored child-care programs in St. Louis, Missouri; university-based programs in Hawaii; a parent-run child-care/school program in Ohio; a child-care program in midtown Manhattan; and a state-funded mobile fleet of vans, whose drivers are Montessori teachers, servicing family day-care homes and child-care centers in Oklahoma City, Oklahoma.

Copies of papers describing these programs can be obtained from the American Montessori Society, 150 Fifth Avenue, New York, N.Y. 10011.

The last chapter in part 3, "Montessori and the Middle School Years," by Elisabeth Johnston Coe, describes a unique program, planned and implemented by Coe as a dissertation project. Coe wanted to address a contemporary American problem: developing an appropriate and viable program to meet the cognitive and emotional needs of seventh- and eighth-grade students.

Coe's program draws upon Montessori's views regarding the education of students of this age, as outlined in her description of the *Erdkinder*, combined with strategies drawn from current research on the needs of students of middle-school age, seen as a critical period in contemporary American education.

This section of the book is especially important in highlighting how useful Montessori's insights are in addressing contemporary social and educational problems just as they were in meeting those of an earlier Italian culture. The need to recognize and respect the important strengths of the child's own culture if we are to assist in the development of his or her full human potential is as true in America today as it was in Italy in the early 1900s. The success of the children and their families who are enrolled in these programs in Buffalo, N.Y., and in California attests to the viability of the approach.

12

BEYOND DAY CARE: FULL-DAY MONTESSORI FOR MIGRANT AND OTHER LANGUAGE-MINORITY CHILDREN

ABOUT THE FOUNDATION CENTER

Si planea para un año, siembre una semilla.
Si planea para diez años, plante un arbol.
Si planea para cien años, eduque a la gente.

If you are thinking a year ahead, sow a seed.
If you are thinking ten years ahead, plant a tree.
If you are thinking one hundred years ahead, educate the people.

The Foundation Center for Phenomenological Research, Inc., is a not-for-profit organization committed to educating not only the child but the community. The Foundation Center currently serves approximately 2,000 children in California through funding from the Child Development Division of the California Department of Education. Approximately 90 percent of the families served are non-English-speaking, low-income working parents who have immigrated to this country from Mexico and Central America. Of these, approximately 900 are from migrant agricultural-worker families. The program operates through a network of eighteen centers and thirty family day-care homes in nine California counties (Modoc, Placer, Sacramento, Yolo, San Joaquin, Fresno, Santa Clara, Los Angeles, and San Diego).

The Foundation Center was first organized as a group dedicated to providing training and technical assistance to other not-for-profit organizations and newly forming groups. In 1980, it was awarded a contract through the Child Development Division of the California Department of Education to revamp a program formerly operated by a county office of education. That county office had lost its ability to operate a child development program cost effectively. As a consequence, its facilities had fallen into disrepair. The Hispanic children it served were physically isolated in one of the three buildings the program occupied, and none of its teaching staff spoke Spanish, the dominant language of the children served. The Spanish-speaking aides were left to "teach" the children the primary colors and the three "classic" child development shapes: circle, square, and triangle.

Into this vacuum came the Foundation Center, which previously had not directly operated child development programs. However, it was entrepreneurial in spirit—it was not committed to the hierarchical, militaristic, top–down organizational structure that most American community-based organizations had adopted in the early 1960s. It also had no preconceived notions about how a child development center *should* look, how noisy it *should* be, how *expensive* it is to train staff, and the like.

After reviewing a variety of curricular models (and, ironically, not being able to find any clear reference in the educational and psychological literature to a "successful" early childhood intervention curriculum for, it seemed, any type of intervention was defined as "successful" just so long as it was "used"), the Foundation Center adopted the Montessori method of education. It encountered a situation not unique to it, but nearly so, in making this curricular choice: The Foundation Center had to train its own teachers. There were no Spanish-speaking Montessori teachers in either the American Montessori Society (AMS) or Association Montessori International (AMI) who were available to work with children from working-poor and migrant agricultural-working families—the two predominant types of families that the Foundation Center served.

ABOUT MIGRANT FAMILIES

Before being able to define the elements of a full-day Montessori program for migrant families and families of working poor, we had to consider the impact of their socioeconomic condition on the individual child and the family members. We share the following with you so that you can visualize the enormous pressures that migrant families experience and that we felt we had to address in a full-day Montessori program.

CHARACTERISTICS OF MIGRANTS

The average annual income for a migrant family of five is less than $7,000 a year. Without subsidized child care, families are forced to take their young children and infants to work with them. More often than not, the children are left in cars or at the edge of fields while their parents toil for as long as 8 to 12 hours a day. The length of the work day for any given parent is dependent on the crop being harvested. Often those families who harvest apricots and cherries, for example, must be at the orchard by 5:00 A.M., meaning they have to leave home by 4:30 A.M. Tomato harvest, on the other hand, requires some parents to work late into the night, working under artificial lights.

Next to finding work, migrant mothers report that their second most urgent need is to find child care. A California State Department of Education publication entitled "A Survey of California Farmworkers' Child Care Needs" (1980), reported that there were 358,000 children eligible for the state-subsidized child-care services and that approximately 3,170 were in care. Of these children, **95,000** were considered "at risk," that is, they were reported to be left alone or in the care of other young children for an average of 43 hours per week. Of these 95,000 at-risk children, more than 30,000 were children under the age of eight, and 2,600 children were infants (less than 12 months old!).

The following are some of the painful realities for migrant adults and children (from: Education Commission of the States, 1979).

1 Migrant families live in health and sanitation standards that are comparable to those found in Third World countries today, and those found in the United States 150 years ago.

2 Compared to the national average life expectancy of 73 years, the migrant life expectancy is 49 years of age.

3 Prenatal and postnatal care for mothers and infants is almost nonexistent.

4 The infant mortality rate among migrants is 25 percent higher than the national average.

5 Birth injuries result in many cases of cerebral palsy and mental retardation.

6 The migrant death rate from influenza and pneumonia is 20 percent higher than the national average.

7 Deaths from tuberculosis and other communicable diseases are 25 times higher than the national average.

8 The migrant's hospitalization rate from accidents is 50 percent higher than the national average.

9 The migrant's two most chronic conditions are diabetes and hypertension, both of which require continuous care and follow-up.

10 Poor nutrition causes pre- and postnatal deaths, anemia, extreme dental problems, and poor mental and physical development of children. The height and weight measurements of a sizable proportion of migrant children show the stunting effects of poor or marginal nutrition.

11 The health histories and physical examinations of migrant children reflect the synergistic interaction of marginal nutrition, diarrhea, chronic respiratory and parasitic infections, and exposure to repeated accidents and injury.

12 It is estimated that 80 to 90 percent of all migrant children have an undiagnosed, but treatable health problem. Ten percent have a potentially life-threatening problem.

13 More than 90 percent of migrant children fail to complete high school.

14 Substandard housing is a major health problem. There is a lack of sewage systems, plumbing, electricity, and fresh water supply, in addition to inadequate protection from the elements and pesticide contamination and poisoning.

15 Accidents cause 50 percent of the deaths of migrant children under five years of age. Accidents are the cause of more than 64 percent of the deaths of children between the ages of six and ten years of age.

16 There is a relationship between learning and hunger, undernutrition and malnutrition. Studies demonstrate that hungry children exhibit behavioral changes which may limit responses to learning opportunities and may impair intellectual development.

17 Adequate child care for only the income-eligible families is estimated at $236 million. Adequate health care costs are estimated at approximately $900 million.

The Foundation Center program was designed and developed to address the most pressing needs:

1 Adequate shelter and safe environments.

2 Highest quality food available to address nutritional deficiencies and dental problems.

3 Assessment and referrals for existing and chronic health problems and health education for prevention of reoccurring problems.

4 Enriched educational program (Montessori) to promote school and societal success.

5 Community development and education through development of indigenous staff.

6 Advocacy for provision of adequate resources from policy makers and service providers.

MONTESSORI CURRICULUM

We believe that the child development program leadership and staff must be able to describe and to discuss with parents the curricular philosophy of the program. They must be able to show the unity between what is described as philosophy and what is done in the classroom. This philosophical umbrella must cover topics as diverse as positions regarding the child's "place" in the community to discipline practices and toileting procedures. Staff, in some cases, must be compulsive and consistent with this implementation.

The Foundation Center chose Montessori as the curriculum to be used in its centers and family day care homes for the following reasons:

1 Its view of the nature of the child is consistent with that of the Foundation Center.

2 Its view of the role of the family and the child's perspective in that family is consistent with that of the Foundation Center.

3 Its view of the family's role in the child's education is consistent with that of the Foundation Center.

4 Its view of "education for life" and "education for peace" is consistent with that of the Foundation Center.

5 It has the ability to situate itself within a variety of cultural milieus and use "local languages," as required by the Foundation Center.

6 It lends itself to the cultural values of the families served: independence/interdependence, care of the person, care of the environment, and the like.

7 The Montessori "setting" or environment is an addition to, not a replacement of, the home. From Dr. Montessori's perspective, the task of children from birth to age six is to construct themselves as human beings. In this process of construction, children are oriented to their environment in their time, place, and culture. Again, the home is the primary source of the raw material for this self-construction. The Montessori environment complements (in Dr. Montessori's sense, "throws light on") and thereby helps children to discover and focus on

aspects of their culture. For this reason, the Montessori environment provides practical life materials appropriate to the culture; uses botanical, zoological, and geographical examples from the child's own surroundings; and offers the best examples of music, art, language, and the like. Children can therefore accomplish this self-construction with the help of the best possible building materials the culture has to offer (Miller).

STAFF TRAINING

Why Montessori? The assets were obvious: language and cultural compatibility, access to community support, development of local role models, long-term commitment to children and families, and the opportunity for genuine community development . . . planning for a hundred years from now.

Also Montessori had a very special benefit: unlike Highscope and other curriculum models that are theoretical, it was clearly possible to "install" Montessori over a period of years. A traditional child development/day-care center could have "components" added to the program and over time the entire children's program could be revamped. Individual teachers could study in meaningful and manageable "blocks" while working full time. The Foundation Center could budget and plan for the costs and logistics related to long-term installation of the model. "Philosophy" assures us that we have our own wisdom and encourages us to expand our worldview. "Practical life" meets many real and present needs of the children and is very familiar and inviting to the staff. "Sensorial" is "intriguing" and calls out to a sensitive period of the teacher in training. "Math" is wonderful, a game that everyone can enjoy. "Language" speaks to our souls and frees us to sing from our newfound self-worth. "Cultural Arts" put us in touch with the rest of the world and bring us back to our own roots in nature. (A student at an annual staff party spontaneously stood up and recited the whole of *The Desiderata* ("you are the child of the universe, no less than the trees and the stars, you have a right to be here"). Everyone cried and laughed and danced.) The assets are fabulous!

Success is real, but so are the obstacles: staff members come to us with limited educational backgrounds, self-doubt compounded by cultural chauvinism and resistance to change, varying degrees of cultural "self-hatred" (brought about by acceptance of the dominant culture's negative attitudes about language, cultural minorities, and low-income people), varying degrees of home support for personal development, and more. And it takes time. This is not a quick fix.

If the multifaceted efforts had not been attempted, if we had simply struggled to employ other-culture and other-language Montessori teachers, we would have surely failed. The teachers had to be of and for the child's community. We see the child as a plant: the parents and family members as its roots, the soil in which the plant grows as its environment. If children are taken from their environments and their roots are weakened or removed, no matter how rich the soil and how beautiful the new pot or garden, they will surely die or wither away. But children have feelings, as do their family members. These feelings contribute to the sense of community well-being and vitality. If children are detached from family and community, they suffer emotionally and spiritually but do not simply die quietly. In the child's emotional/spiritual death, much harm comes to others, including the "gardeners." We all pay the prices in the 50 to 90 percent drop-out rates among Hispanic, Indian, and African-American children; the climbing incidence of teenage pregnancy; drug and alcohol addiction; the crime and self-destruction related to poverty; and the lack of opportunity afforded these children and their families.

Our commitment to train staff was consciously extraordinary. Training from the "bottom up"—from janitors and aides—meant a policy against "the career teacher aide." The teacher aide in our program is seen as the next teacher and ultimately the next education director. The training is both on the job and college credit–based so that the person is not only competent but accredited.

The Foundation Center employs more than 240 individual women and men serving more than 2,000 children each year. All of these individuals are enrolled in Pacific Oaks College credit courses that lead toward California children's center permit Certification and the American Montessori Society credential, be it preprimary or infant-toddler. Approximately 90 percent of these individuals are indigenous to their communities— whether they be Mexican migrant workers, seasonal agricultural workers, garment and produce workers in downtown Los Angeles, sales and fast-food workers, urban or rural dwellers, black, brown, white, or red. Course work is offered and completed in the home language of the individual student. Approximately 80 percent of those employees are Spanish dominant and prefer Spanish-language instruction. All costs related to the course work and college credit are paid by the Foundation Center. The individual student is on regular salary when participating in the training. On March 29, 1989, the Foundation Center graduated 50 students with the AMS credential. Of these, 37 are individuals whose families continue to be migrant workers, seasonal farmworkers, and immigrants and refugees from Central America. Each year, the Foundation Center will see another group graduated until all 200 employees have completed their course work and are awarded their AMS credential. Each year, as we expand our services to other communities, we add new indigenous staff to the training. The Foundation Center believes that good-quality Montessori and child development services for children will benefit the entire community. We believe that college begins in preschool.

Our training effort is a partnership between institutions: the Foundation Center, the Comite Hispano Montessori, the Montessori Teacher Education Center of San Francisco/Bay Area, Pacific Oaks College, the Gloria E. Montejano Teacher Education Program, and the families of the students.

PARENT PARTICIPATION

Parents also believe that college begins in preschool. For example, migrant parents at the three centers in San Joaquin county requested the development of an English as a second language (ESL) program at their centers in the evening. Now, several years later, the ESL classes continue to thrive, GED classes at the center subsequently were developed, and by June 1989, we had celebrated the graduation of more than 75 parents and young adults from these GED classes. A large number received "honors" and one woman received "national honors" for near perfect scores on all exams. Soon it is hoped we will be able to offer our first off-site college course, which will serve to bridge GED and regular college courses. In our view, this is parent education and community development occurring as the direct result of a child care center.

The Foundation Center was invited to present a paper in October 1988 at a workshop sponsored by the National Resource Center for Children in Poverty, Columbia University. The questions we were asked to address were: "In parent education/family support programs how should teaching be matched to parents' learning styles? What aspects should be emphasized? When should interventions begin?" The following principles serve to guide the process of parent education in the context of child development.

1   *The child, as a member of a family and as a member of a community, cannot be educated in isolation. The goals and the values of the child's family and community must be enriched as a result of the child's experience in the preschool or day-care setting.*

Unfortunately, subsidized early childhood education programs (including day care) prepare the child to be more successful in later school experiences without any regard to the impact of the school experience on the home. The implications are that the home has been somehow unsuccessful and that intervention is necessary to correct deficiencies—be they linguistic, behavioral, or social. By allowing their child to participate in the program, the parents are admitting that they are preparing their children inadequately for school and society. The language that we use to refer to the families we serve—"at risk," "in need," "target"—concretizes this philosophical position: we're OK and they're not.

2 *There is a fundamental need to define success for the child from the parents' perspective and from their value base.*

The practitioner must avoid getting caught in the trap of the deficit theory's definition of the child development center's relationship to the family and child, i.e., the family is not okay. The solution for the Foundation Center has been to identify with the community. How is this achieved? How is it put into practice? First, staff help the child develop within the structure and needs of their family. To understand what this really means in terms of appropriate programming, we must redefine success for the child from the perspective of the family. What do the parents need? What do the parents want? What would make the child/parent relationship more successful? In other words, what does the family value?

In our eight years of operation, we have found that parents value social cooperation—they want their children to behave (*que se porten bien*). They want them to be respectful of their teachers, other adults, and other children. This translates into such skills as knowing how to greet others (*saludar a la gente*), being polite (saying *por favor* and *gracias* when appropriate), sharing but not requesting anything unless it is first offered, not accepting more than one's share (*no gracias, con esto tengo*, [No, thank you. This is more than enough for me.]), not bothering anyone—that is, taking care of oneself and one's own needs (using the bathroom without adult assistance, dressing and changing without help, eating without making a mess ([*mira no mas que grande estas y todavía no puedes ir al baño solo;* Just look at that! You are so big and still can't use the bathroom by yourself])). At two or three years of age, when most children enter a preschool program, they have not yet developed these social skills. Parents are afraid that their child will be a burden to the teachers. They caution us, "*No le hagas caso, es muy chillon*" (Don't pay attention to him. He's just a crybaby!) or "*Es muy tímido*" (he's very shy) or "*Simplemente no le hace caso a nadie"* (he just doesn't pay attention to anyone). Every day, parents ask the teacher, *"Se portó bien?"* (Did he behave well?)

Parents can judge the success of the program by observing the child's competencies at home. They see their children become proficient in practical life. The child is polite and greets others, speaks clearly when addressed (*"no es ranchera"*), and talks to parents, grandparents, and other adults (*"Dile lo que estas haciendo en la escuelita"* —Tell them what you are doing in school).

The child is independent. She can use the bathroom without forgetting to use toilet paper, and he can flush the toilet and wash his hands. The children can serve themselves and clean up spills without a great deal of adult intervention. They enjoy brushing their teeth, doing household chores, and being generally helpful.

As these basic needs are met, the parents can anticipate other skills that will help their children be successful. Now they begin to look at what we call "school readiness" skills. The parents' expectations become higher. By this time, the parents have seen that the teachers and staff are concerned with the welfare of the children and the interests of the parent. The parents know that their children are building a relationship with the center's teachers in the same way that relationships with their extended families are constructed ("Your *tía, la maestra"*— Your aunt, the teacher).

The next step is to support the parents' desire for their children's success, to make visible the children's potential, and to predict their actualization. For example, a teacher might say, "She is going to be a great artist someday. Look at her poster painting!" Or, "What a wonderful architect she will become! Look at that structure, that design. You must be very proud of her work. Don't let her talent go to waste. We need minds like hers!"

3 *Adults learn as much, if not more, from informal contact with the center's staff and teachers as from formal experiences.*

Through consistent and routine contacts with the center's teachers; through newsletters, bulletin boards, and the like; and through their daily visits to the center, parents learn about the philosophy and values of the center. They also learn about how the staff and program value their children. From a phenomenological perspective, the parent is receiving repeated messages about the staff's and program's feelings about and behaviors toward their children. The power of these messages cannot be supplanted by the formal messages that parents receive through parent meetings, special workshops, and the like.

4 *Language must not be an issue. If the child learns best in his home language, then the parent will be better informed if communications are in his or her home language.*

We recognize that "translators" are only needed until fluent speakers are available. The home-language speaker may not be Hispanic. The Spanish speaker who is not a native speaker brings to the parents and children an authentic model of cultural and linguistic pluralism and becomes an important cultural "broker." It is as important for parents and children to interact with bilingual non-Hispanics as it is for them to interact with bilingual Hispanics. The sociopolitical message is clear. It becomes important to take the opportunity to model pluralism and equality across cultures in the child's home community.

Although presenting all written material to the parents and children in their home language may frustrate administrators, it signals a significant commitment to the concept of community education.

5 *The majority of the staff members (teachers, center director, cook, health care providers) who work with the children and their families should be members of, or native to, the children's community.*

6 *Parent education should begin with health issues. To parents, their children's health comes before schooling and education. An individual child's state of health (anemia, dental caries, low birth weight, and other chronic and untreated maladies) is often simply a mirror image of the family's overall health profile.*

The process of assessing and obtaining services to address children's and families' health needs builds strong bonds between the caregivers and the parents and legitimizes the work of the caregiver from still another perspective. Discussing and working together to solve health problems build relationships similar to those of extended family members. The bonds are intimate and long lasting.

The Foundation Center's health program begins with a parent and family health carnival or fair, where all members of the child's family undergo physical examinations. The services provided include height, weight, blood pressure, temperature, hemoglobin, urine dip, vision and hearing screening, nutrition analysis, immunizations, and—for women— pap smear and breast examinations. The parent health carnival is followed within days by a children's health clinic, where children go through the physical examination accompanied by their parents. We find that nutritionally based conditions such as anemia are generally found among more than one member of the family; health education and treatment is therefore familywide. Many of the fathers have not had a physical for most of their adult lives. Serious life-threatening illnesses—including hypertension, diabetes, and major hearing impairments—have been detected in about 25 percent of the fathers.

The child development program models good nutritional habits and standards for its families. Organically grown fruits and vegetables are served, and no canned items are used. At each parent meeting, the cook presents a recipe and actually prepares the dish. After the meeting, the dish is used as part of the "social time," and parents are invited to take copies of the recipe home with them. Only juices made from organically grown apples, pears, oranges, and the like are served. On cultural holidays where piñatas are used, they contain no sugar candies, and parents are advised about the problems of sugar and dental caries.

The strong stand taken against junk foods and the "overselling" of some food items (such as milk—ingestion of more than four glasses each day can block the very young child's processing of iron and so can contribute to anemia) require constant vigilance. For the first two years or so of a staff person's employment with us, she or he is likely to dismiss concerns about nutrition and to approve purchasing candies for piñatas. The same consistent attention is also required with parents.

7   *Parents respect and trust commitment to ideals and standards. The "anything goes," eclectic curriculum appears suspect to parents. They can tell when you don't know what you are doing. If the child development program purports to be educational, it must adopt a curriculum that is philosophically consistent with its goals for the community.*

8   *The expectations for parents' involvement and participation should be as high as for children. The enthusiasm of the staff establishes the boundaries of their participation.*

If the staff believes that the parents are "too tired," "too stressed out," "too apathetic," or "too resistant" to participate in the daily joys of the center or in formal parent meetings, the parents will surely meet their expectations.

9   *Parents learn from observing their children interacting and working in their environments.*

The Foundation Center's staff learned early on that working parents simply do not have the time in the morning to linger and observe their children at work. In talking with parents, however, staff members found that they would love to see their children at work. Many had noted their child's work at home and their curiosity was sparked, but they were concerned that their schedules would never permit them to make such observations.

The Foundation Center therefore put into place its "full-day Montessori program"—instead of scheduling the children for outdoor free play after the afternoon snack they can work in any of the learning centers: practical life, sensorial, language, math, botany, zoology, geography, and other cultural subjects. When parents arrive, they then have the opportunity to observe their child at work on a particular task.

Parents will often stand a slight distance from their children, watching them manipulate the golden beads or work at the metal insets. Sometimes they actually join their child at work. (During the monthly parent meetings and during individual formal and informal conferences with parents, staff members demonstrate how to use the materials.) It is not unusual for some parents to spend as much as one half hour with their children one or two days a week.

In addition, teachers advise parents about having quiet places for children to look at books, listen to music, draw pictures, and so on. They tell parents that children need order and routines and that parents should make time in the morning, if at all possible, to have a leisurely, not rushed, start to the day.

The Foundation Center has eliminated other contradictions prevalent in many day-care and preschool programs. For example, child development and day-care staff might encourage parents to buy "educational toys" for the children, yet allow violence and sexist toys in the dramatic play corners. They might encourage parents to buy a few good books, yet have on hand stacks of Cabbage Patch Kid books, Disney character books, and other blatantly commercial "junk."

In addition, the environments must be consonant with the organization's philosophy. In a Montessori environment, jobs are attractive, visually appealing, complete, and clean. To the greatest extent possible, the classrooms are light and airy, yet warm and comfortable in the winter months. Carpets are sanitized routinely, and linoleum and sheet vinyl have a "hospital shine." Shelves with the children's materials are noninstitutional with teak finishes and were purchased from home furniture stores. Materials are not "begged, borrowed, and stolen." Air filters and negative ion generators are in each room to help reduce pollens and other airborne irritants to children and staff. Consistent with the Montessori philosophy, the Foundation Center's environments are beyond "teaching from trash-ables" and avoid "poverty program" stereotypes that so embarrass parents.

10   *Celebrations cement relationships and make real our successes; they are ways we chronicle our history together.*

Through the vehicles of parent meetings, parent conferences, and our positive message program (messages that begin: "Something really nice happened with your child today. We thought you'd like to know, and we wanted to share it with you," which the teacher then individualizes), we record the history we share.

11   *Maximize cultural courtesies that demonstrate respect of all members of the child's family and community.*

This is not difficult for our program to do because our staff are them-selves members of the communities we serve and are, therefore, as sensi-tive to these issues as the parents themselves. In downtown Los Angeles, for example, our children, families, and staff are Central American immi-grants and refugees primarily from El Salvador. In south central Los Ange-les, our children, families, and staff are new or relatively new immigrants from Mexico. In the San Joaquin Valley, our children, families, and staff are migrants who spend no more than six to eight months in this country following the West Coast migrant stream.

In conclusion, the Foundation Center has been successful not only for its children but for the parents because of its commitment to (1) imple-menting the philosophy (and curriculum) of Montessori, (2) developing culturally and linguistically respectful environments, and (3) supporting activities that empower the community it serves. We have demonstrated that the potential for educational reform of programs serving at-risk chil-dren through Montessori is phenomenal. Let's begin this reform movement by looking beyond day care and promoting the development of full-day Montessori programs for children of migrant families and children whose native language is not English.

13

MONTESSORI IN PUBLIC SCHOOLS: INTERDEPENDENCE OF THE CULTURE OF THE SCHOOL, THE CONTEXT OF THE CLASSROOM, AND THE CONTENT OF THE CURRICULUM

> One afternoon a child brought his menorah to share with his friends. They talked about it on the line. When they finished, the child's teacher, Evelyn, thanked the child and asked if she could keep it overnight for the morning class to see. The child said, "Yes." Evelyn said, "Put it on any shelf." The child looked around, walked over to the picture of Maria on the Sensorial shelf, and placed it in front of her.

The child placing the menorah in front of Maria's picture symbolizes the creative connections that are going on inside the child's mind, an acceptance of cultural diversity, and a reflection of the human community.

Sunday, April 22, 1990, was the twentieth anniversary of Earth Day, a global celebration of Mother Earth. We are calling the nineties the "decade of the environment." And today is Arbor Day in New York State.

Last month, President Vaclav Havel of Czechoslovakia delivered an extraordinary speech to our Congress. He used Lincoln's words—"the family of men"—and reminded us that Thomas Jefferson not only wrote that "governments are instituted among men, deriving their just powers from the consent of the governed but he backed it up with his life" (*Time Magazine* March 5, 1990, Vol. 135, p. 14–15).

As we pause on the threshold of the last decade of the century, we all respond joyfully to these new understandings of our relationships to each other and to our world. How appropriate that we educational theorists and practitioners, government representatives, and business supporters should gather to examine the growth of the movement launched by a woman who symbolized these connections between people and their environment.

My contribution is to help analyze what we have done with Montessori in the public schools, what effect the public school bureaucracy has on Montessori, and what impact Montessori has upon that bureaucracy.

MONTESSORI IN THE PUBLIC SCHOOL

Our school, the Bennett Park Montessori Center, is a magnet school in Buffalo. It was started in 1977 as one answer to court-ordered desegregation. It began with 250 children, ages three to seven, and now has 580 children, ages three to thirteen.

Classes contain multi-age groupings, balanced by age, sex, minority, majority. There are 4 environments for three- to five-year-olds, 5 for five- to seven-year-olds, 4 for seven- to nine-year-olds, 4 for nine- to eleven-year-olds, 4 for eleven- to thirteen-year-olds, and 2 special education classes. We mainstream our special ed children first in art, music, physical education, lunch, going outside, and gradually in the cultural subject lessons.

We are located in the inner city and most of the children arrive on buses—seventeen of them. The school is diverse socioeconomically and culturally. The present configuration is 53.4 percent Caucasian, 39.9 percent Black, 4.2 percent Native American, 2.5 percent Hispanic, and 2.3 percent Asian. Fifty-nine percent of our children receive free or reduced breakfast and lunch. Across the street from us is a high school—the Visual and Performing Arts Academy. We can easily walk downtown, to the public library, to city hall, and even to the lakeshore marina for ice cream.

Our children come to school regularly. Our daily attendance for the past two years has been 95.6 percent and 92 percent, respectively. Approximately 50 percent of each graduating class are children who began the program at age three.

Bennett Park was an idea born at the right time. City leaders were anxious to solve the problem of desegregating the public schools, and professional educators and parents were eager to carry out a dream of public Montessori education.

A few years ago I took a course entitled "Designing Organizations." There I began to realize that the the Bennett Park project of implementing Montessori within a desegregating public system has what Henry Mintzberg in *Power in and Around Organizations* (1983) calls a "missionary configuration." Mintzberg said, "The key to the missionary configuration is the organization's ideology, with all the members in a supporting role." (p. 369). Our project called forth the zeal necessary to implement this ideology among professionals and parents alike. Mintzberg continues: "Members in a mission model typically join the organization not primarily for material inducements, not to build a power base, not to satisfy a social need, but because of an identification with the organization's basic purpose, its ideologic goals" (p. 369).

Our mission statement also expresses who we are:

> Bennett Park Montessori Center consists of multi-aged groupings of children who have a variety of abilities, talents, and cultural backgrounds. Our belief in accepting differences and respecting each other is a shared value. The children actively participate at their level within a structured environment with freedom of movement, choice, and thought. By developing the child's physical, social, and emotional needs, she or he develops confidence and becomes an agent of his or her own learning. As the desire for learning intensifies throughout their development, the children will become functioning and productive members of the world community.

HOW IS THIS PHILOSOPHY REFLECTED IN OUR ACTIONS?

OUTSIDE ENVIRONMENT

We go outside everyday unless it's raining, too icy, or below a −10° wind chill factor. The eleven- to thirteen-year-olds walk down the block to a city recreation facility every Friday afternoon to use the gym and game room for forty-five minutes.

VISITING

Children can visit friends or siblings in other environments. Ground rules concerning the frequency of visits differ depending on grade level. The three- to five-year-olds have color-coded bracelets—two or three in a basket per room—which allow freedom of movement within the building. For example, an orange bracelet means the child is going to the library; a white one is for bird watching.

PROBLEM SOLVING

Because we believe that our children are agents of their own learning, problem solving or conflict resolution is a social as well as an academic value. During our early years, many staff development sessions focused on this topic. Because we work so hard at resolving conflicts, fewer children in our school are suspended formally or informally than in other schools in the district.

OBSERVATION

We encourage our parents, the community, and college students to visit at any time. We are now a site for student teachers from three area institutions.

COMMUNICATION REPORTS TO PARENTS

Our primary means of communication to parents is parent conferences. Conferences are an example of how we make the system fit our philosophy. We do not communicate by A, B, C, or number grades, but rather by extensive written or oral communication. The board of education provides one conference day a year when children do not come to school and parents and teachers meet one on one to discuss the children. On two other occasions, substitutes provided by the board release the teachers from their classes to hold conferences. Each parent conference ends with a written summary of the ideas discussed. If we do not see parents by the third marking period, we send a strong letter urging them to come in. Our final communication is a written narrative reporting work habits and social, emotional, and intellectual development. Reports on the eleven- to thirteen-year-olds indicate grades of city exams and final subject exams in addition to the written narrative.

HOMEWORK

We assign no homework as such. The eleven- to thirteen-year-olds may need to take work home occasionally if it's not completed during their independent work time. We encourage children to read at home, work on projects, continue work from writing workshop, participate in chores, get involved in community or church activities, visit libraries and museums, and develop hobbies.

Homework became an issue about five years ago when the school system developed a Homework Hotline and gave directions for all schools to use it. We researched the topic, had staff meetings, and developed the policy I've just discussed. On this issue, we had to deal not just with pressure from city hall but also from some of our parents who needed an explanation of our beliefs.

STAFF COMMUNICATION AND SCHEDULING

When we first started, our total staff was fifteen; now we are sixty-five. As we grew in number, we moved from occupying one floor of a building to three floors. During this growth, we faced the challenge of preserving the original "missionary" zeal and the close-knit feeling of community that had brought us together at the start. In order to meet this challenge, we really needed communication among the staff. We instituted weekly meetings; although attendance is voluntary, these meetings are well attended because they fill a real need. In addition, our staff at different grade levels meet for planning—some once a week, some daily.

The Montessori curriculum, school themes, and current events are the foundation for the three- to five-year-olds and the five- to seven-year-olds. What goes on in these classrooms is not very different from Montessori classrooms in the private sector.

With the seven to nine grouping, there is a gradual change. The reason is simple. Beginning at this level the children must take city exams in June. Here the Montessori curriculum is integrated with the state education department and local guidelines.

WHAT IS OUR PUBLIC MONTESSORI CURRICULUM?

MATH

The Montessori materials are the primary resource integrated with state and local guidelines. The paper and pencil level is developmentally inappropriate for some seven- to nine-year-olds. It is necessary to do a lot of bridging from the concrete to the abstract. Because of the assessment tool (test) used by the city, it is necessary to "try" to take all children to the abstract level at a certain age, rather than when they are developmentally ready. This makes us sad, but we need to do it.

Figure 13–1 provides a composite picture of Bennett Park Montessori Center. I chose a circle to reflect the connectedness of all the components of Bennett Park. The prepared environment is intellectually engaging; it entices children to interact with the content of the curriculum. The framework is the Montessori curriculum. Teachers' styles, judgments, academic backgrounds, and interests make each environment unique. School-wide themes such as a holiday presentation, a presentation for Black History Month, a weather unit, a study of an author, a book dress-up day, celebrations of holidays in various cultures, and celebrations of Earth Day are planned across the curriculum. This fosters a community spirit.

Current topics—for example, the Berlin Wall, Panama, the Exxon oil spill, Hurricane Hugo, and the like—become units that each classroom teacher constructs and delivers according to the grade level. These topics are presented using the Montessori approach to cultural subjects. Moving from the whole to the part these events are placed within a historical perspective, through the use of time lines, nomenclature cards, music, drama, food, and so on.

READING AND WRITING

This is such an alive area in education today. Part of the missionary spirit continues as staff members attend workshops and take courses in this area. Two of our staff members from the eleven to thirteen level discovered that the process approach to reading and writing meshes beautifully with the Montessori philosophy.

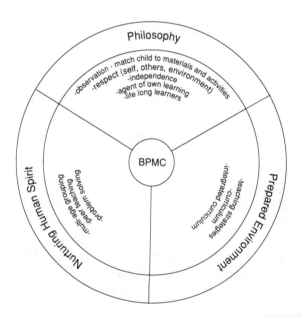

Figure 13–1   Connectedness of the Components of Bennett Park

CULTURAL SUBJECTS (SOCIAL STUDIES, SCIENCE)

The Montessori curriculum is the foundation for instruction in the cultural subjects for all age groups, except eleven- to thirteen-year-olds. At this level, the New York State curriculum is implemented. To retain the integrity of the program, a plan was devised in which the sixth-, seventh-, and eighth-grade state content for social studies and science was put on a three-year cycle. For example, the sixth-grade social studies curriculum is world studies, the seventh is American studies up to the Civil War, and the eighth is American studies beyond the Civil War. This year all students in the eleven to thirteen level are receiving instruction in the seventh-grade curriculum. Next year they will receive instruction in eighth-grade content. The following year they will receive instruction in the sixth-grade curriculum, and then the cycle repeats itself. This cycle allows us to keep the classes multi-age grouped and still address the state curriculum. This arrangement also took a lot of pressure off the staff, who were trying creatively to do it all!

Another reason for concern was that our children take city exams based on the content mentioned above. Because we are on a different cycle than the system, we requested to write our own social studies and science city exams, which was approved by the social studies and science coordinators. It's a lot of work, but it makes sense for our children and they are well prepared when they enter high school.

This decision has also affected the seven to nine and nine to eleven levels. They too integrate this cycle with the Montessori curriculum. Some of the Montessori Great Lessons are rotated every two or three years. Each spring the three grade levels (seven to nine, nine to eleven, and eleven to thirteen) meet and plan the curriculum for the following year.

INSTRUCTIONAL STRATEGIES

Just as Montessori synthesized her knowledge from Rousseau, Pestalozzi, Herbart, and Froebel, so must we draw on many sources. We can't sit and ignore what is going on around us. In devising instructional strategies our teachers draw on Madeline Hunter, with her wonderful interaction strategies; whole language; critical thinking; philosophy for children; and the like. We continually need to make connections, however, to our philosophical base. We need to examine and integrate only what is compatible with our own roots. Regarding cooperative learning, for example, we can incorporate its techniques and strategies for involving children in learning, but we need to reject its competitive aspects.

INTEGRATED CURRICULUM

Integration of the arts—music, dance, drama—is a major component of our program. In this area, being part of a public school system is to our advantage. We are across the street from a performing arts school, and we are frequently invited there to attend plays, dance performances, and concerts. In addition, the music coordinator in city hall knows we are interested in the arts and often calls with opportunities for us in the city. We are able to take advantage of the rich culture in our city.

WHY IS IT SO SUCCESSFUL?

Why does our school continue to thrive thirteen years after it began? The spirit still glows in me personally and in the staff. We have become experts at blending the state- and city-mandated curricula with Montessori.

Our reality is just like yours.

We have meetings before school, during lunch, after school, and in the evening.

We live in a profession that pays the lowest and is respected the least—"You're just a teacher."

We make telephone calls for conferences and problem solving.

We stretch our patience from the egocentrism of the three-year-old to the self-obsession of the adolescent.

We are exhausted every Friday evening—one glass of wine for me at dinner and the evening is over.

What makes us continue to return with positive energy?

We are intellectually challenged by pedagogical problems and issues.

We are never bored—no two days are ever alike.

We look forward to planning interesting lessons, relevant content, manipulative materials, and thought-provoking projects.

We are more compassionate because we know children with physical disabilities, children who live with true fear of physical abuse in their homes, and children whose minds and bodies were scarred during the embryotic stage by alcohol and drugs.

Here are six reasons why Montessori and public education mesh so well:

1 There is a team of Montessori and public school experts working together.

2 Children begin the program at age three, a new option at the time in public school which came about because the superintendent wanted it to be an authentic Montessori program.

3 Teachers are willing to work hard and take risks.

4 It has the backing of the court, which mobilized the whole community. In the beginning, the clergy rode buses; this inspired people to greater efforts for a moral good.

5 The teachers' union has been involved since the beginning. The union enhances the system and does not take jobs away.

6 It has strong parent committment, which even continues for some after their children have graduated.

My words have painted a picture in your mind of our dream that has become a reality. Our picture is not finished, the paint is still wet. I invite you to come and see our picture as it is being painted. And if you ever have an opportunity to paint a picture in your town, say yes!

14

MONTESSORI AND THE MIDDLE SCHOOL YEARS

Early adolescence is a time of dramatic change and growth, when young people are vulnerable to the influences of family, school, and community. The Carnegie report, *Turning Point* (1989), indicates that the middle school years are a crucial time for making life decisions. Yet early adolescents have been largely forgotten by the American society, especially the educational system. *Turning Point* states that there is "a volatile mismatch between the organization and curriculum of middle school grades and the intellectual, emotional, and interpersonal needs of young adolescents" (1989, p. 32). This is evidenced by the rising number of early adolescents using chemical substances, becoming sexually active, losing interest in school, and feeling unproductive in life.

These trends became a concern to a group of parents and students at School of the Woods, a Montessori school in Houston, Texas. They were looking for an alternative to the large, impersonal junior high schools with irrelevant curricula that herded students from place to place every forty-five minutes. They wanted a learning environment that was more in tune with the special needs of early adolescents. In the fall of 1984, research was begun on how to create an optimal learning environment for twelve- to fourteen-year-olds. My investigation included a study of the concepts behind Maria Montessori's *Erdkinder* and contemporary Montessori models, a study of adolescent psychology, and a complete review of the trends and issues in education.

MONTESSORI'S *ERDKINDER*

Dr. Maria Montessori never created an environment for adolescents, but she stated her views about this age group in lectures and papers. Being a physician, she was aware of the drastic physical changes that take place, so she felt young people needed a place where they could be physically safe as they went through the transition of puberty. Along with physical protection, Montessori believed secondary education should "aim at improving the individual in order to improve society" (1948, p. 98). This statement is an example of Montessori's view that the education of the young was the avenue that society must pursue to create a peaceful world. To accomplish this goal, she felt that early adolescents must be respected by society and not treated as children. She thought they needed to learn to be adaptable in order to be able to face the unsure times of the future. Furthermore, she observed that adolescents wanted to contribute to society and to have their contribution recognized. Thus, she recommended that they do productive work in the community, which would lead to self-confidence and independence. This independence included more than choosing courses and materials or earning money; it involved actually choosing to develop a sense of self: ". . . we must consider what is the form of independence at this age which guarantees the development of individuality. We must follow the psychic instincts which present themselves at this period of life" (1937).

Adolescents seek emotional autonomy in order to establish a sense of self. They want to interact with others in order to test and to get feedback on who they are. They are fine-tuning when they comment, "Let me do it alone," "Let me do it with others," "How much?" "How much can I push before I find the limits?" The task of this age group is to learn to be interdependent, to find the balance between needs of self and those of others. Erikson terms this psychosocial task of adolescents identity. It is amazing how Montessori's observations of the needs of children and adolescents are the same as those stated by noted physicians, psychologists, and educators today.

In her works, Montessori (1948) refers to young people going off to live on a farm community as *Erdkinder*, children of the land. She envisioned the farm as the most natural environment for developing a sense of self, practicing community living, and being in harmony with nature. She believed this kind of environment would foster the ultimate goals of creating productive and peaceful members of the world society.

In 1978 Mario Montessori, Jr., grandson of Maria Montessori and a psychoanalyst in the Netherlands, wrote a letter to Phil Gang explaining his viewpoints on a contemporary *Erdkinder* community. Summarized in my words, Mario felt that the European models had lost their original focus and that an ideal model should include the following characteristics: be student-centered, have the support and involvement of the parents, provide activities for development of personal knowledge and individual ego strength, and develop a community for adults and students. He also warned that young people should not be infantilized by giving them the materials that are part of the younger students' curriculum. Further, Mario Montessori encouraged Montessori educators to begin programs even if they would be a compromise of the farm community. By beginning with an experimental model, he suggested, one could observe and develop a program that met the adolescent's inner needs. This, of course, was the scientific procedure that Maria Montessori used in developing the environments for younger children.

ADOLESCENT DEVELOPMENT

Joan Lipsitz (1977) wrote the first comprehensive study regarding early adolescence. She concluded that our society had virtually forgotten this segment of the population. Lipsitz found that educators grouped early adolescents either with elementary children, providing an "enriched" elementary program, or with high school students, giving them a "watered down" or "junior" high school program. To fill this void in knowledge, the Center of Early Adolescence at the University of North Carolina was formed to gather and disseminate information on adolescent development, and subsequently additional research has been conducted and reported by the Carnegie Council (1989) and by organizations such as the National Middle School Association.

TRENDS AND ISSUES

I also reviewed the literature in the trends and issues in education, focusing on the following: history of early adolescent education, the teaching/learning relationship, three modes of learning, cooperative learning, mastery learning, cognitive theory, education reform movements, needs of the future, self-concept, peer teaching, youth service programs, parent-teacher partnerships, peace and global education, whole brain learning, communication skills, and thinking skills. In each area of study, there was plenty of theory available on how things *should* be, but little information on putting these ideas into practice. I knew that my work would be to implement the theory into practice.

From this review of the Montessori philosophy, adolescent psychology, and current trends and issues in education, I decided that the pilot program at School of the Woods should be developmentally responsive, holistic, and empowering. These three characteristics are the foundations of my program design and the basis of my dissertation, *Creating an Holistic, Developmentally Responsive Learning Environment That Empowers the Early Adolescent* (1989).

DEVELOPMENTALLY RESPONSIVE

Developmental stages provide a crucial guide for developing a Montessori program. Respect for children's particular developmental stage and current sensitive period is a foundation of Montessori educational design. The following is an overview of early adolescent biological, cognitive, and psychosocial development, and its implications for the learner.

Early adolescence is characterized by three primary changes, the first of which is biological growth. Next to the first year of life, the most rapid and dramatic growth in a person's lifetime occurs in this period. The body changes drastically. The feet and hands grow first, then the limbs, and finally the trunk. The facial structure changes. No wonder adolescents spend so much time in front of the mirror seeing what they look like! In addition to the external changes in size, shape, and sexual characteristics, there are less obvious internal changes of hormones, heart, lungs, muscles, bones, and blood. These physical changes trigger metabolic changes. That is why many adolescents can be very active one minute, and lethargic the next. These changes have an effect on the nutritional needs, the movement, and the self-concept of the early adolescent. "Physically, early adolescents are at risk with the major causes of death being homicide, suicide, accidents, and leukemia" (California State Department of Education, 1987, p. 145).

The second primary change is a shift in thinking from a dependency on concrete experiences to abstract ideas. Even though theorists don't agree on the processes that cause cognitive growth, they do agree that there is a change in the form of thinking of adolescents that triggers possibility, hypothesizing, and abstract thinking. Piaget defines this shift in thinking as "formal operational" (NMSA, 1988). An important ingredient in this shift is the environment. The environment catalyzes the biologically ready person to change his or her form of thinking. The initial stage is the emergent formal thinking of early adolescence, characterized by the unique behaviors that Elkind (1984) labels as egocentrism, the personal fable, the imaginary audience, and pseudostupidity. Egocentrism, the personal fable, and the imaginary audience relate to the adolescents' perception that the world revolves around their needs, that everyone is watching all their actions, and that they are so special that they are immune to any negative consequences. With the onset of possibility thinking, early adolescents tend to make simple tasks more complex than necessary; this has been identified as pseudostupidity. Possibility thinking also allows young people to engage in systematic inquiry, to participate in complex arguments, and to create many new worries in their life. Hypothesizing is the basis for young people's new quest for perfection. They are seeking the nonexistent perfect parent, friends, school, teacher, and selves. This skill also allows them to set goals, work for those goals, and reflect upon their effectiveness. Abstraction is characterized as second-order thinking that gives an appreciation of word play and abstract ideas. "Intellectually, early adolescents are at risk because they face decisions that have the potential to affect major academic values with life-long consequences" (California State Department of Education, p. 144).

The third primary change is the spoken or unspoken messages that our society gives an adolescent. In American society, some age "privileges" become available to older adolescents, such as getting a driver's license, dropping out of school, joining the service, and working. However, there is not a clearly defined, responsible role for adolescents in this society (Hill, 1980). Biologically mature adolescents must just wait around until they get older to have a productive role.

These three primary changes do not occur in a vacuum, but in the context of relationships with family, peers, school, and community. According to Hill (1980), these changes trigger secondary changes in psychosocial development—identity, autonomy, intimacy, sexuality, and achievement. The early adolescent is characterized by high peer conformity, which is a necessary step in developing identity and autonomy. Young people seek emotional autonomy to prove their capability of taking care of themselves. They begin to develop friendships based on common goals and interests instead of common activities. They learn the give and take of relationships, how to get along with others by asserting themselves, getting feedback, and negotiating. This social task can be done only in small, secure peer groups. The large junior high school does not provide a place where close, trusting relationships with peers can be established. The middle school reforms recommend having teams of students and teachers who work together for several years. These smaller, more secure environments can then foster a sense of belonging and develop the skills of relationship building. A recent National Middle School Association publication (Doda, 1981) indicated that the four Rs in middle school should be Reading, Riting, 'Rithmetic, and Relationships. "Socially, early adolescents are at risk because at no other point in human development is an individual likely to encounter so much diversity in relation to oneself and others" (California State Department of Education, 1987, p. 147). I call this developmental period the "Age of the Mouth," because young people are either eating to keep up with their physical growth, arguing to test their new cognitive skills, or talking—the number one activity of adolescents.

All these changes can be a difficult time for young people, teachers, and parents, because young people move through this growth period at different, irregular rates and in many different kinds of social settings. It is estimated that in an average group of thirteen-year-olds, there will be a difference of six to eight years in physical growth (Lefstein, 1986). The best description of this age is diversity. Perhaps this is why early adolescents have such very special needs. A middle schooler at School of the Woods wrote about his confusion:

> Me
>
> I am rude
> I am kind
>
> I am foolish
> I am wise
>
> I am angry
> I am happy
>
> I am miserable
> I am content
>
> I am varied

All of these changes occur in the context of social systems—the family, the school, and the community. It is imperative that adults in each of these systems become aware of the multiple dimensions of early adolescents and create developmentally responsive programs. These developmental needs and their diversity are the foundations for the program design at School of the Woods.

HOLISTIC

The second theme for my program design is to provide an holistic education. The word *holistic* is another significant element of Montessori philosophy. *Holistic* comes from the Anglo-Saxon word *hal*, which means *whole*, *heal*, and *health*. To Montessorians this means three things. First, the focus of education should be on the whole child for optimal health and growth. Thus, the learning environment should not focus on developing only the cognitive potential but the physical and psychosocial aspects of the person as well. This characteristic made Montessori education unique in the early 1900s. Today it has been accepted as an integral part of early childhood education and was recently the focus of the studies done by the Center of Early Adolescence (Hill, 1980) and the Carnegie Corporation (1989).

Second, the courses of study need to be interrelated so that the student understands the interconnections of life. Dr. Montessori referred to this idea as "cosmic education." Today this theory is labeled "interdisciplinary" or "core curriculum." It's supported by the educational reform theories of Goodlad, Sizer, Elkind, and M. Adler.

Holistic education also has a third dimension. It includes a collaboration with the social systems in which the student operates each day, mainly the home setting. The recent trend in education is to involve parents in the school community; all benefit from this partnership. I have taken this one step further and believe the student should also be a vital member of this partnership. If one of the goals of education is to develop capable, responsible people who are self-directed, life-long learners, then students need to take an active role in developing academic goals and participating in the problem-solving activities. Student-parents-teacher partnerships are important, especially for early adolescents, in creating a complete, healthy optimal learning environment.

EMPOWERING

Young people say, "I want some control over my life, I want to show the world that I can be responsible." Most learning environments, however, have little confidence in the skills of young people, and they tend to tell them what to do, how to do it, and when to do it. At the crucial time of searching for an identity, young people are rarely given any control over their lives. In frustration, many are turning to life-threatening activities to feel powerful. A school environment should respect the young person's quest for self. I wanted to provide a place where early adolescents could develop personal power as well as an opportunity to use this personal power with and for the benefit of others. I believe that is what Maria Montessori meant by a "form of independence at this age which guarantees the development of individuality" (1937). The word *empower* seems to express this thought. Five years ago when I borrowed this word from Paulo Freire (1970), it was a unique word in education.

SCHOOL OF THE WOODS

The program that I will describe was designed for School of the Woods in Houston, Texas. School of the Woods is a nonprofit school founded in 1962. The students come from middle- and upper-class homes representing several ethnic cultures. Since the school has an open admissions policy, the students represent a wide range of academic abilities and learning styles. All core teachers are certified by the American Montessori Society. The school staff believes that the parents should be a integral part of the school so there are many activities that foster a strong partnership with parents.

The campus of two-and-a-half to fourteen-year-olds models the school-within-a-school concept recommended in John Goodlad's A *Place called School* (1984). The PK–8 campus follows some of the recent recommendations for an optimal school environment. Researchers have found that twelve-year-olds who entered junior high school had lower self-concept, higher self-consciousness, and greater instability than twelve-year-olds who remained in a K–8 environment. Girls were more affected by the change in schools than boys (Simmons et al., 1979). Since there are so many dramatic changes occurring at this time, adding a new school environment can be overwhelming to the young person at the crucial age of twelve.

Classrooms at all levels of the school have a multi-aged, heterogeneous grouping of students. This structure is a basic practice of the Montessori philosophy and today is supported by current research as an element for fostering positive self-concept, developing strong social skills, and utilizing the benefits of peer and cross-age teaching. In this structure students are also able to stay with the same team of teachers and students for two to three years, which provides a secure, stable environment.

The daily structure allows for the large blocks of uninterrupted class time for real in-depth learning instead of the superficial, low-level learning that occurs during chopped-up increments of time. This format allows students to have the necessary time to solve problems, to experience the interdisciplinary connections of knowledge, and to create new ideas.

MIDDLE SCHOOL PROGRAM

The middle school program is designed for students twelve to fourteen years and was added to the school in 1985. Sixty students have participated in the program to date representing a wide range of academic abilities and backgrounds. Seven of the students are first generation Americans coming from Ecuador, Germany, India, and Taiwan. Seventy percent of the students had both Montessori preschool and elementary education. The self-contained classroom of twenty-five students has a core teacher and an assistant.

My program design was based on the premise that the program would evolve as I observed the students and received feedback from the students and adults. There are approximately fifty Montessori schools who are in various stages of developing a middle school program. Several schools are replicating my model in both private and public settings. By the number of people who have come to observe the program and/or have requested information on how to start a middle school during these last few years, there appears a growing trend to provide appropriate learning environments for this age group. I believe that there is no one model. I also do not claim to hold all or even most of the answers. I am just willing to share my experiences, research, and model with others.

In describing this program design, I will define the family partnership, the responsibility of the student, and the role of the teacher. The curriculum and instruction will be explained by describing a sample day. The curriculum outside the walls of the typical classroom will then be discussed. Finally, data will be provided to show the effectiveness of the program.

FAMILY PARTNERSHIPS

The year begins with the creation of a family partnership. Before school starts a conference is held to review everyone's expectations for the year and to develop the student's learning plan. The young person, teacher, and parents meet together to assist in developing the student's educational plan. Parents and teacher serve as advisers by setting the minimum requirements and realistic goals. Decisions are made regarding the appropriate vocabulary course, math level, quantity of reading and writing, exploration courses, and independent study projects for the semester. Along with this plan, responsibilities of the teacher, parents, and student are defined. This results in a contract that is then signed by all.

One of the students' responsibilities is to keep their parents informed of their progress. At the end of each month, students complete a summary report that includes all academic areas as well as work habits. This report is reviewed with the teacher, signed by both the student and teacher, and mailed home to parents. The parents are responsible for reviewing the report with their young person and contacting the teacher if there are any concerns. Attached to the summary report is a one-page focus sheet for the next month's areas of study, important dates, and a family challenge.

The three-way conferences are held again in January and May. The students prepare for these conferences by completing a self-evaluation form in which they reflect upon their growth in academics, individual responsibility, and group responsibility. At the conference, students lead the meeting by reporting their progress in each area. They then ask for their parents' and teacher's feedback on each topic. With this information, the original learning plan is reviewed and any necessary adjustments are made for the next semester. During the May conference, students graph their achievement scores so they can see and explain their growth in each of the subject areas. Students have become very accurate in their self-evaluations and create learning plans they are eager to implement.

STUDENTS

Developmentally, early adolescents are egocentric and want emotional autonomy. From their perspective, the world should revolve around their specific needs. Furthermore, they want to prove their independence and individual responsibility. I want the students to experience controlling at least a part of their lives. Thus, I put the responsibility of learning on the students, and they are actively involved with decision-making skills, organizational skills, and time management. The first month of school, students learn about themselves by taking a learning style preference inventory. They learn about the effects of music, various memory techniques, time management strategies, note taking, mind mapping, metaphors for decision making and writing paragraphs, and organizational plans. I present the research behind each of these methods making them aware of a variety of techniques and strategies.

According to Stephen Glenn (1987), a month is an appropriate time frame for adolescents aged twelve to eighteen years to understand the cause and effect of their actions. Thus the work assignments are for a month. There are due dates along the way and tests are taken periodically, but the final drafts of all the monthly work must be pulled together in a comprehensive project notebook according to a specified outline, which includes a cover done with a computer graphics program and a bibliography. Students begin experimenting with the many ways to practice time management by making lists, charts, and schedules. Each morning they create their daily plan. However, the next step of carrying out their plan is not always so easy. They find that their time estimates are not always accurate and they become aware of the distractions that prevent them from completing their day's plan. If they want to work with others, they have to negotiate the time frame and stay on task. They develop a tremendous amount of self-discipline. It is a concrete way to start systematic planning. As the teacher, I am available to assist if my input is requested, and periodically, I meet with students to review their progress.

At the initial family conference, parents agree to allow their student to experience the feedback in learning organizational, decision making, and time management skills. They also agree to bring the student back to school the last weekend of the month if the monthly work is not completed on time. In September and October, I have students spending part of the weekend with me, but as they develop these skills, their work is usually completed on time. This plan helps to provide closure for some students, prevents some from getting so far behind that they can't catch up, and makes all students accountable for time management.

The first Monday of each new work month, students reflect upon what works and what doesn't and discuss their strategies for the new month. It's a constant growing experience. When I introduce new techniques during the year, I always give the supporting research so that they are informed about their choices. To the students, schoolwork becomes important and a personal challenge. It enhances their personal power, and they are actively involved in their learning.

TEACHER

The teacher is said to be the key to a successful middle school program. The teacher should be a consultant to the student, a facilitator of the learning process, and a creator of a positive learning climate. Young adolescents want input from significant adults. They want and need a teacher who is willing to listen actively, to respond nonjudgmentally, and to guide them in their own problem solving. Research indicates that students should have at least one significant adult at school whom they know well and who knows them well. Recent studies (George, 1987) show that early adolescents also benefit from long-term teacher-student relationships. With the multi-aged grouping, this benefit is inherent in the program design.

In the reform movement recommendations, there appears to be a consensus that learners should participate actively, make choices, and take responsibility for their learning. The teacher's role is not to pour in knowledge but to facilitate the learning process. Theodore Sizer in his Coalition of Essential Schools summarizes the teacher/student relationship by describing students as workers and teachers as coaches, instead of teachers as workers and students as sponges (1984). In defining the role of a facilitator, I reviewed M. Adler's three modes of teaching in the *Paideia Program* (1984). The first mode of teaching is didactic instruction for acquisition of organized knowledge. This mode involves having the resources and materials available for the student to obtain the necessary knowledge. In my classroom, I provide the necessary textbooks, library books, videos, materials, and activities and give short lessons to introduce new material. Coaching is Adler's second mode of teaching for the development of intellectual skills. From the didactic instruction, students create a product. The teacher interacts with the student on a one-to-one basis regarding this product by asking leading questions and guiding them in refining their work. The student then revises the work. This is especially important in reviewing math work and editing students' writing. In fact, I believe that the coaching process is such a vital part of the learning experience that all work is checked with the student in class. The third mode of teaching is the Socratic discussion, to increase understanding of ideas and values. This modified process (for true Socratic discussions take hours) is used in the discussion of science, literature, and history to stimulate critical thinking. In this process all ideas are valued and everyone learns from each other.

Teachers create a safe environment for optimal learning. They accomplish this by getting to know each of the students and acknowledging their uniqueness. Because early adolescents test limits, communication with students must be clear and respectful. I use Glasser's (1986) questioning techniques when I need to approach students about their actions. This approach is respectful and establishes a trust—an important issue for early adolescents. I have established a set of ground rules or nonnegotiable limits that remain constant from year to year. Beyond these basics, the students then develop rules for the current year as different situations arise. They take responsibility for the security of the environment and participate in student government.

THE CURRICULUM

The daily schedule provides time for whole group activities, individual quiet work time, breaks, and large blocks of time for in-depth projects that encourage cooperative learning and peer teaching. This approach incorporates the brain research (Buzan, 1983) regarding the best work/rest cycles for concentration, thinking, and memory and the newest information about the effects of music.

The day begins with a community meeting. The students and teacher put their chairs into a circle so everyone is accountable to the group. Members of the student leadership committee conduct the meeting by following an agenda. The student facilitator records everyone's homework and then asks for acknowledgments. Students acknowledge each other for behaviors that they appreciate. The student must "own" the acknowledgment by saying thank you. Group challenge activities, such as a word play or riddle, stimulate abstract thinking, and then I pose a "question of the day" which requires a response from everyone. The purpose of this activity is to listen to many points of view. Daily jobs are reviewed and announcements made. I then give a short lesson or lead a Socratic discussion on history, literature, classroom issues, or current events. The students plan their day and write in journals. At the end of the meeting, the class reviewer acknowledges all students who have demonstrated appropriate group behavior. Once a month each student gives a speech to the group using a podium and microphone. The speeches are videotaped so that the students can evaluate their performances. Since young people are so self-conscious, I find this personal form of evaluation much more effective and less threatening.

Students spend the next hour doing quiet, individual work and the teacher does coaching. During this period, students take any necessary tests, write papers on the word processor, read, or carry out other activities that require concentration. Appropriate music is played. Students have individualized math plans. Each day they read a lesson to the teacher or to a peer teacher and do sample problems. Then they do the appropriate problems for homework. Students have books with the answer keys so they can check their work. It is their responsibility to ask for needed help. After every four or five lessons, a test is taken to check for mastery. The student must achieve 90 percent in order to complete the task. Students are expected to demonstrate 90 percent accuracy in history, vocabulary, science, and math.

Mastery learning gives students time to master particular skills before progressing to the next level of work. The student takes on the responsibility of learning a skill rather than just accepting a low grade and never learning the material. The teacher's job is to break down the learning steps, to offer suggestions for internalizing the skills, and to provide the time to learn the information. The advantages of mastery learning, according to current research, is that it offers clear expectations, fosters mastery of a unit of study, is noncompetitive, encourages responsibility, and gives the message that everyone is capable of learning (Simon & Bellanca, 1976).

After individual work time, students take a fifteen-minute break for movement and relaxation. Students are free to play ball, sit on the deck and talk, or just "hang out." Early adolescents benefit from having periodic snacks—fruit or fruit juice—to meet the needs of their growing bodies. Because the students do not change classes, they can spend time in relaxing breaks instead of rushing from place to place. Students who have not finished the previous day's homework, however, must remain inside to complete it. Further, they may not eat lunch until the homework has been completed. Thus their choice is not whether or not they will do their homework, but when. This approach has produced an on-time homework completion rate of 98 percent.

The next ninety minutes are devoted to the humanities. Students work on projects incorporating history, literature, Spanish, geography, music, and art. The interdisciplinary or core curriculum focuses on one major question: How does this information relate to me and my place in the universe? Each month the study revolves around a historical period. The literature includes legends, poetry, short stories, novels, and dramas that feature the conflicts of young people during different historical periods. The geography relates to the area of the world under study. The writing assignments, speeches, art, music, and exploration classes complement the monthly theme and make the study relevant to their lives.

Lunch is next. Students can purchase a lunch from the salad bar or bring a lunch from home. The salad bar is a class business that is available every day. It is integrated into the math, economics, and Spanish programs. The students plan, buy, prepare, and clean up as well as record the financial matters of the business. As part of our study of Spanish, the grocery list is written in Spanish, and students and the grocery store employees converse in Spanish. This work is done by the salad bar committee. Each student serves on this committee one week out of every five. Profits from the business are divided among students to help finance their class trips.

Following lunch another ninety minutes are dedicated to science and health activities. The science curriculum alternates yearly between life and physical science. Students work in five cooperative groups to learn the scientific concepts. They use their creative talents to internalize the material. Students create videos, games, models, posters, and experiments to demonstrate their learning. These aids are used in their presentations to each other. Each week the students give a group presentation and listen to other presentations on the same content. The creative materials are then donated to the elementary science room for their use. Thus, cross-age and peer teaching occur.

Health classes focus on the health of early adolescents. Students explore topics such as adolescent development, stress management, self-esteem, drug education, sex education, nutrition, and relationships with others. For instance, in one health class, students kept saying that everyone was "yelling at them." After much discussion, it was discovered that yelling had nothing to do with tone or volume; people were asking them to do something they didn't want to do, and they were feeling frustrated. From this need a conceptual framework was developed to help young people decide appropriate communication skills for different situations. The framework was based on problem solving, and eventually the class discovered that many of them really didn't want to solve a problem but just wanted to gripe and complain. This awareness was a good learning experience for all. Now the first question framework is "Do you want to solve the problem or just complain?" One student explained to her friend that the difference between her this year and last is that now she looks for solutions instead of just complaining. Another day students listed forty different kinds of stresses that they encounter. The greatest ones were siblings, parents, and peers, in that order. Because these people will always be part of their lives, the students decided to study various relaxation techniques and to do role-playing activities to practice solutions.

After health, students break again, have a snack, hang out, and organize their belongings to go home. The environment committee makes sure that the environment is restored, and the ecology committee makes sure the recyclable items have been placed in the proper receptacles.

Physical education and exploration classes are alternated during the last hour of the day. All students participate in all sports and the focus is on learning skills and teamwork. Each month a different sport is played, including volleyball, soccer, tennis, basketball, track and field, swimming, and softball. Community resources such as the YMCA are used for some of the sports.

Because young people are changing their thinking styles, they want to try out many new things. One way to facilitate this is through short-term exploration classes. Each month the students may select one of two areas for exploration. These areas vary according to interest and the historical period under study. For example, when students are studying the industrial revolution and immigration, the exploration classes are car mechanics and ethnic cooking. Some other classes are drama, painting, sculpture, computer programming, Red Cross babysitting, and architecture. Parents and people from the community are invited to share their expertise. When using guest teachers, the core teacher is always present to provide stability, to insure student accountability, and to serve as a resource person. If the guest speaker is new, I ask everyone to wear name tags. This has virtually eliminated anonymous inappropriate behavior.

CLASS COMMUNITY

According to research, absentee rate is highest at the middle school level, when students usually change to big, impersonal schools. It is crucial that young people feel useful, important, and part of a group. At School of the Woods the absenteeism is less than two days per student per year. Parents report that students do not want to miss school. Recently when a student was in the hospital for an operation, he called the class at noon the next day to say "hello." The prepared environment is designed so that the student feels part of the classroom community. This process begins the second week of school with a week-long trip to an environment learning camp. The camp is based on the Outward Bound program and offers many opportunities for individual challenge, such as conquering fears by jumping off a thirty-foot pole to catch a trapeze or developing strategies to climb a fifty-foot wall. Other activities are designed to develop trust. After trust has been created, the students work together on many physical tasks that require verbal and nonverbal communication strategies. After each activity, students discuss what they learned from the experience about themselves and apply this knowledge to their everyday life. The program also includes many discussions on ecological issues. Students have a great time and develop a real cooperative spirit.

With this experience students return to the classroom environment better able to work together in team sports; at their salad bar; on leadership, environment, and ecology committees; and on academic tasks. Cooperative learning is an integral part of the classroom; it's not limited to structured group activities. When students have difficulties with others during the school year, the class discusses the problem and comes up with "win/win" solutions. The classroom community is extended through monthly socials. A student committee makes the necessary arrangements. Some of the recent socials have been ice skating and dinner, a sports event and dinner, a play and dinner, and a party with plenty of food. Class trips also reinforce this sense of community. As part of the history curriculum, students take trips to San Antonio and Austin during the year that Texas history and government is studied, and to Washington D.C. in the year of the American history study. Each trip is one week long, because that appears to be the optimal time frame for social and academic learning to occur. Profits from the salad bar, recycling, and babysitting help pay for the trips.

SCHOOL COMMUNITY

Since early adolescents want the opportunity to be productive members of the community, the prepared environment extends beyond the four walls of the classroom. Students have an opportunity to contribute to the school and larger community, by teaching keyboarding to all eight-year-olds, serving as a classroom assistant for a week at Christmas time, giving science lessons and making materials for the elementary students, and planning and leading the schoolwide celebrations such as Earth Day. They also babysit at school functions, supervise the games and make auction items for school fund-raising events, and create the school's sixty-page yearbook. Students know that they make many important contributions to the school. They receive many positive comments and are held in high regard by younger students, staff, and parents.

LARGER COMMUNITY

The students have many opportunities to draw on the resource people in the larger community. Physicians, law enforcement officials, pharmacists, patent lawyers, and artists are invited to share their expertise with the students. As a part of the Junior Achievement Program, a salesperson from IBM teaches Project Business. The students spend one week each year working in a business of their choice—animal clinics, radio stations, theaters, restaurants, architectural firms, law offices, specialty shops, and doctors' offices. Before going to the business, students must write a résumé and a letter to the business stating their goals. The students keep a journal of their experiences. When the group comes back together, they discuss the pros and cons of working in the business world. The adults in the community also have the opportunity to experience the positive aspects of young people.

Students also provide many services for the community. They work with students with multiple disabilities in a local public school, participate in the hunger project fun run, read books for the multiple sclerosis read-a-thon, take in abused animals and nurse them back to health, host the press conference for the State of the World's Children, and do cleaning projects for the Audubon Society. The students have fun and learn a great deal from these projects. In Youth Service (Conrad & Hedin, 1987), it states that these opportunities for young people stimulate formal thinking, develop communication skills, allow problem solving, and enhance self-concept. The Carnegie Council looks upon "youth service as central to the academic program" (1989, p. 45). Students at School of the Woods know that they can make a difference in the world.

EVALUATION

In May, 1988, an extensive evaluation was made of the pilot program using the assessment guidelines created by the Center of Early Adolescence (Dorman, 1984). Data for the evaluation were gathered from achievement tests, the Piers Harris self-esteem inventory, student and parent questionnaires, classroom records, and observations.

The test scores demonstrated that the program is academically effective. Many students were at least two years above level in every area. All students tested higher than the expected year's growth in each subject, indicating a balanced curriculum. Two students who have graduated from the middle school program improved more than forty percentile points in their composite score since they entered the school.

The Pier Harris self-esteem inventory indicated that the students had a very high self-concept score. The mean and mode scores were in the eighth stanine. According to the test, all students gained in self-concept. These are remarkable results, because literature reveals that young people aged twelve to fourteen have the lowest self-concept of any age group (Simmons, Rosenberg, & Rosenberg, 1973). The questions that 100 percent of the students answered positively on the test were

I am a happy person.

When I grow up, I will be an important person.

I am lucky.

I like being the way I am.

I am different.

I am a good person.

I can be trusted.

I am good at my school work.

I like school.

I am smart.

I am an important member of my class.

The questions that were most often answered in a way to cause concern were

I worry a lot. (*yes*)

I cry easily. (*yes*)

I have a good figure. (*no*)

These self-concept results are significant because these young people have a positive self-concept despite the national trend and the questions that 100 percent of them answered positively represent some of the key issues of early adolescents, such as belonging, trust, confidence, satisfaction, and future contributions. It is interesting to note that 90 percent of the students indicated that they worry. This affirms David Elkind's theory that worry prevails during early adolescence because of drastic physical changes and the movement into formal operational thinking. Because this new form of thinking is a sign of cognitive growth, it is a characteristic that cannot and should not be prevented. Students were also vulnerable regarding their physical development, as reflected in their perception of not having a good figure and crying easily. As in the cognitive growth, physical growth with its new hormone production is a necessary developmental task. A supportive environment is of great importance for young people at home and at school during this crucial period of physical, cognitive, and psychosocial change.

The parents and students indicated great satisfaction. One family put off moving for a year so that their young person could finish the program. Siblings continue to be enrolled. Parents feel supported by the parenting class and support groups made available to them. They are constantly commenting on the progress of their adolescent in academics as well as in life skills.

For the middle school parent education night this year, I asked three students to speak. They agreed and as they brainstormed what they would say, one student said, "I want to tell parents that this classroom is a simulation of the real world—nowhere else would you learn to organize your work, practice time management, and have so many real decisions to make. I have also learned so much from having to evaluate myself." Another student said he wanted to tell about the theory behind what we do. He felt that everyone should know the research regarding mastery learning, interdisciplinary curriculum, peer and cross-age teaching, and cooperative learning. The third student wanted to talk about the uniqueness of each subject. Because the students covered all the pertinent information, all I did was the introduction and conclusion. The students spoke spontaneously and answered the parents' questions. By the time the program was over, it was obvious that many parents had been touched by the students' presentation. At the end, one parent announced, "These students are empowered."

Watching the eighth-grade students thank their parents, peers, and teachers at graduation is also a very emotional experience. By the time they graduate, they are self-confident and self-assured. They appreciate the experiences they have had and are looking forward to a new phase in life. The feedback from the high schools is extremely positive regarding our students. In high school, they continue to be active participants in their academic learning as well as in extracurricular activities. Private and public high schools are actively recruiting our students even though we do not give the traditional grades.

In April of last year, *Newsweek* had an article on "How Kids Learn," which I read to my class. At lunchtime the students decided to write a letter to the editor. I believe this letter best expresses their attitude toward the middle school program:

> We are twelve- to fourteen-year-old students in a Montessori school. Our Montessori classrooms are just like the ones you recommended in your article, "How Kids Learn." In fact, even our middle school classroom allows us freedom to learn, to explore, and to create. We feel that this kind of learning environment has given us these advantages:
> 1 We like school and learning.
> 2 We feel good about ourselves.
> 3 We know how to work well with others.
> 4 We know mistakes are good—they help us learn.
> 5 We are independent thinkers and workers.
> 6 We have learned to be leaders and followers.
> 7 We learn from our peers as well as our teachers.
> 8 We get individual attention from our teachers.
> 9 We have relaxed breaks.
> 10 We can work at our own pace so that we can reach our individual potential.
> 11 We will be able to contribute to our world.
>
> We highly recommend this approach to education.
>
> Sincerely,
> Middle school students
> School of the Woods

CONCLUSION

John Goodlad writes, "The single school is the largest and the proper unit for education change" (1975, p. 108). Currently, this middle school model is being replicated by a number of private and public Montessori schools throughout the United States. Each of these schools has been able to take the basic design and personalize it to meet needs of their student population. Many more schools are in the initial stages of adopting this model. My hope is that the middle school program at School of the Woods has taken an important step toward fostering educational change by sharing its model of a holistic, developmentally responsive, learning environment that empowers the early adolescent.

REFERENCES

Adler, M. (1984). *The paideia program.* New York: MacMillan.

Buzan, T. (1983). *The brain user's guide.* New York: E. P. Dutton.

California State Department of Education. (1987). *Caught in the middle: Educational reform for young adolescents in California public school.*

Carnegie Council on Adolescent Development. (1989, June). *Turning point: preparing American youth for the 21st century.* Report of the Task Force on Education of Young Adolescents. New York: Carnegie Corporation.

Coe, E. (1989). *Creating an holistic, developmentally responsive learning environment that empowers the early adolescent.* Doctoral dissertation, Union Graduate School. (University Microfilms International no. 8906565)

Conrad, D., and Hedin, D. (1987). *Youth service: a guidebook for developing and operating effective programs.* Washington D.C.: Independent Sector.

Doda, N. (1981). *Teacher to teacher.* Columbus, Ohio: National Middle School Association.

Dorman, G. (1984). *Middle grades assessment program.* Carrboro, N.C.: Center for Early Adolescence, University of North Carolina at Chapel Hill.

Elkind, D. (1984). *All grown up & no place to go: Teenagers in crisis.* Reading, Mass.: Addison-Wesley.

Finks, H. (1990). *Middle school handbook.* Boston, Mass.: National Association of Independent Schools.

Freire, P. (1970). *The pedagogy of the oppressed.* New York: Seabury.

George, P. (1987). *Long-term teacher-student relationships: A middle school case study.* Columbus, Ohio: National Middle School Association.

Glasser, W. (1986). *Control theory in the classroom.* New York: Harper & Row.

Glenn, S. (1987). *Raising children for success.* Fair Oaks, Calif.: Sunrise Press.

Goodlad, J. (1975). "School can make a difference." *Educational Leadership, 33,* 108–17.

———. (1984). *A place called school: Prospect for the future.* New York: McGraw-Hill.

Hill, J. (1980). *Understanding early adolescence: A framework.* Carrboro, N.C.: Center for Early Adolescence, University of North Carolina at Chapel Hill.

Hoose, J., and Strahan, D. (1988). *Young adolescent development and school practices: promoting harmony.* Columbus, Ohio: National Middle School Association.

Lefstein, L. (1986). *A portrait of young adolescents in the 1980's.* Paper prepared for Building Leadership for Youth: A Shared Vision.

Lipsitz, J. (1977). *Growing up forgotten.* New Brunswick, NJ: Transaction Books.

Montessori, M. (1937). *The Erdkinder and the function of the university.* Amsterdam, the Netherlands: Association Montessori Internationale.

———. (1948). *From childhood to adolescence.* New York: Schocken.

Simmons, D., Blyth, D., Van Cleave, E., & Bush, D. (1979). "Entry into early adolescence: The impact of school structure, puberty, and early dating on self-esteem." *American Sociological Review, 44,* 948–67.

Simmons, R., Rosenberg, F., & Rosenberg, M. (1973). "Disturbance in the self-image at adolescence." *American Sociological Review, 38,* 553–68.

Simon, S., & Bellanca, J. (Eds.). (1976). *Degrading the grading myths: A primer of alternatives to grades and marks.* Washington, D. C.: Association for Supervision and Curriculum Development.

Sizer, T. (1984). *Horace's compromise: The dilemma of the American high school.* Boston: Houghton Mifflin.

PART FOUR

PROJECTIONS FOR THE FUTURE: MONTESSORI BEYOND THE YEAR 2000

INTRODUCTION

This final section of the book begins with a chapter by Marlene Barron, "Montessori and the Twenty-First Century," which describes in fascinating detail the changing characteristics of American culture as we approach the turn of the century. Based on the projected demographics and the dynamics of this new culture Barron proposes a new set of cultural and educational priorities. She then assesses the ability of the Montessori model to adapt to these new cultural needs and to influence the broader educational community. Barron suggests that many aspects of the Montessori model offer solutions and that the proposed reforms in education if implemented will closely resemble the integrated and holistic view of education pioneered by Montessori.

Part 4 closes with a summary of the highlights of the final session of the symposium. Approximately one hundred observers and presenters met in small groups to discuss the subject of Montessori in contemporary American culture. Although there was no attempt to arrive at a consensus, the small groups did provide some sense of closure to the stimulating three days of discussions.

15

MONTESSORI AND THE
TWENTY-FIRST CENTURY

World history is being revised faster than CNN can telecast events. Newspapers have become de facto history texts. There is no doubt that current economic and political events will profoundly affect the way we live our lives in the twenty-first century. Yet for the most part the overpowering problems of today (drug abuse, impoverishment of the young, teenage pregnancies, adolescent suicide, crime, the devastation of the natural environment, and the critical need for good child care) rivet our attention on the here and now.

My purpose today is to stimulate thinking about Montessori's relevance to the future. I plan to do so by identifying societal trends and by highlighting the opportunities and challenges they pose to educators today and into the next century.

During this symposium we've heard different descriptions of the Montessori approach. To this amalgam let me add another—that of Montessori as a mind-set, a constellation of concepts, values, precepts and practices that forms a particular vision of reality. The Montessori paradigm is culture sensitive and highly adaptable. This adaptability is why the Montessori approach is effective in diverse settings. This capacity to accommodate information from a global context to different cultural settings suggests that Montessori will be a worldwide force in the future, in the twenty-first century.

Let me take a few moments to distill the Montessori paradigm into what I see as its basic tenets about people, learning, and the aims of education.

Montessori views each human being as a uniquely endowed whole individual living a whole life in a whole world. Personal, educational, social, and work life are intertwined and inseparable; self, family, neighborhood, and global community are interconnected. To tease out any one component is artificial and academic.

Within this framework, learning and growth are synonymous with living. It is an ongoing, dynamic process of self-construction within a social context. Montessori recognizes the inextricability of knowledge and knowers. Learning is viewed as a transactional process that affirms collaboration and community; participants teach and learn from one another. This socio-contextual approach to learning explains why Montessori is so adaptable.

The aim of Montessori education is to develop each person's abilities to the fullest extent while celebrating and enhancing his or her uniqueness and cultural background. The goal of education is the development of autonomous, competent, responsible (to themselves, other humans, and the environment), adaptive citizens—lifelong learners and problem solvers. Respect, competency, responsibility, self-initiative, and self-management are valued.

On an institutional level, this translates into programs that are responsive to each individual's idiosyncratic needs and interests as well as to community and ecological demands. Diversity of practice within this context is the norm. Montessori programs in migrant worker camps in California look different from programs in midtown Manhattan or rural Maryland. The essence is Montessori, the programmatic pieces are community specific.

On a pedagogical level, the Montessori perspective dictates the inclusion of a rich variety of experiential, meaningful, high content activities. Activities are multisensory, interactive, and engaging. They provide opportunities for innovation, reflection, problem solving, repetition, and collaboration. The setting, the prepared environment, the educative environment, is responsive and supportive and encourages risk taking.

Specific pedagogical practices that support these goals include collaborative learning, cross-age groupings, a focus on "cosmic" education, teacher observations, classroom research, and the design of the learning environment—to name a few. What makes these practices so effective is that they empower all participants (parents, teachers, children, and community members) as collaborators, facilitators, and learners.

I believe that the Montessori paradigm supports attitudes and behaviors needed today and in the future, in the next century. These include personal empowerment and cultural pluralism, global thinking and ecological awareness, flexibility and adaptability, creativity and innovation, respect and responsibility, and competencies of all kinds. Let me support this assertion by now examining some of the societal forces that will affect the way we live our lives.

The common technologies of information, service, and electronics have wrenched us (in just two decades) out of the industrial era and into the information age. Our language (a barometer of how we perceive reality) has already responded to this profound change. The models and metaphors of physics that fit the industrial age are being replaced with those of biology. Physics presents a mechanistic worldview: energy intensive, linear, macro, deterministic, outer-directed. Biology is more information intensive, micro, inner-directed, adaptive, and holistic. As one example consider computer technology. It uses a host of biological references. We talk of computer viruses and worms, and we use a mouse.

In this information age, global economic interconnectedness drives all other changes. In 1992 a frontier-free Europe will come into being. The European community will remove all barriers to the flow of people, goods, services, and money among twelve European countries (and there are others, such as Turkey, clamoring to join). Communist countries have begun to enter the world marketplace. New alliances are being formed and reformed (as, for example, in Germany). And the Pacific Rim countries (Japan, China, South Korea, Taiwan, Hong Kong, and Singapore) have already become a major economic and cultural influence in the world.

In education, the International Confederation of Principals (comprising representatives from eight nations—Britain, Canada, Japan, the Netherlands, Soviet Union, Switzerland, Germany, and the United States) was recently formed as a "logical step for a 'global' society" (Bradley, 1990, p. 12). Its goal is for "school leaders to work together to make students globally literate" (p. 12).

Global economic interconnectedness has lead to a world culture, a homogenizing effect, which has met with powerful countertrends toward ethnic awareness and a new focus on the individual. It seems that the very nature of an information age shifts focus away from the state to the individual and leads to an expanding philosophical and spiritual concept of what it means to be human. The wider our horizons and the more powerful our technology, the greater we value the individual. This is quite different from what happened in the industrial economy when our current educational system was designed. No wonder it is so out of alignment with today's reality.

On the other hand, the Montessori paradigm already fits the demands of the information era. It supports individuality and cultural pluralism within a global cultural context.

The rapidly changing information economy has also created an entirely different workplace from that of the industrial age. The industrial economy needed people who would follow orders (creativity was not desired on the assembly line) and managers who could give orders. The information age needs people who can adapt and change to the fast pace of societal and technological change, people who can do complex mental tasks. Leadership, not management, will be what matters. "Leaders think long term, grasp the relationship of larger realities, think in terms of renewal, have political skills, cause change, affirm values, achieve unity" (Naisbitt & Aburdene, 1990, p. 219).

People in the information age are valued (and paid) for their knowledge; the unskilled and uneducated will have decreasing economic value and fewer job possibilities. "By the year 2000, below average skills will be good enough for only 27 percent of jobs created between 1985 and then, compared with 40 percent of the jobs existing in the mid-1980s" (Swasy & Hymowitz, 1990, p. 6). And most current job categories will be "upskilled." By the year 2000, about 75 percent of workers currently employed will need retraining.

We need to educate children to assume multiple careers (not jobs) requiring complex analytical skills and leadership abilities. The current American educational system is simply not doing this.

Not only have the requirements for active participation in our economic environment changed, but the racial, ethnic, socioeconomic, and gender mix of entrants into the workplace has also shifted. It is projected that between 1990 and the year 2000 only one out of seven new entrants into the workforce will be a white male born in the United States. And our immigration policy continually adds to this ethnic diversity. In 1988 643,000 *legal* immigrants entered the United States—more than entered all other countries combined (Naisbitt & Aburdene, 1990). By the year 2000 nearly a third of new workers will be minorities and nearly half of this group is now considered functionally illiterate (Richards, 1990).

Functional illiteracy is the inability to meet the demands of daily adult life because of a low-level ability to read and write. In 1982, 56 percent of Hispanic and 44 percent of Black teenagers in the United States were functionally illiterate. A contributing factor to this shameful statistic is our school dropout rate. For example, in 1983 in New York City, 61 percent of Black and 62 percent of Hispanic youth dropped out of school (usually in their sophomore year) compared to 39 percent of white youth. Not surprisingly, illiteracy is highly correlated with criminal behavior, unemployment, and receipt of public assistance (New York Community Trust, 1987).

We often forget that these illiterate, unemployed youth have children, the majority of whom live with their mothers. In 1984, 4 percent of family households were maintained by men as compared to 17 percent by women. Sharp racial and ethnic differences also exist in the proportion of these single parent families. In 1989, 44 percent of Black family households, 23 percent of Hispanic households, but only 13 percent of white family households were maintained by women (*Dimensions*, 1990).

The education of those for whom the educational system failed and is currently failing is a top priority if America is to compete in the global economy. The impending labor shortage simply requires their participation. The business community has begun to respond with what they call "remediation" (i.e., in-house courses in literacy, math, technology, and the sciences). These programs, which prepare current job applicants to assume entry level positions, have become a necessity.

When we add to this complex picture of racial, ethnic, and socioeconomic diversity each group's fervor in asserting the distinctiveness of its culture and language, we are faced with the challenge of creating an educational system (both structure and content) that can preserve individuality and the richness of people's experiences while creating an educated, unified citizenry. In other words, we need to restructure the way we deliver educational services from top to bottom. And Montessori educators have met this challenge in individual schools.

Another change that has affected our thinking about education has resulted from more and more women entering the work force. Since 1970, women have taken two-thirds of the *new* jobs created in the economy. Because of the impending labor shortage the population of fourteen million mothers still at home will certainly be aggressively recruited by the private sector. The private sector will have to increase significantly its subsidization of child-care and elder-care programs in addition to instituting flexible work arrangements. Two recently announced corporate moves in this direction are US West's investment of $10 million over the next five years in early childhood development and parenting programs, and IBM's $22 million over the next five years "to increase the availability and improve the quality of childcare in communities where its workers live and work" (Cohen, 1990, p. 7).

It is important to note that elder care is predicated to affect an even wider segment of employees than child care. Although the influx of immigrants keeps our population comparatively young, we are indeed aging. The median age of the U.S. population in 1980 was 31; in the year 2020 it is projected to be over 40 (Levine, 1990). (European countries and Japan are aging even faster, and they aren't letting many immigrants in.) This trend will lead to an increase in the number of elderly people dependent on health care and other expensive services. Even today almost one-third of all working adults are responsible for providing some care for an elderly person, and three-quarters of those who care for the elderly are women. Stride Rite has taken the lead in this area by opening, in March 1990, a joint "day care center" for fifty-five children and twenty-four older people (Teltsch, 1990, p. 1).

The obvious challenge is to increase the availability (both in numbers and in variety of programs, such as sick care) and quality of child-care, parenting, and elder-care programs.

When we now examine the implications of the shift of focus to the individual brought about by the information economy, we find, what some are calling a worldwide spiritual revival, a re-examination of the meaning of life. It seems that when people are buffeted about by change, the need for spiritual belief intensifies. Science and technology do not tell us what life means. We learn that through literature, the arts, and spirituality.

One manifestation of this trend toward a re-examination of the meaning of life is the renaissance in the arts; the other is the worldwide multidenominational religious revival. Let's look first at the arts renaissance.

The arts have replaced sports as society's primary leisure activity. In 1988 Americans spent $3.7 billion attending art events and $2.7 billion attending sports events (Naisbitt & Aburdene, 1990). Twenty years ago, Americans spent twice as much on sports events as on the arts. And this interest in the arts is worldwide. Some of the specifics are fascinating; for instance, in 1988 more people attended one popular Broadway play than all Yankee and Mets games combined.

Leading schools have begun to respond to this trend. MIT is requiring its undergraduates to take a more "systematic study of the arts, humanities and social sciences" (Naisbitt & Aburdene, 1990, p. 76).

In America religious revival is not synonymous with a renewed interest in organized mainstream religions. A 1987 Gallup poll found that mainstream church membership had either dropped or stayed flat (Naisbitt & Aburdene, 1990). People seem to be turning to other religions and other sources for their spiritual needs. In 1988 in the U.S. there were 4 million Muslims, 2.5 million Episcopalians, and 3 million Presbyterians, and in North America more than 3 million Buddhists. And the New Agers (who share a holistic view of life) are 5 to 10 percent of the population, which is more than any one Protestant denomination. In addition, the ethics debates over genetically altered organisms, biomedical issues (organ transplants), and business issues (insider trading) have created a renewed demand for a curriculum that discusses values and ethics. Six state legislatures (Hawaii, Michigan, Missouri, New Jersey, California, and Tennessee) have already made "ethics" a mandatory part of the curriculum. And corporations have even begun to hire in-house philosophers (Naisbitt & Aburdene, 1990).

The challenge is to create educative experiences that extend beyond the 3 Rs and to integrate values and ethics into the educational lives of students. The Montessori curriculum responds to these fundamental needs.

So these are the challenges to educators—now and into the twenty-first century: to develop the unique potential of all our citizens for a world in which critical thinking, knowledge beyond the 3 Rs, self-initiative and self-management, collaboration, ethical values, and global thinking will be valued, and to do this in a variety of settings and with a pluralistic population of all ages, infants through seniors.

Although it is easier to describe the problems than it is to solve them, the adaptability of the Montessori paradigm as well as its beliefs, aims, and practices suggest that it is well suited to meet these educational and societal demands. This now leads me to wonder if Montessori will be a key player in the education/social service universe of the twenty-first century or if it will continue to be "an alternative." Alternative to what? Let's first look at the "to what" issue.

Over the past few years, the United States has been paying more than ordinary attention to its educational system, its way of delivering service. There is a consensus that what is done in the name of education is not working. As Timothy Dyer, the executive director of the National Association of Secondary School Principals, stated, "The restructuring of American education is going to be the debate of the 90's"(A Look Ahead, 1990, p. 30).

In the January 10, 1990 issue of Education Week (A Look Ahead), a sampling of 47 policy makers, practitioners, and pundits responded to the question, "what major issues, trends, and developments will mark education in the 1990s?" by discussing new schooling models. Even in articles that focus on tinkering with bits and pieces of the current educational model the restructurer's voice can be heard. For example, in a New York Times article on items banned in a New York City public school (removable gold fittings on teeth), Roland Barth, project director of the National Network of Principals, states, "To me, it raises the question about the usefulness of schools as we know them . . . maybe we need a different conception of packaging schools" (Lee, 1990, p. 22).

If we look beyond the rhetoric, we can find a handful of restructuring projects, ranging from statewide initiatives, union approaches, and national projects, to locally initiated efforts. Although the focus and approach of these projects differ as much as their definitions of what restructuring means, they seem to share a few features. So far they are all tailored to the needs of individual schools; they are not centralized reforms. They also "depend for their birth and continued existence on the energy, ethics, and creativity of individuals" (Crandall, 1989, p. 7). The beginnings of larger-scale efforts in defining restructuring can be seen in the newly created Northeast Common Market for Education (focusing on this region's restructuring projects) and in the work of a handful of national groups (National Governors' Association, Education Commission of the States, and Council of Chief State School Officers), each of which is seeking to make clear what school restructuring is and how to go about it.

Unfortunately, the American phenomenon of trivializing issues has reached a point where meaningful debate and decision making have become almost impossible. Ideas are not discussed, public opinion is based on "common sense" understandings of how things work, and national leadership is lacking. The resultant faddism in school reform leads to many ill-conceived changes being instituted. The selection and implementation of proposed innovations are often based on superficial tinkering with bits and pieces of the structure. The fundamental issue of dismantling the bureaucracies that inhibit real change in individual schools and classrooms is not addressed. Missing from most reform attempts are meaningful discussions of the intrinsic worth of education and of how learning takes place.

The American need for fast, clean, immediate solutions has created another problem for those committed to restructuring public education. It seems that the incremental improvements resulting from most school reforms are intolerable to many. There is a societal impatience to see and document immediate changes—even with long-range projects. This results in methodological schizophrenia in researchers. As they acknowledge, their assessment tools do not assess what needs to be assessed nor do they measure what they claim to measure. Nevertheless they continue to use them even as they work to create new ones (e.g., performance assessments). As a result programs and reforms are prematurely abandoned.

In addition, educational decisions made so as not to offend important groups (e.g., unions) often turn into political decisions. Consider the watered-down legislation that protects teacher's transfer rights—regardless of the resistance of the receiving schools and principals—forced by the teachers' union in Chicago's restructuring of its school system.

In the rush to do something, supporting infrastructures (faculty training and ongoing in-service support)—a must for new programs—are either not created or are poorly designed; consequently, new initiatives falter.

Last, control and accountability decisions often ignore reality. For example, few theorists have explored the possible outcomes of parents' indirect control of schools through their exercise of "choice"—although our society has many institutions that respond to competitive marketplace demands.

What can we expect in the next decades? I foresee a proliferation of independent innovations (including interactive computer technologies) as more and more communities experiment with various kinds of educational structures and models in their public schools. These new initiatives will expend enormous energy dealing with bureaucratic inertia—an important issue in all restructuring projects.

Broad-based community, business, and foundation linkages will be formed to provide services that extend beyond the public school's traditional mandate. For example, in the area of science and math education, grass-roots alliances are now found in virtually every large community, and their number is growing rapidly. In science alone about five hundred sizable partnerships have been identified, a few of them statewide (Atkins, 1990, p. 36). The lines between formal and informal schooling will continue to blur as schools become less insular and interact more with their communities. And we, as educators, will need to learn how to work in coalition with groups outside the education arena.

Similarly, the child-care and elder-care universes will experience an explosion of innovative initiatives driven by both private sector and government monies. The expansion of Headstart programs, the new Workfare program (which will establish child-care services for poor, unemployed adults), and Title XX programs are the current governmental funding strands. Unfortunately these state and federal efforts will not come close to meeting the needs for child-care and family preservation services of this population. In 1986, 27 percent of the three- and four-year-olds from low-income families were enrolled in school, compared with 42 percent of those from more affluent families. President Bush's proposed budget for fiscal year 1991 will enable only 27 percent of all eligible children to participate in Headstart programs. Private, community-based coalitions will be needed to provide the child-care and support services so desperately needed by all these families.

In addition, the expansion of corporate and private child-care and elder-care programs will present a variety of challenges: sick care, night care, 24 hour care, drop-off centers (for days when schools are closed), and intergenerational programs—to name a few.

Certainly many of these new initiatives will use the Montessori model. I believe that these will be efficacious and long lasting, however, only when accompanied by the following: the reconstruing of Montessori tenets and practices in a language understood by others and the formation by Montessorians of coalitions and linkages with other similarly minded groups (other educators, foundations, family preservationists, and social welfare groups). In this way we can begin to address the fundamental issues and spark meaningful public debate.

Unfortunately the lack of a shared language among professionals who work with children and families presents a barrier in forming these coalitions and instituting a national dialogue on these issues. Allen Sheldon suggests that perhaps it's time to create a new language, "kinderspeak" (A Look Ahead, (1990, p. 32). He may be right.

Moreover, none of these opportunities can be taken advantage of by Montessorians if the critical need for Montessori teachers is not met. The availability issue of potential teacher candidates might be alleviated when the money the business community dedicates to these initiatives reaches a critical threshold. Only then will we see increased teacher salaries and prestige, and a focus on teacher education.

Certainly the challenge of preparing teachers from diverse backgrounds will need to be addressed, not only by Montessori teacher education programs, but by all teacher preparation institutions. The advent of the information age has resulted in a changing definition of what needs to be learned by teachers as well.

Teacher preparation for any kind of comprehensive, integrated approach is time and resource intensive; it cannot be taught through a series of workshops. For example, the American Montessori Society's teacher education programs require more than 300 academic (contact) hours plus a full year internship. During the academic phase, teachers (1) learn how to design, adapt, and work with a wide variety of materials—both commercially available and teacher designed; (2) gain an understanding of child development; and (3) complete detailed, extensive resource manuals. During the internship phase, student teachers, working under a master teacher, learn how to adapt instruction to a student's individual needs. They learn how to assess what children know as well as how they are construing information. This teacher training model empowers teachers as true facilitators in the teaching/learning experience, and it is costly. I wonder if we, as a society, are willing to pay this cost. Do we have a choice?

This again leads me back to the "to what" issue. I can only speculate that many of the emerging educational models will look very similar to Montessori; they will contain many of its essential elements. In fact the questions that will be asked Montessorians in the future will be: "What makes your program Montessori?" "What is it about your program that makes it distinctive?" As many of Montessori's tenets and practices have been incorporated into developmentally appropriate early childhood programs, so will it happen in many of these new models—whether Montessorians take a leadership role in forming these new programs or not. The question Montessorians have to address is what are the nonnegotiable components of their model.

I've explored some of the issues facing educators as we move into the twenty-first century. For Montessorians, it is clearly a time of opportunity and growth. The Montessori paradigm is the best and most comprehensive approach to meet individual and societal needs. However, understanding and discussing societal issues, articulating the Montessori model to diverse populations, forming coalitions and linkages, taking advantage of high-tech learning tools, and demonstrating Montessori's effectiveness in diverse settings will be the strategies needed to "mainstream" the Montessori model over the long haul.

On a national level, Montessori professional organizations, like the American Montessori Society, will need to form broad-based national linkages with other similarly minded groups, create backup resources and support networks for individuals working in their communities, and support research projects. In its seventy years of existence, Montessori practice has accumulated a wealth of practical information that needs to be digested and then disseminated. They need to make this valuable knowledge available to the educational community. The risk to Montessorians is not one of assimilation, of being co-opted, or of being "watered down"; the danger is of being perceived as too different or too specialized to offer important and practical insights to the broader educational community.

The challenge for Montessorians will be to look beyond the distinctiveness of the Montessori perspective and encourage national debates on deeper educational issues, such as the aims of education and what learning is all about.

I do believe Montessori will survive as a viable model in the next century. It will exist along with a few other models in American education that will have much in common with Montessori. They will be intensive, comprehensive, and well planned. They will view children from a holistic, socio-contextual perspective. They, like Montessori, will not only use interactive, manipulative materials, but will also effectively employ adults and other students as facilitators and collaborators in the teaching/learning process. And it will be these essential elements in all these models that will make the difference in creating an educated, well-served populace.

REFERENCES

NEWSPAPER ARTICLES

Education Week, Wynne, E. A. (November, 1989). "Examining 'faddism' in school reform." p. 32.

———, (January, 1990). "A look ahead: Education and the new decade." pp. 29–32.

———, Mitchell, R. (January, 1990). "Performance assessment: An emphasis on 'activity'." pp. 36, 25.

———, Cohen, D. (February, 1990). "$10 million for parenting programs set." p. 7.

———, (February, 1990). "Dimensions: Women who maintain families." p. 3.

———, Walker, R. (February, 1990). "Single definition of 'restructuring' remains elusive." p. 15.

———, Bradley, A. (February, 1990). "Principals in 8 Nations join to address 'global' issues." p. 12.

———, W.S. (March, 1990). "Union urging principals in Detroit not to volunteer for reform effort." p. 4.

————, (April, 1990). "Theodore D. Kimbrough: At the top of a 'bottom up' experiment in Chicago." April 18, 1990. pp. 16–17.

New York Times, Teltsch, K. (March, 1990). "For younger and older, workplace day care." Vol CXXXIX. No. 48, 170. pp. 1, 8.

————, Lee, F. R. (March, 1990). "Can a change in rules alter young lives?" Vol CXXXIX. No. 48, 171. p. 22.

————, Levine, R. (March, 1990). "New York area's population growing, but graying faster." Vol CXXXIX. No. 48, 178. pp. 1, 30.

————, Atkin, J.M. (April, 1990). "Commentary: On alliances and science education." p. 36.

Wall Street Journal. Swasy, A. and Hymowitz, C. (February, 1990). "The workplace revolution." The Wall Street Journal Reports: Education. pp. 6–8.

————, Richards, B. (February, 1990). "Wanting workers." The Wall Street Journal Reports: Education. pp. 10–11.

MAGAZINE AND JOURNAL ARTICLES

Crandall, D. (December, 1989). "Here today, here tomorrow." *The Regional Lab Reports.* MA: The Regional Laboratory for Educational Improvement of the Northeast and Islands. pp. 7–8.

Edelman, M. W. (January, 1990). "Our challenge for the 1990s: Making it unAmerican to allow child suffering." *CDF Reports.* Washington, DC: Children's Defense Fund, 11, 6. pp. 1–2.

BOOKS/PAMPHLETS

Naisbitt, J. & Aburdene, P. (1990). *Megatrends 2000: Ten new directions for the 1990's.* New York: Morrow.

New York Community Trust (April 1987). *Public education in New York City: A review of issues and strategies for grantmaking.* NY.

SUMMARY OF THE FINAL
SMALL-GROUP DISCUSSIONS

The discussants were generally surprised at the broad range of areas in contemporary American culture in which Montessori's educational ideas were influential. Both Montessori parents and educators and those from outside the Montessori community, who represented a variety of disciplines and organizations, were impressed by the diversity and by the innovations described. (Although only a few representative examples have been included in this book, many other exciting programs from schools and child-care centers around the country were presented through panels and papers at the symposium.)

Concerns were expressed that as Montessori education became a greater force in mainstream American schools, the very characteristics that make it so attractive to parents and teachers may become diluted and changed, because its integrated educational approach does not fit easily into the bureaucratic and compartmentalized system of traditional public education.

Participants discussed how to insure that this will not happen and made several suggestions, including (1) the view that Montessori educators must become more involved in mainstream educational organizations and issues, and (2) the suggestion, receiving much support from discussants, that since the use of specialized Montessori terminology often leads to misunderstandings with others it is important to translate Montessori concepts and strategies into more common educational and psychological terms.

The symposium provided an exciting and appropriate vehicle for initiating a long overdue dialogue with the wider American educational community. Discussants suggested that other forms of public discussion and exchange should be sought in order to continue the dialogue, and a variety of subjects for further examination was offered.

Discussants suggested that other forms of public discussion and exchange should be sought, such as making presentations at local, state, and national meetings to parents and educators, as well as submitting articles on different aspects of Montessori to a broad range of magazines and educational journals. The importance of Montessori educators becoming active and involved participants in educational groups outside the Montessori community also was stressed.

Although all participants were weary at the end of the three-day meeting, many expressed a reluctance to end the meetings. Although no consensus was reached or sought on the many issues discussed, there was satisfaction that differing opinion had been heard and respected.

EPILOGUE

A great deal of thought and planning went into the design and the implementation of the symposium upon which this book is based. The goal of the effort was to bring together a group of persons to examine the many facets and applications of Maria Montessori's thought in as objective and rational a way as possible. The participants from outside the Montessori community who were invited to present papers had differing views of Montessori. All had expressed some interest in her ideas in their writings or in their own work, but none were Montessori advocates. Instead, they were considered knowledgeable persons in their own fields who would accept the challenge of examining Montessori's influences, both pro and con, in contemporary American culture.

Whether this has been accomplished, we'll leave to the reader to decide. Of one thing we can be sure, however. No longer can people complain that "there's nothing new written on Montessori."

This epilogue would not be complete without thanking all those who have helped create this book. We are extremely sad to report that one of the contributors, Ann Neubert, died of a heart attack at age forty-five before the book's publication. Since Ann was a bright and energetic young teacher and researcher who recognized the importance of objective examination of educational ideas, we would like to dedicate the book to her.

AUTHOR INDEX

SUBJECT INDEX